# MEN, MESSAGES, AND MEDIA

# MEN, MESSAGES, AND MEDIA

## A Look at Human Communication

**WILBUR SCHRAMM**
Stanford University

HARPER & ROW, PUBLISHERS
New York, Evanston, San Francisco, London

Sponsoring Editor: Raleigh S. Wilson
Project Editor: Cynthia Hausdorff
Designer: T. R. Funderburk
Production Supervisor: Valerie Klima

**Men, Messages, and Media: A Look at Human Communication**

Library of Congress Cataloging in Publication Data

Schramm, Wilbur Lang
  Men, messages, and media.

  Bibliography: p.
  1. Communication.    2. Mass media.    I. Title.
P90.S375          001.5          72-12469
ISBN 0-06-045797-X

# Contents

# Acknowledgments

The task of writing on a gigantic topic such as this could never have been undertaken without good friends and colleagues —so many of whom have been of help that I cannot possibly name them, though they all have my deepest gratitude. To two organizations, however, I must give my thanks for special assistance: the Ford Foundation, which made possible some time for writing, and the East-West Center, which provided a roof over my typewriter and me while the writing went on. All these friends and helpers are blameless for what should be better, and responsible in no small measure for what is good, in the following pages.

Stanford, 1973                                    Wilbur Schramm

# MEN, MESSAGES, AND MEDIA

# i.
# How Communication Developed

As I write these lines I can look up from my paper at the jagged green mountains of Hawaii. If I look down the horizon to the seacoast, I can pick out the place where man is supposed to have first stepped ashore on these islands. He came out of the Stone Age, twelve hundred years ago, riding in an outrigger canoe that he had fashioned with the crudest of instruments. He came to Hawaii at the end of an incredible 5000-year journey from Southeast Asia, carrying his gods, his children, his foods with him, hopping from island to island over thousands of miles of open sea, living in a rapport with wind, water, and earth such as we could hardly expect of modern man. He landed on a lava island, planted his seeds and his culture, and made the land his.

That first Hawaiian was already a skillful communicator. He could read information in the skies and in the waves, and use it to navigate. He had a well-developed language. True, he could not write it, although he recorded some information in pictures and carvings. But he used his spoken language as a powerful instrument. With it he created a viable government and a pleasant family life. He expressed wonderfully subtle ideas and relationships. He persuaded others to accompany him on voyages over the horizon and reassured them in moments of discouragement. He carried with him all the lore of ocean sailing, the beliefs and rituals and customs of life as he wanted to live it, and passed all this on to his children, without writing. When he landed on Hawaii and felt the earth shake and saw smoke and fire in the mountains, he had information that helped him recognize Madam Pele, the Goddess of Fire; and he knew how to communicate with her, too, with prayer and offerings and dances.

## The Meaning of "Communication"

But pause here a moment. "He knew how to communicate with her." What does that mean?

When the critic and philosopher Kenneth Burke sent a book to press in 1935, he proposed the title *Treatise on Communication*. The publisher vetoed the name because, so he said, readers would expect a book on telephone wires! That is how one of Burke's most important volumes came to be called *Permanence and Change*.

We cannot quarrel with multiple uses for a term that is so pervasive in our thinking and our behavior, but we must at least make clear what it is we are talking about when we use the term *communication*. This book is not—at least not directly—about telephone wires, nor transportation (as it might be if it had been written by an economist), nor Reading and Writing (which is what my children studied under the name Communication in primary school), nor freshman English and Speech (which their baby-sitter was studying at the same time in a college course called Communication), nor *successful* communication (which we are talking about when we say, "He really communicates!"). Indeed, we will find some of the failures of communication as instructive as the successes.

This book is about the fundamental human social process. Communication is the tool that makes societies possible and, by its nature, chiefly distinguishes human from other societies.

In an eloquent chapter written fifty years ago, the sociologist Charles Cooley called communication "the mechanism through which human relations exist and develop—all the symbols of the mind, together with the means of conveying them through space and preserving them in time."[1] And the anthropologist Edward Sapir wrote with great insight in the first edition of the *Encyclopedia of the Social Sciences,*

> While we often speak of society as though it were a static structure defined by tradition, it is, in the more intimate sense, nothing of the kind, but a highly intricate network of partial or complete understandings between the members of organizational units of every degree of size and complexity, ranging from a pair of lovers or a family to a league of nations or that ever increasing portion of humanity which can be reached by the press, through all its transnational ramifications. It is only apparently a static sum of social institutions; actually, it is being reanimated or creatively affirmed by particular acts of a communicative nature which obtain among individuals participating in it. Thus the Republican party cannot be said to exist as such, but only to the extent that its tradition is being constantly upheld by such simple acts of communication as that John Doe votes the Republican ticket, thereby communicating a certain kind of message, or that a half dozen individuals meet at a certain time or place, formally or informally, in order to communicate ideas to one another and eventually to decide what points of national interest, real or supposed, are to be allowed to come up many months later in a gathering of members of the party. The Republican party as a historical entity is merely abstracted from thousands upon thousands of such single acts of communication, which have in common certain persistent features of reference. If we extend this example into every conceivable field we soon realize that every cultural pattern and every single act of social behavior involve communication in either an explicit or implicit sense.[2]

Society is a sum of relationships in which information of some kind is shared. Let us understand clearly one thing about it: Human communication is *something people do*. It has no life of its own. There is no magic about it except what people in the communication relationship put into it. There is no meaning in a message except what people put into it. When we study communication, therefore, we study people—relating to each other and to their groups, organizations, and societies, influencing each other, being influenced, informing and being in-

formed, teaching and being taught, entertaining and being en-
tertained. To understand human communication we must understand how people relate to one another.

Two or more people come together, trying to share some
information. They are likely to be very different people. Because their life experiences have been different, the signs that
carry the information are likely to look different to them. The
more different the experiences, the more different the information that is likely to be read into them. Ideas like "pain" and
"hunger" have a fairly good chance of being understood in
common because all of us have experienced these things—
though even in this case the "stiff upper lip" tradition of one
culture is likely to be misinterpreted in a culture where feelings
are more openly expressed. But words like *freedom, communism,* and *apologize* obviously are going to cause trouble when
people come from different life patterns, especially if they come
from different cultures.

Note carefully, however, that communication is not conducted entirely, or even mostly, in words. A gesture, a facial
expression, a pitch pattern, a level of loudness, an emphasis, a
kiss, a hand on the shoulder, a haircut or lack of one, the octag-
onal shape of a stop sign—all these carry information.

It is not a simple relationship. Kingsley Davis wrote, as long
ago as 1949, about the indirectness of the communication relationship, in which "one person infers from the behavior of another . . . [the] idea or feeling the other person is trying to
convey. He then reacts not to the behavior as such but to the
inferred idea or feeling. The other person then reacts to his
response in terms of the idea or feeling—the meaning—behind
it."[3] All there is to go on are the signs—the print or sounds or
movements—and it is always necessary to infer what lies behind
them. Not what *they* mean but what *he* means. Or, to put it
more precisely, what is *inferred* from what they mean as to what
he means. And, therefore, in the communication relationship
one always listens with a "third ear."

When this relationship works well, it results in a kind of
"in-tune-ness" that is one of the remarkable experiences of man.
When it works poorly, it results in misunderstanding, sometimes
in hostility, and often in behavior far different from what was

intended. However it works, this is the process that allows us to form the images in our heads that map our environments and guide our behavior.

This process, the way it is used by man, and its effects upon man and society are what this book is about.

## The Dawn of Communication

Now back to that first of all Hawaiians, who landed from his outrigger canoe sometime between 750 and 800 A.D., liked what he saw, and decided to make it his home. He was relatively far advanced in the long history of communication. He was, let us say, at about 2359 on the 24-hour communication clock running from one-celled animals to Alfred North Whitehead.

It may be stretching the point to say that communication began with primitive one-celled creatures, yet these too could process some information—which is the essence of communication. They could at least map their environments in terms of what was nutrient and what was not. But their messages were chemical. Nobody has recorded the communication history of the great leap upward from the level of chemical information to the level of animals able to take in information with their sense organs and give signals with their bodies. Yet compared to the greatest of Olympic high jumps, that leap—from information-processing bacteria, as we see them in a petri dish, to animals capable of two-way communication by means of sense organs, central nervous systems, and musculatures—required a run down a cinder path for hundreds of millions of years; it cleared the great barriers of self-identity, processing information from the environment, and establishing relationships with other identities. And when that height was cleared, living creatures were still only at the threshold of what we think of as modern communication.

None of us doubt that a dog can communicate. But, as Kenneth Boulding said in his wonderfully wise and witty book *The Image,* so far as we know a dog is not aware that there were dogs before him and that there will be dogs after he is gone. Dogs certainly communicate messages while chasing a cat, but so far as we know they never stand around afterward and say, "That was a fine chase, but not so good as yesterday's." Or,

"If you had blocked that alley, he wouldn't have got away!"[4] But the Stone Age man who came to Hawaii could do all that. He could process information so as to criticize and improve his own behavior. He could conceive of a past in which he had not lived and a future in which he would not participate. He could deal with abstract notions like goodness, evil, power, and justice. Furthermore, his skill with communication was such that he could make an image of his environment in terms that were relevant to his needs and goals, and tinker with that image in his head until the image would help change the environment while the changing environment altered the image.

What happened between the first two-way-communicating animal and the first communicating man who landed on Hawaii was a continuing process of extending the senses farther and farther so as to command more information; extending the voice and gestures farther and farther so as to deliver more information; making one's messages always more portable, more separable from oneself both in space and time. Considered that way, Marshall McLuhan's metaphor of the media as extensions of man is sound history, although the process was under way long before there were any media as we now know them.[5]

## The Beginnings of Language

Somehow, somewhere, in the primeval shadows, human animals took doubtless hesitant but gigantic steps. They developed language. Animals must have communicated with each other for millions of years before any of them developed an ability to generalize on the signals they had learned to give. When an animal growls, he can communicate dislike of or warning about something at hand. But at some magical moment some animal learned to make that signal portable, so that it would apply not only to the particular creature he was growling at but to a whole class of creatures or events or things. That is, he learned to say, "I don't like cats" or "Stay away from my woman," without having to point at a cat or his woman.

How did language start? We can only guess. As with many other great events, we can be fairly sure that no one recognized it at the time as a great event. But somehow, somewhere, humanizing animals developed sound-signs that could be carried around and used to mean the same thing everywhere, without having to point at the subject or stand next to it or snarl at it. Word-signs began to supplement signals. How? We have only speculation to go on.

Some of the speculations have given rise to ingenious and amusing names. There is the "bow-wow" theory, for example, which suggests that words came into being through the imitation of natural sounds like the barking of a dog or thunder or the waves. There is the "poo-poo" theory, which seeks to explain speech as growing out of involuntary expressions of emotions—pain, pleasure, fear, satisfaction. There is a whole set of theories based on the supposition that words came into being in close association with other movements of the body. A Soviet scholar, Marr, speculates that the first word-sounds were merely accompaniments to gestures; when the sounds became detachable they retained the meanings of the gestures.

Other theorists have advanced a "sing-song" theory—that words grew out of primitive and wordless chants communicating emotions and celebrating events. Still others have suggested the "yo-heave-ho" theory, in which words developed from the grunts of physical exertion. There is also the "yuk-yuk" theory—that words arose from chance sounds that happened to be associated with events of special importance or excitement. For example, perhaps a humanizing animal happened to be making the sound *yuk*—playing with his vocal system as he did with other parts of his body—when he bit into an especially tasty clam, and thereafter *yuk* came to be associated in his memory with a clam or with something good to eat.[6]

There is no way of deciding among these speculations. The facts are buried too deep in the past. And it is not really necessary to choose among them, because essentially they are all the same. They all say that certain humanizing animals began to associate certain sounds with certain experiences or behaviors. These sounds picked up some of the meaning of the original experience they were associated with. This makes sense to us because it is the way children acquire many word-meanings today. They see an animal and pet it, listen to it, perhaps smell it. Someone says "dog," and when that occurs often enough the sound *dog* calls up in their minds the animal they have seen, touched, heard, and smelled. In the same way, at the dawn of civilization human animals must have gone around the world associating names with elements of their environment.

How did they learn to abstract from these first associations so that *yuk* or something like it began to refer to *all* tasty clams rather than one? How did they then find a sound to mean "eat" or "things to eat" rather than just one kind of food? How did they find a sound to refer to all good things rather than one kind of good thing? How did they learn to string sounds together so as to fasten actions and relationships to names? How did they learn to express highly subtle relationships such as those that distinguish what was from what is or will be? The point is, they did. Slowly and painfully, over many thousands of years, they must have added to their repertoires the basic conventions of language that any child now learns in three years. It must have been this humanizing skill, and the intellectual growth related to it, that enabled one group of animals to gain an advantage in the race for survival. With their new linguistic tools they could survey and catalog their environment more efficiently, bring reports back for decision and make decisions in terms of information previously stored, organize their social relationships more efficiently, pass what they had learned on to new members of the society—in other words, process information more efficiently than other animals.

There are no fewer than three thousand languages and major dialects still spoken in the world. Once there must have been many more than that. It is hard to believe that they all evolved from a single ur-language. More likely, they came from at least six major original sources corresponding to the main families of present-day languages. Still more likely, they represent many starts at language in many places. In retrospect it seems an almost insuperable chaos. No matter how many starting points there were, languages must have been evolving in countless tribes and tribal groups that had little contact with each other and therefore little need to develop compatible languages. Each of these tribal languages must necessarily have mirrored the experience and the developing culture of the people who spoke it.

How did all these separate forms shake down to the three

thousand used today and to the dozen or so, like English and Chinese, that are understood by large portions of the world's people? It must have been the effect of increasing contact among peoples: easier travel, the growth of trade and commerce, the development of cities and later of city-states and nations, conquest, empire, and the more subtle influences of power and ideas and prestige. This process made it necessary to find common languages, and the process continues, inevitably though slowly, toward a single world language.

## The Beginnings of Writing

Along the path of history, up the long incline, perhaps hundreds of thousands of years beyond the beginnings of language, lay another landmark: writing. Having learned to separate sounds from their referents, man now learned to separate them from the speaker as well and consequently made them even more portable.

We know approximately when writing was first introduced —in the fourth millenium B.C.—but little more about how it was introduced than we know about language. We are confident that it developed in more than one place, grew out of trial and error with a number of visual devices, and doubtless came from man's older experience in drawing pictures. No animal except man has ever been known to draw unaided a picture of his environment, although some chimpanzees, given human encouragement and materials, have produced abstract paintings. These have quite deservedly been sold and exhibited, though they are not representational pictures but only abstract patterns of line and color. But for thousands of years before he could write, man covered cave walls and tools and ornaments with pictorial designs and representational pictures that showed high skill and were sometimes very beautiful.

This skill was not restricted to any tribe or place. Excitingly beautiful pictures of hunters and animals have been discovered as far apart as the caves of southern France, the inner Sahara, and the aboriginal areas of Australia. Many of these pictures must have had a magical purpose; they served as totems or were intended to ensure that the animal painted in the cave would also be available on the hunting grounds. Perhaps some of the pictures recorded great achievements, and some may have been left behind by unknown early Van Goghs and Cézannes who wanted to set down some of the beauty they saw in the world around them. Whatever their uses, these pictures may be thought of as the first written communications, and if so, the dawn of writing may be set at twenty to thirty thousand, rather than five to six thousand, years ago.

As language arose from the need to abstract upon events and experience, so must writing have come from the need to abstract upon pictures and to make word-signs last longer than the fleeting second during which they could be heard. Many devices apparently were tried for this purpose. The custom of tying a piece of string around a finger to remind oneself of something to be done reaches back thousands of years to the time when early man tied knots in string in order to count and keep records. Darius the Persian, for example, gave his commanders a string with 60 knots in it and said to them, "Men of Ionia: Every day from the day you see me march against the Scythians, undo one of these knots. If I do not return before the last knot is undone, gather your supplies and sail home. . . ." Just as we pound stakes into the ground to mark off a mining claim, so did ancient man use stones or wood, often marked with an individual sign of identification, to indicate the boundaries of his land. Men marked with stones the shadow of the sun at its most northerly and most southerly points, and checked off the days of the sun and moon cycles with scratches on a rock, much as we count ⫻⫻ or 正 today. Thus he made for himself a calendar. And his word symbols apparently made use of these counting signs and of his pictures.

The hieroglyphs of Egypt and Crete were mostly pictures, although each one stood for a word-sound. Some six hundred Chinese ideographs are mostly pictorial and representational, and many others show signs of pictorial origins. The ancient Maya writing is largely pictorial in style. It is difficult to trace modern written signs back to pictorial origins because there must have been a constant effort to simplify the pictures, conventionalize them, and make them widely applicable and easily portable. To write a sentence in pictorial form required an artist and a great deal of time. What was needed was something that could be written quickly and economically, and that would relate to the sophisticated spoken language already in use rather than going back to the direct representation of reality. Gradually, therefore, the pictorial signs must have come to stand for sounds rather than a scene or an event.

The hieroglyphs did just that. They were abstracted and conventionalized. A writer had merely to set down a series of sound-signs; he did not have to paint a mural or draw a storyboard. When writing emerges into history it is already stylized in this way, although in many cases it retains some additional meaning from its pictorial form. Thus, in a language like Chinese there are more ideographs than sounds, and the pictorial nature of one ideograph helps distinguish it from others. Many Chinese, Japanese, and Korean names, for example, sound alike but carry personally identifying characteristics in their appearance.

Because writing came when there was already more travel and more frequent contact among peoples, and also because many spoken languages to this day have never developed their own written languages, there were fewer types of writing than of spoken language. Nevertheless, the written languages, like the spoken ones, reflect not only the flow of human contact and the effects of conquest and ideas and larger social groupings but also, and much more important, the cultures out of which they came. Even the basic worldwide division among writing systems —the sign-syllabic systems that probably originated in the Fertile Crescent of the Middle East and spread over the Western world and the word-ideographic systems that originated in eastern Asia and spread through China, Japan, and other Asian countries—seems to reflect cultural differences, or at least we can speculate that it does. The sign-syllabic system, in which every sound in a word has a different written symbol, is easier to learn, easier to use, easier to change, and may well represent the Western concern with change and growth. The word-ideographic system, on the other hand, in which every word has a different symbol and which requires a child to master about a thousand signs (rather than 26 or 30) before he can read relatively simple prose, seems to go with a need for stability and a deep sense of the past. Perhaps as some scholars have suggested, the serene atmosphere of the long Chinese dynasties was conducive to such a system.

Be that as it may, the invention of writing, which was probably taken for granted in its own time, seems in retrospect to be one of the earth-shaking events of history. It made it possible to carry information over the curve of earth, farther than a speaker could go, or smoke signals or pennants or monuments could be seen, or drums could be heard. It preserved events and agreements for later times so that man could store some of his experience without having to strain to remember it. Therefore he was able to spend more time processing current information and planning for the future. And it must have speeded up enormously man's ability to change his way of living when he so wished.

The ancient civilizations typically credited the invention of writing to one of their gods—the Egyptians to Thoth, God of Wisdom; the Babylonians to Nebo, God of Destiny; the Greeks to Hermes, herald and messenger of Olympus. So much they valued it.

## The Beginnings of Mass Media

Animals communicated with each other for millions of years before any of them developed language. Human animals spoke to each other for tens of thousands of years before any of them learned to write. Knowledge and ideas were shared and preserved in writing for thousands of years before there were mass media.

When did the mass media come into being? The Acta Diurna, written on a tablet and posted after every meeting of the Roman senate, may claim to have been the first newspaper, although it appeared in only one copy. As papyrus, vellum, rice, and other materials began to provide a supply of paper and the skill of ink making moved westward from Asia, artists carved wood blocks containing both text and pictures. Block print books and scrolls were in existence at least half a millenium before Gutenberg. Any rich man or monastery that could pay for it could have one. Long before "printing," any rich man in Western Europe could have a handwritten and illustrated book if he could pay a scribe to make it. We know what some of these handwritten books cost. In the early thirteenth century, for example, it took the equivalent of about $3000 in modern currency to copy a thin volume as a birthday gift for a French princess.

What happened in the mid-fifteenth century in the city of Mainz, Germany, was that a man named Johann Gensfleisch, commonly known as Gutenberg, put together some materials and procedures that were already generally available and produced religious documents in numerous copies. He used ink and paper that depended on skills developed first in East Asia. The press he used was adapted from the wine press of Western Europe. The movable metal type from which he set his text by hand was not really new either, because the Koreans had used something of the same kind, but he had found an efficient way to cast it, and he had a syllabic rather than an ideographic language with which to work. Putting all of these elements together, he created a viable way of making multiple copies of written texts, often very beautiful copies, at relatively low cost. And thus the early 1540s (for printed documents) or about 1456 (for the Gutenberg Bible) is as good a date as any to celebrate as the beginning of mass communication.

Technically what Gutenberg did, and what all the mass media have done since his time, was to put a machine into the communication process in such a way as to duplicate information and to extend almost indefinitely a person's ability to share it. The communication process was little changed, but because man lives by information this new ability to share it had a profound effect on human life.

In some of the new countries that are now just emerging from an oral into a media culture, we can see five hundred years of mass media development foreshortened. There are still many villages on the earth where roads do not reach, where no one reads, and where radio has not penetrated. Life in these villages often seems to have a charming, unhurried quality. Time tends to be measured by the sun or by bodily needs rather than by a clock. Even though life is sometimes harsh and brief in a traditional village of this kind, still we can see farmers on their way to the fields or fishermen on the way to their nets stop to watch the antics of a young animal or enjoy the early sun on a mountainside if they feel so inclined—and we think rather ruefully about commuter trains, appointment calendars, class schedules, and other modern devices that keep us hurrying around the modernized world.

Knowledge is power in a traditional village as elsewhere, but in a premedia culture that form of power tends to reside with the old men who can remember the wisdom of the past, the sacred writings, the laws, customs, and family histories. When radio and print enter a traditional village, or even when a road is built, the change is often spectacular. For one thing, the amount of available information is enormously increased. Communication comes from farther away. Almost overnight horizons move back. The world stretches farther than the nearest hill or the immediate horizon. Villagers concern themselves with how other people live. Power passes from the men with long memories to those who command relevant information from distant places. The past, when it is written down, becomes common property. Attention turns to information that might be used to bring about change rather than to preserve changelessness. New concepts and images flow through the communication channels—crop rotation, insecticides, vaccinations, elections, family planning, engineering. Thus, as Harold Innis has so brilliantly pointed out, the life of the village, when it passes from an oral to a media culture, comes to center on space rather than on time, what can be rather than what has been, and the wheels of change are set in motion.

The mass media are both great multipliers of information and long pipelines for information; we will have more to say about them in later chapters. Here let us merely note that they also become powerful gatekeepers along the pathways of information, with a great deal of power over what travels along those pathways. Thus they supplemented or replaced the personal gatekeepers—the priest, the traveler, the old man—who performed this function before the development of media. But the communicating machines are able to gather so much information, multiply it so fast, and come into use so pervasively that they represent a quantum jump in the ability to control and circulate information and focus the attention of human beings.

Mass media have come into use only in the last second of

the long day of life on earth. Yet in that time printing and reading have reached every corner of the earth. The airwaves over every populated part of the earth are full of radio signals. More than sixty countries have television. Hardly a country in the world is still unacquainted with film. In the cities these media are taken for granted, but anyone who has seen African boys running through the bush shouting the news that the film van has come or watched a father proudly urging his son to write his name for a visitor, thus demonstrating that for the first time in that family a child has learned to write—anyone who has seen sights like these will never doubt the phenomenal appeal of mass communication.

Where the mass media are readily available today, people typically spend more time on them than on any other daily activity except work and sleep. Many children in North America devote as much time to television in their first twelve years of life as they spend in school. Almost all news comes through the mass media, and consequently almost all of our images of our distant environment. A high portion of the entertainment in a media-rich society is delivered by those channels. The mercantile systems are geared to advertising in the mass media, and tastes are at least to some extent shaped by media offerings.

Thus, the communicating organizations that grow around the communicating machines—news agencies, newspaper and magazine staffs, broadcasting stations, publishing houses, film studios—have come to be extraordinarily powerful gatekeepers on the information pathways. Knowing as we do that only perhaps 2 or 3 percent of all the news that starts from India ever gets to a reader in Indiana, and holding some doubts about the completeness, accuracy, and depth of the news coverage in the first place, we have reason to be justifiably concerned about the images we form of our faraway but important environments. When we consider the power of the media to focus our attention on one subject or one person rather than others that might concern us, we have good reason to ask how these gatekeeping decisions are made and under what controls. For the modern media are inextricably intertwined with modern life.

Whether the Revival of Learning stimulated the development of printed media or printing stimulated the thoughts and ideas of the Revival is not a very important question. Neither is the question of whether mass media stimulate change in the traditional village or change in the village stimulates the introduction of media. There are a series of interactions. The book and the newspaper moved hand in hand with the Enlightenment. The newspaper and the political tract were involved in all of the political movements and popular revolutions of the seventeenth and eighteenth centuries. The textbook made public education possible on a wide scale at a time when there was a growing hunger for knowledge. The news sheet first, and the electronic media later, made it possible for ordinary people to be informed about politics and to participate in government at a time when there was widespread dissatisfaction with the locus of power.

Without channels of mass communication the Industrial Revolution of the nineteenth century could hardly have transformed our way of life as it did. This technical revolution, in turn, added the camera, the projector, the microphone, the tape and disk recorders, the transmitter, and the computer to the available tools of communication—all within a little over a hundred years. And in the developing regions today, where, as we have pointed out, this entire process has been foreshortened, the information media have stimulated a revolution of rising aspirations and are themselves among the goals of these aspirations.

It is no accident that we have used the word revolution in talking about social interactions with mass communication. The media have been involved in every significant social change since they came into existence—intellectual revolutions, political revolutions, industrial revolutions, and revolutions in tastes, aspirations, and values. They have taught us a basic precept: Because communication is the fundamental social process, because man is above all an information-processing animal, a major change in the state of information, a major involvement of communication, always accompanies any major social change.

The rate of change in the style and form of human communication is therefore itself a social datum of importance. From language to writing: tens of thousands of years. From writing to printing: thousands of years. From printing to films and broadcasting: four hundred years. From the first experiments with television to live television from the moon: fifty years.

What comes next? Some new forms of media are on the horizon, and we will say more about them in later chapters. But it is rather clearly evident that we are entering an age of information, in which knowledge rather than natural resources may become the chief resource of mankind and the prime requisite of power and well-being. Peter Drucker points out that as many books have been published in the past twenty-five years as in the five hundred years before 1950; that perhaps 90 percent of all the scientists about whom we have records are alive today; and that workers engaged in providing knowledge to the public now outnumber farmers and industrial workers in the United States. During the next half-century man will finally have to come to terms with his extraordinary ability to process and share information. He will have to learn to use it for his own good rather than for his own destruction, and for further humanization and socialization rather than alienation or regression. At this moment in history, therefore, it seems reasonable to take stock of what we know about human communication.

# ii.
# What Communication Does

We are communicating animals; communication pervades everything we do. It is the stuff of which human relations are made. It is a current that has flowed through all human history, constantly extending man's senses and his channels of information. Now that we have achieved broad-band communication from the moon, we are looking around for other creatures on other worlds to talk to. Communication is the most human of skills.

But let us look a little harder at this idea. What does communication actually *do* for us, and what do we actually *do* with it?

The question may sound as silly as "Why eat?" or "Why sleep?" One eats because he is hungry. One sleeps because he is weary. One shouts "fire!" because the house is burning. One says "Pardon me!" because he has bumped into someone.

To an individual, communication is a natural, necessary, omnipresent activity. A person enters into communication relationships because he wants to relate to the environment, especially the human environment, around him. As Sapir wrote in the passage we quoted earlier, society is a network of such relationships maintained chiefly by communication.[1] To an observer communication seems to flow through the social system like blood through the individual cardiovascular system, serving the whole organism, concentrating now on one part, now on another according to need, maintaining contact and balance and health. We are so accustomed to living in an ocean of communication that we can hardly imagine living without it.

Try to think of a society existing without communication. A world society? During recent years a stony official silence was maintained between the United States and China, but communication went forward through many channels: statements through the mass media, political action obviously intended to convey messages, third countries, intelligence-gathering on both sides. It even proved necessary to arrange "unofficial" meetings at the ambassadorial level in a neutral country. An extraordinary set of ambassadors was exchanged—Ping-Pong players—through whom the high officials of one country were able to speak with remarkable openness to the people of the other.

A group society? A "silent" Trappist monastery prohibits conversation but not communication. The monks depend on countless acts of communication: a glance or a smile, administrative actions, adherence to a schedule, the kind of commitment and solidarity that members communicate through acts of devotion.

Suppose a hermit retires from the world to meditate in his cave on a mountainside. He is trying to avoid communication with other human beings—unless they come to seek his wisdom. But the very act of meditation implies internal communication. The hermit is dredging up stored information from his past, adding information from his nonhuman environment, thinking, talking it over with himself. He is in communication with his breviary and his books—and, in a sense, with all the men whose ideas have influenced him. He is communicating a message to mankind in general by retiring to his cave. And like St. Francis he may talk to the birds.

Even in extreme cases, therefore, communication goes on. For most of us most of the time it is largely unconscious, until we become self-conscious about it. A professional may be highly self-conscious and self-critical about the article he is writing for a magazine. A politician may be self-conscious about the speech he is rehearsing. But a child wanders through life, sending and receiving messages naturally, behaving with his whole organism, not thinking much about how he does it. He knows his parents reward him for saying "Daddy" and later for saying "Please," but even these behaviors merge into his natural patterns. He enjoys watching television and goes back to programs he enjoys more than others. He goes to school and becomes a bit self-conscious about the themes he has to write or his first telephone call to a girl. But unless he develops a speech defect or deafness or some other painful difficulty, he simply communicates in the ways that come naturally to him, using the behaviors he learns by trial and error to bring about the results he wants.

Even when the child grows to adulthood and becomes more conscious of the effects of his communication and the consequences of doing it in different ways, he still finds it hard to verbalize why he communicates as he does. Some years ago, when New York newspapers were on strike, Bernard Berelson took advantage of the opportunity to ask a sample of New Yorkers what they missed in the newspapers they were not receiving. His purpose, of course, was to try to find out why they read what they did. But they had extreme difficulty saying even what they missed. They could tick off some information services they were no longer receiving—the weather forecasts, the movie schedules, the evening broadcast lineups—but missing these was not what chiefly bothered them.

Many were afraid they were missing some specific information of importance to them: Several elderly respondents thought that some of their friends might have died and been buried without the respondents knowing anything about it. Still more bothersome was a vague sense of something absent in their lives: "Contact with the world," some said, "a feeling of being in touch," or simply "something I did every day." Perhaps the most significant finding of the study was how fully the act of reading the newspaper had been incorporated into people's daily lives, how natural this communication behavior had become, and how deeply the reasons for adopting it in the first place had disappeared into the shadows of the past.[2]

This is one reason why "what communication does" is hard to verbalize. Another is that the reasons for using communication are often highly complex and not necessarily on the surface. Still another is that the *manifest* (intended) functions of communication do not always take account of the *latent* (unintended) functions.[3] The language is Robert Merton's, and he is saying, in effect, that the actual consequences of communication are not always the intended ones. For example, a warning about cancer may result not in sending a person to seek a medical checkup but rather in frightening him away from the clinic. A cheery good-morning could lead not to good fellowship but to a suspicion that the speaker is going to try to borrow money. And finally, since most of our analysis of communication functions has to be done from the outside, we find ourselves always trying to look into the black box.

But we have access to at least one black box each: our own. For what purposes do *you* communicate? Why do *I* communicate?

I came out of my house this morning, saw a man in a sport shirt, smiled, and said "Good morning." If someone were translating that literally into a tribal language of New Guinea, he might have difficulty. Was I saying it was a "good"—that is, a fair—morning? No, it was a foul morning, with rain squalls scudding down from the mountains and threatening to soak me. Was I commenting on the goodness of the morning in a moral sense, as we say "Good Friday"? No, it was a day like other days. Was I wishing him a "good"—i.e., a pleasant—morning? To some extent, but he looked perfectly competent to manage his own morning, and as a matter of fact I felt rather irritated because he could spend this morning beside the sea while I had to go to work. What was I really saying to him? The most reasonable explanation I can give is that I was conducting our own tribal ritual. I was communicating that I belonged to his group and his culture, and was not an outlander or a rebel or a threat. In other words, I was confirming a comfortable relationship.

He said to me, "How are you this morning?" I doubt that he was much concerned about my health. He was doing what I was—communicating social membership and a certain degree of friendship. He expected me to say "Fine," and I did. In effect, we seemed to be casting around us our social radar beams, as ships do in the fog or airplanes on instruments, confirming our identity and that of the other person who appears on the radar screen, confirming our membership in a friendly culture group, doing what we had long ago learned was expected of us. The authors who have written about human relationships as "ships passing in the night" were not writing about our closest and most intimate relationships but rather about the kinds of contact I have just described, which constitute a large portion of the contacts we have in life. And for all of these communication serves us as radar, identity signal, and early warning. Or at least that is how it looks to an observer.

Another example: Amid the smoke and chatter of a cocktail party, a young man says to a pretty girl, "Cigarette?" On the surface, he is inviting her to take one of his cigarettes. Actually, he is communicating interest and doubtless hoping she will respond in the same way. He is communicating membership in a culture by offering her a cigarette, and he probably hopes she will confirm her membership by taking a cigarette or at least rejecting it with a smile rather than slapping his face because she doesn't believe in smoking or doesn't think a boy should speak to a girl without an introduction. In other words, it is the same situation as the one we have just described: radar, identification, early warning. If the girl responds favorably, his next question is likely to be, "Haven't I seen you somewhere?" —which really has nothing to do with whether he has actually seen her; rather, it is an opening move to find out a little more about her, perhaps to estimate whether this chance acquaintance might become a more lasting one. In other words, radar behavior merging into tool behavior.

Still another example: When I am home in California, I usually hear church bells at about six every evening. I listen to them because it is hard to ignore them but even more because they have a pleasant tone and blend well with sunset or late-afternoon shadows. They give me a sense of pleasure and warmth. Moreover, they tell me the time. If I am still working, it is time to begin thinking about a late-afternoon swim and a cocktail. The evening is beginning; it is time to recall the plans or engagements I have made. In addition, the bells remind me that religion is part of my culture and that some of my fellow residents are at that moment practicing it. And they raise pleasing pictures in my mind of a church and candles and an organ and plainsong and people in humble postures.

What is St. Mary's Church trying to communicate by means of those bells? It is calling the faithful to worship. But most of the people at that particular service would probably come with or without a bell. The bells are perhaps meant to communicate a presence, an availability in case someone needs the kind of spiritual assistance the bells symbolize. Perhaps they are intended to reach sinners like me and remind us of our religious obligations, even though we have seldom been inside St. Mary's. And perhaps St. Mary's is communicating its own membership in an ancient and honorable tradition in which bells have served as a sign for centuries.

Thus, the full significance of acts of communication is seldom on the surface. Every act of communication, every communicator and receiver, has an individual set of purposes and reasons. But we cannot be satisfied with that explanation. Acts of communication are more similar than they are different. Human communication deserves a more systematic explanation of what it does.

## Human Communication—Explained by Three Psychologists

Some very able men have written about the functions of communication. Jean Piaget, a Swiss child-development psychologist, distinguished between what he called social and egocentric speech in a child. When a child uses speech socially, Piaget said, "the child addresses his hearer, considers his point of view, tries to influence him or actually exchange ideas with him. . . ." In the other kind of speech, "the child does not bother to know to whom he is speaking, nor whether he is being listened to. He talks either for himself or for the pleasure of associating with anyone who happens to be there."[4] Later research, however, has indicated that much more of a child's speech than Piaget thought—perhaps 90 percent—is apparently socially intended. And although children play with their vocal mechanisms as they do with other parts of the body, there is little agreement with Piaget's conclusion that social communication usually appears around the age of seven. It actually appears much earlier. Very early the child discovers that his vocal behavior can be used as a tool. He learns what kind of vocal behavior is rewarded and soon discriminates among kinds of behavior and kinds of rewards.

Nevertheless, if we analyze our own supposedly adult communication behavior we find that a rather surprising amount of it is largely for our own satisfaction. I hit my finger with a hammer and say some strong words until the pain begins to go away. I sing in the shower, enjoying it thoroughly and rather hoping no one else will hear. I get a quiet enjoyment out of recalling an incident that I could probably never communicate fully to anyone else. All of these actions are using communication as a tool for my own satisfaction without intentionally involving anyone else.

A number of psychologists have recognized that much communication is tool behavior. Edward Tolman, a psychologist of learning, once described human speech as nothing but "a 'high-faluting' 'tool' not differing in essence from other tools such as strings, sticks, boxes, and the like." For example, he wrote, "this is quite obvious in the case of a command. What happens in a command . . . is that by means of it the speaker causes one of his fellows to do something. Instead of the former having to take the latter by the scruff of the neck and actually push him through the desired act, the speaker by means of a command accomplishes the same result."[5] A child learns this without difficulty. When he cries, he is likely to be picked up and fondled; if he is not, he makes less use of that particular communicative act. A smile gets him a smile. Certain sounds earn him food or a toy to play with. He learns names and finds not only that this brings social approval but also that it replaces harder physical labor.

As we have suggested, even talking aloud to oneself often has a tool use. The spicy words one says after hitting a finger are functional not only in relieving tension but also in avoiding other, less acceptable ways of expressing feeling, such as weeping. All of us know that inner discussion, inner talk, plays a part in many difficult decisions. Lorimer wrote about an 18-month-old child he observed in a verbal battle between a command not to touch some objects in a chest and an understandable curiosity as to what was in the chest. "For ten enormous minutes," he said, "I watched with fascination the battle between the impulse and the inhibition, as the little hand reached toward the things in the chest and withdrew to the verbal accompaniment 'no! no! no!' uttered by the child herself. Then the battle subsided, called to close by the distraction of other interests."[6] Thus, even the most apparently egocentric communication often has a tool purpose also.

In some contrast with this is William Stephenson's approach in *The Play Theory of Communication*. He concentrates not on the communication tool behavior intended to bring about change but rather on the part of communication that is not intended to accomplish anything except a sense of satisfaction and well-being.[7] Following the Dutch scholar Huizinga (in a book entitled *Homo Luden*[8]—Man Playing) and the pleasure theories of the Hungarian psychiatrist Szasz,[9] Stephenson bases his thinking on a sharp distinction between play and work: "Work deals with reality, with earning a living, with production. Play, on the contrary, is largely unproductive except for the self-satisfaction it provides."[10] Corresponding to these are two kinds of communication behavior. One is illustrated by a conversation between two people that seems to serve no apparent purpose: Neither is trying to convince or put down or get anything out of the other; they expect nothing of each other except conversation. But they enjoy the experience. The result, in Stephenson's words, is communication-pleasure. Quite different is communication that is intended to bring about action—for example, a command, a cry for help persuasion, demand. Stephenson calls the effect of this communication-*un*-pleasure, communication-pain. It takes work to get something done; play is just fun—in communication as in other behavior. Social control (of which an example might be the formation of public opinion) is work. Work is a function, he says, of all social institutions, but the central concern of the mass media is not with work but rather with communication-pleasure: making it possible for people to free themselves from social control and withdraw into the land of play.

"Playing is *pretending*," he says,

> a stepping outside the world of duty and responsibility. Play is an *interlude* in the day. It is not ordinary or real. It is voluntary and not a task or a moral duty. It is in some sense disinterested, providing temporary satisfaction. . . . Play is secluded, taking place in a particular place set off for the purpose in time or space. The child goes into a corner to play house. And play is a free activity, yet it absorbs the players completely.[11]

This description is very much like what others have written about television-viewing behavior. Yet Stephenson does not credit work-communication and debit play-communication. Quite the contrary. He feels that communication-pleasure is psychologically useful. It is "an enrichment of individual aspects of self." It is "self-developing and self-enhancing." It provides "opportunities to exist for ourselves, to please ourselves, free to a degree from social control." When mass communication is used for social control, it has to face firmly embedded beliefs and attitudes that are very difficult to change; when it is used for play it can "suggest to the masses certain standards of conduct, . . . provide for the leisure of such peoples, . . . make life easier for them." He feels that other theorists have tended to approach the mass media with "heavy loads of conscience . . . bent on doing good in terms of their own values," and therefore tending to view with alarm the trivia, the violence, the invitation to "escape" from real problems provided by the entertainment media. He emphasizes that he sees nothing nefarious in this. He feels that mass media play behavior is useful and that it has been a mistake to study mass communication largely in terms of persuasion and social effect; it should rather have been studied in terms of its play and pleasure elements. For this reason, he chose to develop "a play theory and not an information theory of mass communication."[12]

If Stephenson's book had been easier to read, and if he, like McLuhan, had been a coiner of phrases, the commercial entertainment media might have chosen to lionize him rather than McLuhan. His play theory presents a better justification for prevailing media content than does McLuhan's global village.[13] After once exposing oneself to this brilliantly conceived theory, one can never again ignore the importance of the play-pleasure elements in communication. And yet this theory leaves something to be desired as a general explanation of communication functions.

Undoubtedly a considerable portion of communication behavior can be described as play, just as other considerable portions can be described as tool behavior and still others as egocentric behavior. The distinctions between these are far from sharp. Much egocentric communication is play, and it is not hard to conceive of certain play as tool behavior also. A little scene from Mark Twain's biography combines them all. Twain was known for outbursts of colorful profanity, into which he put the same imaginative quality that readers found in his writing. His demure little wife tried to shame him by repeating some of his language. Twain listened in some surprise and then realized what was missing. She wasn't relieving inner tensions by saying what she said; she wasn't talking to herself; she wasn't enjoying, as any writer would, the flow of words and imagery that he could put into a few well-turned and thunderous phrases. Twain chuckled, and told his wife that she had the words but not the tune!

These are single-factor approaches. Each one helps illuminate a *part* of communication behavior. By choosing to detour attention from the information function, Stephenson ignores the quality that chiefly distinguishes communication from other behavior. His chief interest is in the use of the mass media; consequently, he pays less attention than we might wish to interpersonal communication or to the use of the media for such tool purposes as instruction. His existential position toward the entertainment media is doubtless highly congenial to the media because it tends to sidestep the critics who come with "heavy loads of conscience," yet this too leaves out an important part of thinking about the functions of the communication system. In other words, it is a useful, but partial, theory, which ought to generate important propositions for future research on communication effects.

The trouble with most such single-factor theories is that they may explain so much that they explain nothing. Explaining the function of communication in terms of work and play runs into the fact that these categories blur into each other. For example, one can enjoy saying "Good morning!" and at the same time meet his social obligations. The very hard work of creative writing also has important components of play. The really interesting distinctions may be within rather than between such very broad categories. Is there not possibly an important difference between the kind of play-pleasure to be derived from, say, passing the time of day with a friend, escaping into a Walter Mitty fantasy life, allowing oneself to be massaged by the words of an orator, experiencing the catharsis that Aristotle felt was the chief reward of a Greek tragedy, agonizing or weeping over a football game, enjoying the aesthetic beauty of the Bolshoi ballet, or playing with the sounds and images of a poem one is writing? Is it not possible that there may be a useful distinction between the kinds of pleasure derived from playing with the medium—reading, speaking, viewing, listening, simply filling in time, or the like—and the pleasure derived from playing with the message—for example, enjoying a particular bit of writing, turning a particular phrase, or capturing a particular idea? Stephenson concludes, after some impressive arguments, that "newsreading is a communication-pleasure, sans reward." But is it really helpful to fit into his category of newsreading as play behavior, without differentiation, such different sub-behaviors as reading the grocery ads, reading about the pollution of one's swimming place, reading about a public boner by an elected official, reading a humorous feature story, reading the Pentagon papers, reading about the assassination of a leader, reading about the death of a friend, reading an interpretation of a Supreme Court decision—and to consider that play is a sufficient umbrella to cover all of their different functions and consequences?

## The Social Functions of Communication

When we try to understand what communication does, we tend to shift back and forth between the individual and society like a zoom camera alternating between wide-angle and close-up pictures.

Piaget, Tolman, and Stephenson were all writing as psychologists concerned primarily with individual functions of communication. When we turn to the wide-angle lens and look at what political scientists, sociologists, and economists have written about the functions of communication, we find somewhat more differentiated theories.

In a classic essay, Harold Lasswell, a political scientist and a pioneer in communication study, identified three social functions of communication: (1) surveillance of the environment, (2) correlation of the different parts of society in responding to environment, and (3) transmission of the social heritage from one generation to the next.[14] Three groups of specialists, he says, are important in carrying out these functions. "Diplomats, attachés, and foreign correspondents are representative of those who specialize in the environment. Editors, journalists, and speakers are correlators of the internal response. Educators in family and school transmit the social inheritance."[15]

Translate this picture of political communication back to Stone Age men in their caves. They station a watchman to survey the environment for dangers and opportunities. When the sentinel brings back his report (an approaching war party, a herd of game animals), there may be a council of war or a meeting of the best hunters to make plans. The decision is passed along. These uses of communication are timely, centered on events as they occur. But there is a continuing need to teach the children of the community to play their part in it. The boys must learn to hunt and to read a footprint; the girls, to sew and prepare food. So the best hunter becomes a teacher, while the girls learn at their mothers' knee. In our time much of the task of surveillance is taken over by the news media; much of the coordination by government, political leaders, political reporters and analysts, and pressure groups; and much of the transmission of heritage by the schools.

Charles Wright, sketching a sociological perspective on communication (*Mass Communications: A Functional Approach*), added a fourth function to the Lasswell categories—entertainment. Lasswell had doubtless omitted that function as not an essential part of the political process, although history might argue with him. Wright called the second category, coordination, "interpretation and prescription," and the third one, transmission of the social heritage, by its sociological name, "socialization."[16]

In his book *Theories of Mass Communication,* Melvin DeFleur, another sociologist, added to these categories although not essentially changing them. The communication act, he said, is "the means by which a group's norms are expressed, by means of which social control is exerted, roles are allocated, coordination of effort is achieved, expectations are made manifest, and the entire social process is carried on. . . . Without such exchanges of influence human society would simply collapse."[17]

No economist has written with comparable specificity about communication functions in the economic system, yet it is possible to put together a set of economic functions from the work of economists like Boulding. For one thing, communication must meet the need for an economic map of the environment so that each individual and organization can form its own image of buying and selling opportunities at a given moment. Some of this will be done through advertising, some by means of price lists and business analysis. For another, there must be a correlation of economic policy, whether by the individual, the organization, or the nation. The market must be managed and controlled, and manufacturers, merchants, investors, and consumers must decide how to enter it. Finally, instruction in the skills and expectations of economic behavior must be available. The social scientists' maps, therefore, look like the table at the top of the next page.

These are no more satisfying than the single-factor approaches previously examined. The categories blur. And it is rather startling that no more attention has been given to the social function of entertainment. Perhaps the most encouraging feature of these social science approaches is the degree of agreement among them.

## Social Functions of Communication
## As Applied to the Individual

Let us go back to the high-definition lens and see what kind of individual map we might construct on the basis of the social functions just enumerated. We might think of four basic functions—no more perfect, no more mutually exclusive than

| Political system | Economic system | Social system in general |
|---|---|---|
| Surveillance (gathering intelligence) | Information on resources and buying-selling opportunities | Information on social norms, roles, etc.; acceptance or rejection of them |
| Coordination (interpretation of intelligence; making, disseminating, enforcing policy) | Interpretation of this information; making of economic policy; operation and control of market | Coordination of public understanding and will; operation of social control |
| Transmission of social heritage, laws, and customs | Initiation into economic behavior | Transmission of social norms and role prescriptions to new members of society |
| | | Entertainment (leisure activity, relief from work and realistic problems, incidental learning, and socialization) |

the classes of functions we have been reviewing but taking more account of the fact that human communication is both an individual behavior and a social relationship.

Each of these functions has an outward and an inward aspect, like all communication: One seeks or gives information, one receives and processes information. And therefore we might construct a sort of index to our map, like this:

| Function, which has an | Outward aspect and an | Inward aspect |
|---|---|---|
| Social radar | Seek information, inform | Receive information |
| Manipulation, decision-management | Persuade, command | Interpret, decide |
| Instruction | Seek knowledge, teach | Learn |
| Entertainment | Entertain | Enjoy |

The analogy to social radar is not bad. A ship in a fog at night must know where it is: Who is out there? Where are the rocks and shoals? Where are the sea lanes to safe harbors? All of us, too, must maintain continuing surveillance of an environment that grows more complex year by year. Who's there? Friend or foe? Local or stranger? Danger or opportunity? We have a deep need for a sense of belonging, for being part of our culture and our society, feeling a degree of stability and familiarity in our surroundings and life patterns. The historian Arnold Toynbee often exhibited acute unease in a new place until he had a map in his hands and could locate himself on it. And so every day we revise and update our working maps; the more unfamiliar the location or the experience, the more we depend on our social radar.

Primitive men, huddled together in their caves against cold and danger, asked the same questions: Where am I? Who or what is out there? They wanted to know what dangers and opportunities and threats were hidden in the dark. Were there enemies? Were there game animals? We ask the same things as we grow up or when we move into a new town. We seek friends and allies. We try to locate the points where we are in danger or where we can find rewards. We interpret the radar blips and make our maps. Stone Age man, as we have said, stationed a watchman on a hill; today we depend on interpersonal communication to make our close-by maps and on the mass media to look over the hill.

At one end of the scale, social radar behavior is very specific. The merchant wants to know the prices in a city. The farmer wants to know whether it is going to rain on the day he intends to plant. The boy wants to know whether a new girl is one he could try to date. At the other end it is very general. Berelson found a great deal of this in the people he talked to about missing the newspaper. Some individuals were uneasy because their radar was not registering its customary blips. One husband complained he had to look at his wife instead of at the news; several wives complained that they had to look at their husbands rather than at the crossword puzzle. When interviewers probed below that level, they found that a sensation of unease came from a feeling that one was closed off from the world

—wondering what was happening, even though when they had access to a newspaper, they barely scanned the headlines and seldom found a story of great interest. Old people whose families have moved away and who have lived beyond their friends in their own generations and consequently have few individuals to talk to, often turn to the mass media for a sense of belonging to the events and society around them. By keeping up with the news and the battle of ideas, even though they do not participate in any of those events, they combat the cold and dark of loneliness and alienation.

So all of us use communication in different ways as our social radar. We also use it for *manipulative* purposes. Think of all the times in the course of a day when we call upon communication in lieu of other methods to bring about behavior we desire in others. "Mrs. Miller, I want to dictate a letter." "Johnny, go outside and bring in the newspaper." "Please pass the sugar." "STOP." "No left turn between 3 and 6 P.M." "Vote Yes on Proposition A!" "Patronize your local merchants." "Don't be a litterbug." "Let's go to a movie." All of these substitute for physical force or more tangible rewards in getting people to do what we want them to do. This kind of tool behavior comes to a peak during a hot election campaign, when every channel of information and trick of persuasion is employed to manipulate decisions and voting in a desired direction. In every family it comes to a lower but significant peak at a time of decision: Should Johnny have the car tonight? Should Mary's allowance be raised? Should we go to the mountains or the seashore for this year's vacation?

For the other side of manipulative communication is *decision*. Sometimes this is very easy: No great effort is necessary to decide to pass the sugar. At other times it may be very difficult—for example, deciding whether to vote Yes or No on Proposition A, or whether or not to marry a particular person. A President decides to enter an undeclared war in Southeast Asia but then has the greatest difficulty manipulating the decisions and behaviors of his countrymen to implement his policy.

Decision and manipulation are usually two sides of the same coin. Any decision of importance is usually the outcome of competitive manipulation; any decision involving others will require some manipulation to put it into effect. Together they constitute a kind of communication *management*.

There is another large class of communication uses that we call *instruction*. This includes what the teacher does in a class and what the students do—not only exposition but also guidance and practice and problem solving. It includes not only what happens in class but also instruction outside school. We explain to someone how to follow the best route to our house. We teach our children to say "Please," mow a lawn, make a bed. An extension agent instructs a farmer in the use of a new seed. Cuba sends out schoolchildren to teach mountain people how to read. By failing to laugh or respond, we teach an uncouth person that there are some places where one does not tell dirty jokes. (At a point like this instruction and manipulation are very close.) We read the directions before we use a new blender. We look at the road map before we drive across the island to the surfing beach. (At this point social radar and instruction are very close.) This process goes on all the time. As I wrote this paragraph I took part in three acts of instructional communication: (1) A young man appeared in the doorway and asked where he could read about communication satellites. (2) Another young man looked in to ask whether Dr. Lerner was here today. And (3) the mail brought a rather formidable brochure about how to make out the Hawaii income tax.

These uses of communication tend to overlap. The income tax brochure was both instructive and manipulative: The tax collectors want to make sure I know how to pay so that I *will* pay. In particular, all of the tool behaviors are likely to have some entertainment mixed in. Every public speaker knows that he must lighten his message with humor or narrative. Every teacher knows, as Horace said, that he must both teach and please. Herta Herzog discovered by interviewing members of the audiences that soap operas, although intended for entertainment, are used by many listeners for advice, insight, and reassurance regarding their personal problems.

A startling percentage of mass communication is used primarily for entertainment. Almost all American commercial television, except news and advertising (much of which tries to entertain); most large-circulation magazines, except the adver-

tising pages; most radio, except news, talk shows, and ad
ing; most commercial movies; and an increasing porti
newspaper content—all are aimed at entertaining rather than
enlightening. And as Stephenson has argued convincingly, almost the entire content has a generalized function of play or
pleasure. It may be significant that man uses much of his everyday, interpersonal communication for orienting himself—answering the questions, Where am I? Who is out there? How shall
I respond to my immediate environment?—and on the other
hand fills his formalized and mediated communication pipelines largely with materials that relieve him at least temporarily
from worrying about those questions.

It is likely that these functions have changed hardly at all
since the birth of human society, although different institutions
have come into use to do these jobs. Notable among them are
enlarged and professionalized forms of government, formalized
school systems, and the mass media. But the government is
doing what government always has, the schools are socializing
the young people as their parents and the skilled craftsmen used
to, and the mass media are an extension of personal communication. This is how the map changes:

| Communication function | In oral society | In media society |
|---|---|---|
| Social radar | Personal contact, watch-men, town criers, travelers, meetings, bazaars, and so forth | Personal contact, the news media |
| Management | Personal influence, lead-ers, councils | Personal influence, lead-ers, institutions of government and law, opinion media |
| Instruction | Teaching in the family, by expert example, and by apprenticeship | Early socialization in family, educational sys-tem, instructional and reference media |
| Entertainment | Ballad singers, dancers, storytellers, group participation | Creative and performing arts, entertainment media |

## Summary: The Functions of Communication for Man

What does such a map of communication functions tell us about man as a communicating animal? Man moves through life always in touch with and touched by communication. He uses it as his individual radar both to look for what is new and to seek reassurance and guidance concerning his relationship to the society around him, and at the same time to confirm to others his identity and his understanding of relationships. He uses communication as his own management tool, for decision making and to persuade and manipulate others. In his small way he joins in society's larger program of decision making and then receives, interprets, and reacts to the signals that tell him what society has decided and expects of him. He is especially concerned with passing on knowledge, skills, and norms to the new members of his society—the new class of "barbarians" who enter the world each year and must be socialized within twenty years or so to become useful members of the social group, comfortable and safe to live with, prepared to take over the responsibilities they will be handed.

In seeming contrast to these tool uses of communication, man engages in much of his communication in a spirit of pleasure seeking and relaxation from the demands of social control. This spirit, as Stephenson points out, is a form of play. Indeed, man probably views a relatively small part of his communication behavior as "work" and is very unlikely ever to verbalize the ponderous functions we have credited to communication. He seeks an enormous amount of entertainment in the mass media, and even in his most serious public spokesmen, even in his most serious newspaper or newscast, he values a light touch.

Thus, as all philosophers from the Greeks to the French Academy have decided, man is neither entirely Godlike nor entirely animallike. His communication behavior proves him to be really quite human.

# iii.
# The Process
# of Communication

We have just credited communication with performing some very important functions. How does it do these things? In other words, how does human communication work?

Let us begin with a few examples of everyday human communication and try to analyze what is going on:

A driver studies a road map.

A sentry's voice rings out in the night.

A traffic light changes from red to green.

A picture tube flickers on. We look over the shoulders of three newsmen who are asking polite questions of the President of the United States. The President speaks over their shoulders to us.

The girl is 13, blonde, blue-eyed, with a heart-shaped face. The boy is tall, lanky, with arms and legs that seem longer than necessary, as they usually do at age 13. He moves toward the girl; his face is rather red. He says, "Linda, would you like . . ." and stops in embarrassment. She smiles up at him. "I'd love to," she says.

A man buys a morning paper, climbs aboard a commuter train, finds a seat, and settles down to read the story under the black headlines.

These are all communication incidents, manifestations of the flow of communication through society. What is common to them all is *information*, a communication *relationship*, and the special kind of behavior that handles information and takes place only in communication relationships, which we call communication *acts*.

## The Nature of Information

Information is the stuff of communication. It is what distinguishes communication from, say, swimming or bouncing a ball (although information about one's watery environment and about the position of the ball one wants to bounce is a necessary part of each of those behaviors). All of the incidents just described exist for the purpose of conveying, sharing, or processing information in some way.

Precisely what do we mean by information? Obviously we are not just talking about "facts" or "truth" (if anyone can be sure of the truth in a given situation). We do not mean only news or instruction or the kind of data we find in an encyclopedia. We are using the term in a way not unlike that in which Shannon and Wiener used it when they wrote about information theory and cybernetics: anything that reduces the uncertainty in a situation.[1] This is an idea that has influenced the thinking even of scholars who know very little about physics and engineering, and have never looked an information-theory formula in the face.

"Twenty Questions" is an information game. When one asks, "Animal, vegetable, or mineral?" the answer reduces the uncertainty about that particular question to zero and contributes to reducing the total uncertainty about what the game is supposed to discover. If one receives the answer "Animal" and then proceeds to ask "Human or nonhuman?" (answer: human), "A particular human or a kind of human?" (particular), "One human or a group of humans?" (one), "Male or female?" (male), "Living or dead?" and so forth, he is progressively reducing the uncertainty in the system with which he is dealing.

There are formulas in Shannon's mathematical information theory by which to calculate the entropy of a given system and the information required to eliminate uncertainty from it. In natural science entropy means "shuffledness," complexity, the opposite of simplicity or organization. When any social scientist encounters the term *entropy*, he has reason to be excited, because this is one of the great general ideas used for a long time by natural scientists to describe the world. Eddington said that if it were possible to make a film of the developing universe, the only way a scientist could tell whether the film were running backward or forward would be to observe whether entropy increased or decreased. One of the great principles in evolutionary science is that *entropy always increases*. That is, more types appear. Separate types are mixed in different combinations. The universe becomes more complex. And inasmuch as information is the tool that reduces entropy, it would require more information today to describe the spaceship earth and its flora and fauna than would have been required, say, two billion years ago.[2]

The possibility of applying concepts like these to human communication is what made the publication of Shannon's *The Mathematical Theory of Communication* and Wiener's *Cybernetics* at the end of the 1940s such an exciting event for communication scholars.[3] And although it soon became clear that direct application of the mathematical treatment was limited because the universe of human information is less simple and less finite than the mathematical and electrical universe for which the formulas had been created, still the effect of the new electronic and mathematical approaches was to open a series of important new insights on human communication. One of the most important of these was on the subject we are now discussing: the nature of information.

The information any individual seeks from most communication (if he is seeking information rather than the play that Stephenson describes) is whatever content will help him structure or organize some aspects of his environment that are relevant to a situation in which he must act. Consequently, information will make his decision easier. In locating point A it helps him to know that A is southeast of B. If he can find out that it is 25 miles southeast of B, that is still more helpful. If he learns that it is near some mountains, that information contributes further. And if he can discover that it is on Route 37, he finds that very useful indeed if he plans to go by automobile. All this information reduces the uncertainty of the situation. Note, however, that although it helps him make the decision it does not make the decision for him. He still must decide such things as whether to go through C or D to A if there is a choice. He must decide whether to take the most direct route or the most scenic one. He must decide whether it is worth going at all and if so, when. These decisions come out of his internal information processing, the other information (for example, his schedule, the condition of his automobile, and the like) he has stored up, and the values he has developed out of previous experience.

Take the case of the sentry who called out in the night. He must have heard a footstep or seen something move. Thus, suddenly his picture of environment and situation had changed. Most communication arises, indeed, because someone's image of his environment or of his own needs changes. So the sentry called upon whatever communication behavior he had learned that was appropriate for the new situation. If he had been playing Twenty Questions he might have said, "animal, vegetable, or mineral," but he was on guard duty, so he called, "Halt! Who goes there?" He was communicating by his words that this is a guarded place, that the intruder, if any, must identify himself or risk danger. If the intruder answers, "Friend," as they do in fiction, the sentry learns a certain amount of information. But he proceeds to try to reduce the uncertainty further. Perhaps he says, "Advance and identify yourself." If he then learns that the visitor is Sergeant Brown, Company A, serial number CZ14689732, he has a great deal of the information he needs. If the visitor moves into the light so that he can be recognized as a Marine sergeant with brown hair and brown eyes, about six feet tall, and dressed in field green, the uncertainty is reduced still further.

The boy who was so embarrassed got the information he was looking for. Suppose the girl had said, "I'm busy now—maybe tomorrow." That would have given him less information than if she had said Yes or No but more than he had before he asked. If she had said, "I'm busy now, but come by in an hour," that would have further reduced his uncertainty; he would have been fairly sure that she was not merely giving him a brush-off.

Consider a different kind of information. I can remember a boy who grew up on the plains and at the age of about 11 was taken for the first time to the mountains. He had seen pictures of mountains, read about them, heard about them, but as he rode toward them he became increasingly excited because he was going to see them for himself. And when he finally came to the place where he could look over a lake toward a snowy range, he gazed hard and said at last, "I thought they were higher, but I didn't know they were so beautiful!" The information he got, then, modified the image of mountains he had carried in his head.

We are talking about the most human skill—the ability to process information and share it with others. All animals process information to some extent, but man has developed the skill much more fully than has any other animal. He has learned to abstract his information into language, to write language and store it and multiply it so that it can be carried around to be used in his absence and so that he will have information from other people available to him in their absence. He has learned to process information that sometimes does not proceed from any other person—for example, the nature of mountains—and to use that as a basis for communication with other people and to help govern his behavior. In other words, man is above all an information-processing animal.

The internal processing takes place in the black box, and we can only infer it. But the relationship and the acts are out in the open.

## The Communication Relationship

The relationship in which communication takes place seems simple: Two people (or more) come together over a set of informational signs that are of mutual interest to them.

What can we say about this relationship? Let us return again to the situation in which the boy is talking to the girl. Who are the participants in this event? A teen-age boy and a teen-age girl? Not really. The relationship is a matter of images.

A boy, as he sees himself, is speaking to a girl as he sees her. The girl, as she sees herself, is responding to the boy as she sees him.

It is very likely that these images are by no means congruent. The boy's image of himself at that moment may be of an oafish, awkward creature whose arms are too long for his coat sleeves and who doesn't know what to do with his hands. Let's imagine that he sees the girl as beautiful, serene, queenly, and wonders how she could ever be persuaded to dance with someone like him. The girl, on the other hand, may very well be thinking of herself in quite different terms. She is perhaps wishing she were more popular with boys than she is, hoping that nobody will notice the little pimple on her chin. She may see the boy not as ungainly and awkward but as rather "cute," coming up to her as he does with his flushed cheeks and embarrassed speech. It is these images, rather than any objectively seen "boy" and "girl," that are operative in the relationship. And if we describe it from the outside, we can only describe what *we* see—a third set of images that are doubtless different from those held by either the boy or the girl.

In *The Republic* Plato wrote a beautiful description. People are in a cave, bound so that they face only a wall rather than the world outside. Behind them a bright fire burns. From time to time people move in front of the fire, and their shadows are cast on the wall of the cave. The watchers never see the people and know them only from their shadows in the flickering firelight.[4]

This is an excellent analogy to what happens in human communication. It is a shadow game. One participant never knows another as that person knows himself or knows himself as others know him. (As Robert Burns wrote, "Oh wad some power the giftie gie us to see oursels as others see us!") There is no objective fact or truth involved. Even between a husband and wife who have been married many years and doubtless feel that they know each other pretty well, even between a psychiatrist and a patient whom he has studied through many sessions, even between a reader and a skilled writer like Proust who spread his intimate thoughts and experiences over many volumes of *A la Recherche du Temps Perdu*, there is still no bridge over which one individual can walk to make contact directly with another. With communication and observation the shadow figures may become sharper and clearer, but they are still abstracted from the reality. It is still a shadow play.

There are other shadowy figures in this relationship. There is the girl's mother, who taught her how a young lady should act. There is the boy's mother, who insists that he brush his hair carefully, straightens his tie, and occasionally gives him a few last-minute directions about manners with girls. There are the girl's friends and the boy's friends, from whom both of them have probably learned more than from their parents about how young people act in social situations, and who may now be watching to see what success the boy has with his invitation. And behind the family and peer groups stand a long line of still more shadowy figures, many of whom are forgotten but who have left an imprint on the images of behavior and values that the boy and the girl carry in their heads. These include the people they have admired enough to want to imitate, those who have taught them skills or beliefs, those who have rewarded them for a certain kind of behavior and thus helped teach them customs and habits.

Into the communication relationship, therefore, each participant brings a well-filled life space, funded and stored experience, against which he interprets the signals that come to him and decides how to respond to them. If two people are going to communicate effectively, their stored experiences have to intersect over some topic of common interest. If the circles below represent A's and B's life spaces, the overlapping area, AB, is the setting for their communication.

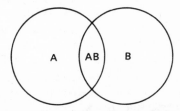

Both the boy and the girl have sections of their life spaces devoted to social manners and behavior with the opposite sex.

The motorist and the Department of Highway Safety have experience that intersects over the meaning of and expected responses to traffic lights. But if they did not—if, for example, one could imagine a motorist who came from a place where there were no traffic lights, who had never heard about traffic lights— the relationship would be a rather difficult one. And when one realizes that two life spaces are never perfectly congruent— meaning that no two individuals have ever had identical experiences and learned identical values and behaviors—it speaks well for the adaptability of the human organism that most communication relationships work out as well as they do for all of the participants.

## The Communication Contract

In a sense, the participants enter into a communication relationship with a kind of contract governing their performance. The motorist, on his part, contracts to stop when a traffic light is red, go when it is green, slow down when it is yellow. But he expects the light to go through that cycle so that all cars will have a fair chance to get through the intersection. If he waits for ten minutes while the light stays red, he will become frustrated and irritated because the motor vehicle department apparently is not living up to its side of the contract. The kind of radar behavior we described in the preceding chapter reflects a kind of social contract between individuals to identify themselves, to respond in the way expected, to confirm their social membership and sociability.

Social radar behavior is usually conducted under an implicit contract. That is, when we ask road directions we expect a simple and helpful answer. On the other hand, the person who is directing us expects us to listen carefully and to be grateful for what he has told us. When we read the news in the newspaper, we expect full and accurate coverage and a selection of topics that will be interesting, perhaps important, to us. On the other hand, the newspaper staff members expect us to buy their paper and to know enough about it to comprehend the conventions of their craft—for example, the way headlines are written. I saw a headline this morning that would certainly have mystified any reader unfamiliar with headline style. It read: CONTRACT PLAN

REPORT EYED. A person who had studied English as a second language might well conclude that he had come upon a third.

Perhaps the best way to see the significance of these unwritten contracts is by looking at the expectations people bring to relationships established to serve the communication functions we described in the previous chapter. In informational relationships the unwritten contract calls for one party to be a good reporter and the other to come in a mood to seek and test reality. Entertainment, however, requires of one party a willing "suspension of disbelief." The entertainment seeker does not require of his communication partner full and accurate reporting; he does not come prepared to be skeptical of anything that checks poorly with his picture of reality. Rather, he is prepared to go along with a story or a spoof or a good joke, to identify and agonize with a character who never lived, perhaps never could live as described. Instead of expecting simple, clear, unambiguous writing, he expects a certain kind of artistic ambiguity and is prepared for latent meanings. Poetry, for example, often uses figures of speech and incidents that would never be accepted in news, because they can be, indeed need to be, interpreted variously by different readers. Poetry wouldn't be any fun if it were as clear and definite as a road sign.

The news writer is expected to be clear and accurate; the form in which he writes or speaks is secondary to that requirement. But the way the entertainer writes or speaks is itself expected to give pleasure. He should be imaginative rather than efficient, write richly rather than clearly, tell a good story, turn a phrase or build a scene expertly. His part of the contract requires him to be, on his own level, an artist. Even a luncheon club storyteller must be an artist—skillful at imitating dialects, knowing how long to string out a narrative, knowing how to put over a punch line.

The other party to the entertainment relationship is expected to have a certain empathy with fictional characters, to go along with the conventions of films or broadcasts, to enjoy ambiguity and incompleteness rather than letting himself be frustrated by it. The old primary school question, "What did the author mean?" is out of style and perhaps never was in style with sophisticated readers or teachers. The question is rather, "What does it mean to you?" In fact, it is in works of art that one can most easily appreciate that the signs of communication exist separately from the person who made them. For nearly three thousand years people have enjoyed the *Iliad* and the *Odyssey* without knowing much about Homer. For four hundred years viewers of *La Gioconda* (the Mona Lisa) have enjoyed the portrait and read their own interpretations into it without knowing what it meant to da Vinci, who painted it.

Consider the type of communication relationship in which persuasion is the main objective. Here the persuader operates under no such contractual restrictions as the informer or the entertainer. He is on his own. To accomplish his purpose, he can select the information that fits his point and package it as he thinks best. He can use entertainment to attract atention to his messages (for example, television programs as showcases for commercials); he can try to preempt the perceptual field with large type, loud voices, parades, rallies, well-known names, and big events. He can argue, threaten, promise. He can even reward people on occasion for role playing, the way sponsors of some causes offer prizes for essays with a desired viewpoint. He is free to advance his ideas or sell his product. Caveat emptor!

But the other party to the relationship is expected to come with his defenses up. He has faced persuasion before and should be prepared to be skeptical. He is expected to ask hard questions about the claims made, especially to ask what's in it for him. He is not even required to pay attention. If the other party is someone he respects, he may well subscribe to a social contract that requires him to give attention to the arguments; for example, our social norms encourage us to listen to the arguments of the Presidential candidate of the opposing party. But we have no such obligation to listen to a salesman at the door or to a telephone pitchman, or to read "junk" mail if we do not wish to. The contractual arrangement provides that persuasion is a buyer's market.

Persuasion is distinguished from, say, the use of force or a training process like operant conditioning by the fact that it is primarily a communication process. It consists simply of introducing some information with the intention of leading the user to revise some of the pictures in his head and consequently, perhaps, some of his behavior. Therefore, it is a shadow game like any other communication, and the enormous effort and budget expended by merchants and advertisers to find out more about their audiences shows how shadowy their perception of the other participants really is.

Let us consider one more type of relationship: instruction. This clearly presupposes a contract between teacher and pupil. On his part the teacher contracts to give the pupil a systematic view of useful knowledge and to provide opportunities and guidance for him to practice what he needs to learn. These days the contract would undoubtedly specify "relevant" knowledge. The pupil, on his part, contracts to bring to the relationship a certain amount of trust in and respect for his teacher's guidance, and the willingness to engage in some learning activity. Supposedly, he comes *wanting* to learn. But one of the teacher's responsibilities is to feed the pupil's motivation. If the pupil is not motivated to learn or the teacher is unable to motivate him, one or the other has abrogated the contract.

Thus, for each of these relationships the ground rules are different, and what happens in the relationship will also take a different form.

What brings people into a communication relationship? Many times it is chance. Whom does one see on the street? What policeman happens to be on duty when one needs to ask a policeman for directions? What attractive girl is still available? What teacher is assigned to the seventh-grade science class? But it is also partly need—either a long-felt one or one that is aroused by a change in the situation. One needs to ask where 1044 Ala Moana is. One decides he needs a salable skill and signs up for a course in computer programming. One sees a tempting window display of baked goods and realizes he is hungry. And so on. Basically it is one's estimate of the probable reward of entering into a certain communication relationship as opposed to the difficulty of doing so. The reward of social radar behavior is often relatively slight—but then it is very easy to speak or nod to someone you see on the street, and it is socially expected. It might be very rewarding to own an encyclopedia, but if it costs $300 to $500 one might think hard before entering into that particular kind of communication. It would fit one's image of politeness to write a thank-you letter to Mrs. Parkman for her dinner party, but writing that kind of letter is difficult and a bit boring, and one must get ready for a lecture tomorrow, and besides it would be more fun to watch a program on television, and the pen is not working very well, and also one hates to write with pen rather than typewriter, and the typewriter is at the office, so. . . .

## The Acts of Communication

What happens inside the communication relationship? There are communication acts and a set of informational signs. (A sign is the element of communication—a sound, a gesture, a written word, a picture—that stands for information. We will discuss signs at length in the next chapter.) One participant in the relationship puts out the signs. The other makes some use of them. That, in simplest terms, is the communication process.

But it is evident that some internal activity precedes and accompanies the offering of the signs. One must feel a reason for communicating in the first place. Then, inside the black box, there must occur some information processing that results in encoding a message and giving orders to the musculatures of the body that produce the signs—spoken words, written words, gestures, or whatever. For clarity, let us call this a Type A communication act.

Information processing is also required when someone makes use of the signs—which we will call a Type B communication act. That is, someone must direct his attention to them, extract certain information from them through his sensory channels, and (in his black box) process that information, make what changes appear necessary in his stored images and his priority list of what needs doing.

When the late Wendell Johnson described this process from his psychological viewpoint, he said:

1. An event occurs . . .
2. which stimulates Mr. A through eyes, ears, or other sensory organs, and the resulting
3. nervous impulses travel to Mr. A's brain, and from there to his muscles and glands, producing tensions, preverbal "feelings," etc.,

4. which Mr. A then begins to translate into words according to his accustomed verbal patterns, and out of all the words he "thinks of"

5. he "selects," or abstracts, certain ones which he arranges in some fashion, and then

6. by means of sound waves and light waves, Mr. A speaks to Mr. B,

7. whose eyes and ears are stimulated by the sound waves and light waves respectively, and the resulting

8. nervous impulses travel to Mr. B's brain, and from there to his muscles and glands, producing tensions, preverbal "feelings," etc.,

9. which Mr. B then begins to translate into words, according to his accustomed verbal patterns, and out of all the words *he* "thinks of"

10. he "selects," or abstracts, certain ones, which he arranges in some fashion and then Mr. B speaks, or acts, accordingly, thereby stimulating Mr. A—or somebody else—and so the process of communication goes on, and on. . . .[5]

Johnson's beautifully simple exposition is aimed directly at describing what happens when two people talk together, but the process is the same whether it is a two-person group, a lecture session, a discussion group, a message carried by telephone or one of the mass media, or a President in a press conference. At the minimum there is a Type A communication act, a set of signs, and a Type B communication act. And one of the characteristics of the process is that at some instant the signs are completely separate from and out of the control of either participant. Thus the process has three distinct and separable components that can be observed, and to some extent analyzed, without having to go into the black box.

For a moment it may seem strange to think of the signs as being separate. Yet if we recall one of our common experiences with communication—mailing a letter or a manuscript and then wishing one had it back to make some changes or perhaps to reconsider whether to send it at all—we can understand this situation. When a word is said it cannot be unsaid. When a sentence is printed it cannot be unprinted. When one's facial expression conveys a certain emotion, one can't take it back. But suppose the other person in the communication relationship has not yet noticed the expression or in the split second before the sound waves travel to his ears has not yet heard the spoken words, or that the sentence is on paper yet unread, or that the Dead Sea Scrolls are waiting in a cave for someone to find them. In this interval of time, long or short, there are only light waves or sound waves or ink on paper, quite separate from either participant in the relationship.

Sometimes the process of communication seems like coaching a football team and then sending it out to play without its coach, or training and equipping an army and sending it into battle without its general. The similes are not too far off. The communicator does all he can to prepare the signs he is going to send out. If he tries to speak or write carefully, he will make use of all the strategies and skills he has learned. But then he can do no more about his signs. When he has sent them out, they are on their own. And many a message has been sent—many a letter, for example, has been carefully written and posted—leaving the sender to wonder how it would fare. Like the general, he was wondered whether his soldiers would come home with their shields or on them, whether they would do what he had intended, whether they would even attack the intended objective.

Of course, a football coach can send in a substitute or an entire new team. A general can order up reinforcements or air support. And this is also true of the communicator. He can send more words after the first ones to change his tactics. He can write another letter. He can try to express the feeling that his facial expression or manner apparently did not convey. Just as the scoreboard or the tabulation of yards gained and lost tells the coach whether his game plan is succeeding, just as the general learns from field intelligence how his tactics are working, so the communicator gets "feedback" from the other person or persons in the relationship.

Feedback is another idea derived from engineering communication theory. It means a return flow from the message. In human communication, a speaker hears his words at the same time, or practically the same time, that the other party hears them. He can then judge for himself how well he has spoken. Moreover, even before he gets a formal response from the other person he can derive some information from other behavior. If he is speaking to an audience, he can very quickly make a judgment as to how much interest they are showing and on that basis decide whether to tell a story or give an example or change his tactics in some other way. Then when the other party answers, it is rather easy to tell whether his message has been comprehended or has been persuasive. If he asks road directions and someone answers, "Yes, it is a nice day!" he has reason to think something has gone wrong, and he had better send another message to reinforce the first one. If he asks directions in English and a policeman responds, *"Je ne parle pas Anglais,"* he had better change languages. If he is talking to his wife at breakfast time and she keeps working on her crossword puzzle, he has evidence for concluding that his communication is not as compelling as it might be.

Feedback is thus a powerful tool. When it doesn't exist or is delayed or feeble—as, for example, in mass communication, when the audience is far away and personally unknown to the communicator, or when a class is required to listen to a lecture without the opportunity to ask questions—then the situation engenders doubt and concern in the communicator, and frustration and sometimes hostility in the audience. This is why the mass media and their advertising sponsors spend so much money ascertaining who is in the audience and what they think of the programs; why a few letters or telephone calls may have an effect on a broadcasting station or network quite out of proportion to their number; and why great efforts are made to supplement large lecture courses, when there must be large courses, with small discussion sections and office hours and other opportunities to question or clarify or object.

Note that feedback operates like any other communication process: It is merely a reversal of the flow, an opportunity for the communicator to react quickly to signs resulting from the signs he himself has put out. In other words, having performed a Type A communication act, he is offered the opportunity for a Type B act. He can process the information he gets from listening to his own words, rereading his own print, observing the person he is talking to, or finding out his program rating.

## The Circuit and the Acts

Studying communication behavior is like studying the sea: It may be done at any level and beyond a certain depth must be done in darkness. Yet what happens in the communication process does not have to be mysterious, nor does it need to be described in charts or diagrams. We have appended to this book a note on some of the models that have been influential in this field (with some diagrams). You may or may not want to read about those models. If you do, you are likely to find them provocative and stimulating. But here we are going to get along without any very great complexity.

Let us take as an analogy the difference between what happens on an electric light circuit and on a telephone circuit.

First, the electric light. A switch is turned, closing a circuit. This taps a source of energy, and electrons flow along a wire to a light bulb. They enter the filament and heat it, and it radiates energy that we see as light.

Is this communication behavior? Was it a *message* that flowed along the wire?

Forty years ago many people would have described communication in just that way. They believed in a "hypodermic" theory of communication—that a skillful communicator, especially if he could use the all-powerful mass media, could "inject" ideas or beliefs into an audience so as directly to control behavior. This long-abandoned belief is reflected in the term "thought transference," which the Educational Resources Information Center (ERIC) of the U.S. Office of Education, adopted to explain what they meant by their index term *communication*. ERIC should know better, because thought transference is precisely what does *not* happen in communication. One's thoughts are personal and private. Some parts of them are abstracted into signs from which another person may stimulate his own thoughts.

If there is one thing we know about human communication, it is that nothing passes unchanged in the process, from person to person. Consider the difference between the electric light circuit and what happens when two people use a telephone.

Someone picks up the phone and dials a number. A bell rings at the other end of the circuit. Someone else picks up the phone there and speaks into it. His words leave him as "sound waves" (impulses in the air), which strike a diaphragm, activate a carbon microphone, and set off electrical impulses that travel over the wire. In time they reach another instrument, where they are recoded into movements of a diaphragm that set off impulses in the air. These, if anyone chooses to listen, are perceived as sound and are in turn decoded into words and other information to be processed by the receiver. In other words, the flow is transformed at various points and "triggers" further activity.

Now, note the difference. When we turn on the light circuit, it is unbroken from the source of energy to the light filament. There is no coding or decoding, no interpretation, no change in physical nature. The energy that flows over the wire does not carry a message; it acts directly. The bulb is a passive partner. Until it wears out it responds in the same way whenever a current of adequate size and nature reaches it.

The human analogy to the light circuit is a physical act like a fist to the chin. If the blow is hard enough, it will knock the recipient back; it may knock him down. In general, the laws of conservation of energy will apply: For each action we may expect an equal and opposite reaction. The motion and force of the fist will simply be transferred to the chin.

But this does not describe human communication. True, it may be loud or obtrusive. It may have a startling effect. But it does not operate like a blow to the jaw. The sequence of cause and effect is not a simple transmission of motion from one body to another. Rather, it is a triggering effect, a catalytic process. A tiny communication may have an enormous effect, and on the other hand all the resources of national propaganda may go unheeded by the people on whom they are used.

The disproportion between the impinging force and the action produced in the receiving organism is often so spectacular that some physical scientists have questioned whether ordinary causal laws can be applied to behavioral responses like those triggered by communication. Among them was Julius Robert Mayer, one of the discoverers of the law of conservation of energy in physical transformation. He felt that the triggered reaction was an exception to ordinary physical laws and proposed a distinction between "true" causality and another sort "wherein the cause is not equivalent to the effect."[6] Suzanne Langer quoted the philosophically minded German chemist Wilhelm Ostwald as observing "that the action triggered by a stimulus drew its energy from the organism, not from the receiver, and that the physical effect, elaborate and sometimes violent as it might be, indicated the existence of complex and labile structures within the organism in which great energies were chemically bound and could be released by a small catalytic contact."[7] He suggested that there was a special kind of energy that obeyed the unknown laws of this kind of causality.

The idea that something "flows," untransformed, from sender to receiver in human communication is a bit of intellectual baggage that is well forgotten. It is better to think of a message as a catalytic agent with little force of its own except as it can trigger forces in the person who receives it. What does happen is illustrated better by the telephone than by the light circuit.

Let us go back to the telephone analogy. There is no unbroken circuit from sender to receiver. There is current flowing over the wire, it is true, but this has been transformed from sound impulses to physical movements—to electrical flow—and is transformed back into physical movements and sound waves. There would have been no sounds to encode in the first place without a person acting at the sending end of the circuit. There will be no meaning in the sound waves at the receiving end unless someone acts upon them—attends to them, interprets them, processes them, decides what response, if any, to make. And his response is limited only by the differences among individual human beings.

Therefore, it is not the electrical energy that acts on the listener, as it does on the light bulb. In fact, nothing really acts on him. The telephone circuit makes available to him a set of communication signs on which he acts as he wishes and can. He may decide to pay attention or not. He may decide to interpret what he hears in a way quite different from what was intended. He may react explosively or not at all.

Permit me to suggest a homely analogy. I have a friend in India who gets up at dawn to bake cakes, which he then sells in the marketplace. Of course, he tries to bake the kind of cakes that people have shown they like. He tries to display them attractively. He puts them out where passers-by are likely to see them. Then it is up to the patrons. The crowds move past. Some people see the cakes; some do not. Some will be hungry, looking for food; some will not. Some will be looking specifically for cakes, others not. Some have bought good cakes from this baker in the past and will consequently be more likely to buy from him again; some have not had this experience. Some will see the cakes, find their appetites stimulated, and reach into their pockets for coins; they may or may not find any. And if they buy, they may or may not eat the cakes. For example, they may suddenly be invited to lunch and may give the cakes to someone else.

Any analogy falls short. But the acts described in this last account do have some resemblance to the two different acts of communication. There is no automatic transfer of a cake from the oven of the baker to the stomach of the buyer, any more than there is automatic transfer of a message from the mind of one man to that of another. As the cake must be baked and offered, so must information be processed and offered in the form of signs. As the buyer must decide, so must the receiver of the message. He must weigh the desirability of buying and the desirability of eating. And whether he enjoys the cake, if he does eat it, will depend both on what the baker has put into it and on what he likes in cakes.

We will have more to say on this subject. But let us conclude this chapter with a few additional notes about the nature of communication acts. The most obvious quality that distinguishes them is that they are information-processing acts. A fist to the jaw may convey information, but that is not its chief content. On the other hand, a shout of "Fire!" may take as much energy as a roundhouse right, but it does not work like a blow.

Moreover, acts of communication are acts of the whole person. In her monumental work, *Mind: An Essay on Human*

*Feeling,* Suzanne Langer says that this kind of act leads one to deeper and deeper roots, and ultimately to events that belong to chemistry or electrochemistry and involve the whole organism.[8] One communicates with his whole body and draws upon all of his resources in interpreting the information he receives.

Finally, there is a symmetry, a certain wholeness, about an act of communication. Dr. Langer has written with her usual insight about this, too: the building of a store of tension that has to be spent; the beginning and the acceleration of meting out that tension, a turning point, and a closing phase or cadence in which the tension is resolved. Even in a simple act of communication, therefore, we have the model of communication as art. Even such a simple sign as a gesture may be given more artistically by a professional actor than by an amateur. A practiced speaker or writer will "turn a phrase," build symmetry and balance into a sentence so as to add a bit of beauty to its raw meaning.

## Summary: How Communication Works

Let us sum up. The process of social communication requires at a minimum two people who come together in an information-sharing relationship over a set of informational signs. The purpose of the relationship—information seeking, persuasion, instruction, entertainment, or whatever—determines the roles the participants play. For example, a person who comes for entertainment is willing to "suspend disbelief"; one who anticipates persuasion comes with his guard up. But whatever the roles, one participant, drawing on his cognitive needs and resources, and his communication skills, encodes some informational signs and offers them to the other participant. We call this a Type A communication act. If the signs are written, they may be long-lasting; if they are gestures or facial expressions or spoken words, they may be fleeting. In either case, at one point in the process they will be separate from *both* participants.

The second participant, drawing on his own cognitive needs and resources, and his communication skills, decides whether to accept the available signs, and if he does, he processes them according to his own cognitive map. We call this a

Type B communication act. The second participant is likely to encode some informal, largely involuntary signs in the form of facial expressions or other indications of interest or disinterest, belief or disbelief, understanding or lack of understanding, which the first participant can decode as feedback. If the situation calls for it, the second participant may then himself formally encode some signs and carry out a Type A communication act that may evoke a Type B communication act from the other participant. And so forth.

In other words, there is no way that a message can *directly* cause overt behavior. As we have said, it is not like a current that travels on a wire to a certain place where it turns on a light bulb. Some responses are so built into us that the action is almost automatic; for example, we respond very quickly to an automobile horn or a cry of "Fire!" But still there are intervening steps. We must hear it, and we must interpret it: "Is he blowing his horn at me?" "Where is the fire?" The only way an external sign can affect behavior is by changing one's images of the situation. Therefore, if one decides to make any use whatsoever of the message when one processes it against one's own stored images, the result is usually a confirmation of the existing picture, a slight redefinition, or clarification of some point. A complete change is as rare as conversion. But conversion does occur occasionally, and so do abrupt changes in one's perception of a situation. For example, if one is informed that one's house is on fire, that will obviously change his picture of the situation and lead to a precipitate response.

The other day I heard a sad little tale that comes closer than the fire alarm story to illustrating typical communication behavior. A wife became suspicious that her husband was more interested in a detective story he was reading than in the neighborhood news she was trying to tell him. She concluded her newscast abruptly: "And the horse ate up all our children!"

"That's fine, dear," he said, after a moment.

"Henry, did you hear a word I said?" she demanded indignantly.

"No, dear," he said, turning the page.

# iv.
# The Signs of Communication

Some years ago Arthur L. Campa recorded a little vignette that came from his long experience with teaching modern languages: the story of a Spanish-American schoolboy named Juan.

Take the case of Juan in a school somewhere in the Southwest. He has a certain amount of "amorproprio" which is mistranslated as "pride," and then because it does not mean the same in English, Juan is said to have "false pride." One day he gets into trouble with Pedro, one of his schoolmates and, there being no word for "compromise" in their vocabulary nor in their culture-content, they resort to physical arguments. The teacher insists that Juan "apologize" to Pedro for what he did. "Go on," she insists, "apologize to him." Again Juan doesn't know what to say, because there is no word in Spanish for it, nor does the apologizing custom exist. The teacher is assuming that just as words are linguistically translated, so are cultural patterns. She continues, "Tell him you're sorry." This he refuses to do because he is a product of a realistic culture, loath to change the realism of the past by the instrumentality of mere words. So he stays after school for being stubborn, disobedient, and generally incorrigible. Juan still doesn't know the meaning of "apology," but if he is intellectually curious he may look up the word in a Velasquez dictionary where he will find it mistranslated linguistically as "apologia." Not knowing this half-dollar word he looks it up in the Academy dictionary where he finds to his amazement the following definition, "Discurso en alabanza de una persona" (an utterance in praise of a person). Now he is mad at the teacher![1]

What is going on behind this sad little comedy? The teacher is trying to "communicate" some information to Juan: what she thinks of his behavior and wants him to do. She has no way of letting him look directly into her thoughts and feelings. All she can do is use certain signs that she hopes will make clear to him what those thoughts and feelings are. "Signs" is a good word because what she shows Juan is just as separate from her thoughts and feelings as a sign beside the road would be. She uses the kinds of signs available to her: English words, doubtless backed up by stern facial expressions and tone of voice. She hopes Juan will "read" in those signs the message she intends him to get.

What has gone wrong? The signs do not mean the same thing to the teacher as to Juan. Perhaps the messages of face and voice are understood more in common than the words, although even in this case the teacher probably feels that her manner indicates righteous indignation or parental disappointment, whereas Juan merely thinks she is being unreasonable. But the word-signs especially are far from being understood in common. Note that there is no more direct connection between the "communicator" and the receiver than if the teacher had handed the boy an orange or a book. The words do *not* resemble a current flowing over a wire from battery to bulb, nor do they flow like a hypodermic injection into the receiver. They are simply signs intended to carry meanings that would be responded to with certain desired behavior. And the meanings the teacher thinks she is sharing are not by any means those derived by the boy.

## The Nature of Signs

In other words, Juan and his teacher were having trouble with the signs they were using. Therefore, let us try to understand clearly what signs are.

They are the elements of human communication that stand separate and alone between the participants in the communication relationship—the elements that stand for something in the mind of one participant and, if accepted, will come to stand for something in the mind of the other. Some scholars prefer to call them *symbols*; some, *significant symbols*. Whatever they are called, they are the elements in communication that can be decoded into "meaning."

Our dictionaries are repositories of verbal signs. If we look up *signs* in *Webster's Second International*, here is part of what we find:

> Sign (OF *signe*, fr. L. *signum*; prob. akin to L. *secare*, to cut. . . .)
>
> A conventional symbol or emblem which represents an idea, as a word, letter, or mark. . . .
>
> A motion, an action, or a gesture by which a thought is expressed, or a command or wish made known. . . .
>
> A lettered board, or other conspicuous notice, placed on or before a building, room, shop, or office to indicate the business there transacted, or the name of the person or firm conducting it; a publicly displayed token or notice.
>
> In writing or printing, an ideographic mark, figure, or picture . . . conventionally used to represent a term or conception. . . .
>
> Something serving to indicate the existence of a thing. . . .

It is worth thinking a moment about how the dictionary arrived at those definitions. The editors were not arbitrary. They were not *creating* meanings. In recent years some Indian scholars have done exactly that in trying to "purify" the Hindi language by expunging words that came from Persian and inventing new words from Sanskrit roots to replace them. But *Webster's* could not get by with that. Its editors are *recording* the meanings that society has agreed upon for particular signs: common meanings. These meanings are not inherent in a sign; they come out of a public consensus on what sign shall be used to represent a particular meaning. The dictionary records something we might call the central tendencies in society's use of a particular sign.

If we read down the page in *Webster's,* we find that there are many special meanings for *sign* used in particular situations or by particular social groups. *Sign* can be used to indicate a heraldic or military device such as a banner. It can mean a constellation or a signal. It can mean a remarkable event: The ancients often thought they saw a "sign" of some deity's pleasure or displeasure. It can mean a portent or an omen. It can refer to a trace or a vestige (for example, a sign of habitation). It can be a sign of the zodiac. It can be a trace in hunting (a sign of the bear). In mathematics it is used to indicate positive or negative quantities (plus or minus sign). In medicine it is used in a rather special way (a sign of a disease). In philology it sometimes indicates an inflectional ending. In theology it sometimes refers to a manifestation of something spiritual or supernatural.

The existence of so many special uses suggests that even "common" meaning, socially agreed-upon meaning, varies considerably with experience and by social group. When one student asks another, "What is the sign of the correlation?" he is calling up a quite different meaning from that of an evangelist who says, "God has given us a sign," or for that matter from what we mean when we say that a communicator encodes a message in a set of signs—although in each case the central idea is that the sign represents something.

The central idea in all that we have quoted from the dictionary is *representation*: A sign represents "an idea," "a thought . . . command, or wish," a "conception," some otherwise hidden information such as the name of the person occupying an office. A sign stands for something.

The idea of a sign merely representing something is not an easy one. Among primitive people especially, names are often thought of as an inalienable part of whatever they refer to. In such a culture one can therefore treat names like things: Practice magic on a name and it affects the person. Vigotsky, a Russian psychologist, tells the story of a peasant who was listening to two astronomers talking about stars. The peasant said, "I can see that with the help of instruments men could measure the distance from the earth to the remotest stars and find their position and motion. But what puzzles me is: How in the devil did you find out the name of the stars?" To the Trobriander, as Wendell Johnson has pointed out, the word *ghosts* is not an abstraction for something inside his own head; it is not merely an inference and therefore testable. It is reality: There *are* ghosts.[2]

But this type of thinking is not restricted to the primitive or the uneducated. Political oratory is full of it. Symbols like the flag, words like *victory* or *national dignity* or *patriotism*, concepts like "good guys" and "bad guys," take on a life of their own that makes it extremely hard in popular usage to distinguish between the symbol and the reality behind it. This was one of the chief lessons the general semanticists taught in the 1940s and 1950s—that words are not things, maps are not territory, names are separate from what one calls by them.

How does a sign come to represent a certain meaning for us? From experience. Beginning very early in life, perception seems to be organized and meaningful. We do not for very long see pinpoints of light, formless shadows, blurring masses of color, moving and stationary masses. Krech and Crutchfield have argued this point vividly.[3] These stimuli blend into recurrent patterns. "Facts" occur but once; as Heraclitus said, a man never puts his foot into the same river twice, because the river he touched before has moved on. It is inefficient, indeed impossible, to store away and retrieve many of these momentary experiences. Therefore, one tends to observe recurrent and related patterns of experience, and very early in life one discovers the utility of having signs to call them by.

We have spoken earlier in this volume about the way signs are learned. A child is rewarded for learning them. Saying "Daddy" or "Mama" is rewarded with love and laughter and fondling and sometimes food. And gradually one comprehends the relationship of the sound one has learned to make, to the sensory impressions; "Mama" to the warmth and the perfume, the softness of skin and hair, and the source of food; "Daddy" to the booming voice, the pipe smell, the strong arms, the experience of being lifted high in the air to look around. So the sign becomes a tool to call upon the creatures who can produce these sensory impressions, and a little later when one hears the sign spoken by someone else one feels some of the same sensations as when Daddy or Mama were actually present.

For any individual, then, the meaning of a sign is the set of pictures, emotions, glandular and nervous activities that the sign calls up in him. These are similar, but not identical, to the responses called up by the referent itself. The response to hearing the name of a girl with whom one is in love is not identical to the response one makes to the girl in person. It is less, both in detail and in strength. It is abstracted from many direct experiences with the girl. It is probably contaminated somewhat by experience with other girls who have the same name as the beloved one. But the responses are still sufficient to serve as a kind of shorthand for the girl herself. One can therefore talk about her when she is not present. One can recognize her name signed to a letter. One can even say her name to oneself under a full moon with sensations somewhat different from those one would expect from repeating the name of another female—for example, Carrie Nation.

But Mary or Natasha or Akiko, or whoever she is, is a particular individual. She exists in one copy only. One can therefore classify her given name, her social security number, or some other individual designation. How does one learn the meaning of a word like *chair*, standing for something that exists in many copies. This meaning, too, must be abstracted from experiences with particular chairs. One is told, "This is a chair." He is told at another time, "Sit down on the chair," although it is a different chair. He sees his father standing behind his mother when she is seating herself at the dinner table, and his mother explains, "See how polite your father is. He pushes in the chair for a lady." And so after a while he has heard the sign often enough to know that it refers to "chairness," the common qualities of the dining room chair, his high chair, the big soft chair in the living room, the reclining chair on the porch, the picnic chair, and others, and whenever he meets the sign *chair* it calls up in him a set of responses he has learned to make to something to sit on a couple of feet above the floor.

Suppose he has lived all his life in a tent or an igloo and has never seen a chair or even a picture of a chair. Then he will not have any meaning to associate with that particular sign until someone shows him a chair or explains to him by means of other signs—pictures, words, demonstrations—what a chair is. As we grow older we learn many signs in this way. Without the ability to learn signs from other signs, we would never be able to make any practical use of words like *purity, infinite,* or *tomorrow.*

Suppose a person has lived all his life in the Arctic Circle and has never seen any kind of dog except an Arctic husky. And then suppose he is brought together with a man who has lived all his life in Central America and has never seen any kind of dog except a tiny Chihuahua. If both these individuals have learned English, they will surely have the greatest difficulty in making joint use of the word *dog.* The southerner will find it unbelievable when the northerner talks about a dog pulling his sled over the snow, and the northerner will listen with astonishment if the southerner speaks of holding his dog in his lap.

Yet this kind of misunderstanding or lack of common meaning is not far from what happens whenever two cultures meet. The difficulty experienced by a Wall Street banker and a black ghetto activist in making themselves understood to each other does not arise because they use different signs (at least not a large number of different signs) but rather because the signs mean different things to each.

We have talked about sharing. It is the *sign* that is shared rather than the meaning. Meaning is always individual, built of personal experience, a combination of responses that are doubtless not the same for any two individuals (and that we can't test completely for sameness anyway). The meaning of a sign to any individual is much more than the dictionary common meaning. Meaning is endless. The individual puts all his psychological state into the task of encoding signs. The receiver responds with his total organism. It is therefore impossible to codify or summarize meaning in its entirety. A sign is shorthand for the state of the encoder at the moment with respect to a particular matter or topic. Literally, the sender encodes himself, and that is why most communications include meaning far beyond that of the words if one is skillful enough to read the other cues. Similarly, the sender decodes his sensory impressions of the sign with his total capability. Meaning is his cognitive state at that moment, resulting from experiencing the sign.

Signs, of course, are imperfect vehicles. They are necessarily abstracted from personal experience. No set of signs can ever convey all that a person feels, all that is occurring within him. As Wendell Johnson emphasizes in *People in Quandaries,* we can never be sure we "know" how another person feels.[4] We can ask questions. We can observe actions. At one level this is relatively easy. The response to the words "Kiss me" or "Pass the potatoes" or "Send in the coupon today" will tell us quite a bit about whether the basic meaning has been understood. But this is only the tip of the iceberg; the depths of meaning that lie below any simple response to an important question are forever hidden, except as empathy and insight can support good guesses and as very skillful encoding can make the task easier.

In a sense it is two lives that are intersecting when two people share a sign. Each person brings to that relationship his stored-up experiences, the pictures in his head, his value judgments and attitudes, the responses he has learned to make to particular sensory stimuli—the personal qualities we call his frame of reference. It is hard to conceive that this would ever be exactly the same for any two human beings. And consequently meanings of signs will to some extent be different for different people, in different contexts, and even for the same person at different times. Spectacular differences in frames of reference (for example, Arctic experience vs. tropical experience) usually cause us less trouble than the small and delicate individual differences. For example, the man who knew only huskies and the man who knew only Chihuahuas would be able to reach an understanding on how to talk about dogs once they realized what the trouble was. Suppose the Chihuahua man had never seen snow; he and the man from the Arctic would probably learn how to talk about that, although one would always have a far greater depth of feeling and knowledge about it than the other. It is far from impossible for the banker to understand some of the differences between what "police" means to him and what it means to the activist from the black ghetto. It is possible

for an American journalist and a Soviet journalist to comprehend the differences in their response to the concept of press
freedom. But it is the tiny discrepancies in experience and evaluation that most often tie up human relationships. These lie
deep in experience, are sensitive and hard to explain, and often
hold people apart without either of them being quite aware of
the reason why.

A certain amount of meaning is shared widely in any society. Members of a society must agree on enough details of
denotative meaning (the kind that identifies something by nam-
ing it and can be specified in the dictionary), or else they cannot communicate. Similarly, any society must have a certain
degree of agreement on *connotative* meanings (the emotional
and value reactions—what are the pejorative words, what are
the value concepts, who are the good guys, and so forth), or
else its members would find it very uncomfortable to live
together.

In his brilliant work on measuring connotative meanings,
Charles Osgood has found that within any given culture there
are broad areas of agreement on ways of thinking about connotative as well as denotative responses, although there are
often wide differences in value judgments.[5] Osgood's approach
to this problem was most ingenious. Beginning with a large
number of polar scales or "yardsticks" such as *good-bad, strong-
weak, new-old,* and so forth, he asked people to judge a great
many word signs against each of these scales. He found that in
the United States judgments tend to cluster around three main
factors, which he called goodness, potency, and activity. Most
connotative meanings seem to be describable (in large part) in
terms of how good or how bad, how strong or how weak, how
active or how quiet the referent of a given sign is judged to be.
Judgments vary for different words and for different individuals,
but there is considerable agreement within cultures. Osgood
even considered the possibility of a "connotative dictionary,"
which would consist of average scores for different words on a
number of connotative yardsticks. Such a dictionary would
probably have to be different for each culture, although Osgood
has made studies of connotative meanings in a number of dif-

ferent countries and has found a rather surprising amount of agreement in the connotative factors used.

On the one hand, therefore, a sign triggers an individual response that is made by the whole organism out of its total funded experience and therefore is necessarily unique to each person. In that sense meaning is clearly individual and can never be expressed or shared in its entirety. On the other hand, we necessarily have to share a certain basis of denotative meanings so that members of a society can talk together, and a certain degree of connotative meaning so that the society can live in peace and comfort.

The practical significance of this is that two people are never talking to each other about exactly the same thing. If they come from different cultures, they may find important differences even in the common, socially shared meanings of signs. Until this is recognized, for example, a journalist from the Soviet Union and one from the United States will have the greatest difficulty trying to discuss concepts like "democracy" and "freedom." And even if the socially shared meanings are held sufficiently in common to avoid serious difficulty with them, still the picture a sign calls up on Mr. A's mind is never quite like the picture it calls up in Mr. B's. If one is unaware of these differences, the results may be quite unexpected!

## The Nature of Nonverbal Signs

A sign can be verbal or nonverbal, visual, auditory, tactile, olfactory. It can be speech or writing or print or picture, a gesture or a smile, a hand on the shoulder, a laugh, or a whiff of perfume. Ray Birdwhistell, one of the chief students of gestural communication, which he calls *kinesics*, has estimated that 65 percent of the "social meaning" of a situation in two-person communication is carried nonverbally. How he measures this is not entirely clear, but it is obvious that a very large part of the information derived from any human communication is derived from cues other than words.

However, there are certain restrictive features of nonverbal signs that need to be considered together with figures like those mentioned above. Albert Mehrabian, another scholar who specializes in the study of nonverbal signs, has usefully pointed out that whereas language can communicate about anything, non-verbal communication is limited in range.[6] That is, with non-verbal cues a person can indicate very subtle shades of liking or disliking, feelings about the importance of the subject being communicated, personal reactions and emotions, and the like. Pictorial cues—from line drawing to film and television—can communicate a rich combination of concrete information. Much better than words, they can tell us what something or somebody looks like or acts like, how one actually operates a machine, what one sees from a spaceship or a bathysphere, and the like. But the more abstract the subject, the more difficult it is to present it without words. Why one pushes a certain button rather than another or why a circuit is designed as it is can be explained more efficiently with words than with pictures alone, although an accompanying picture provides an unequalled practical guide for a person who actually intends to push the button or wire the circuit. "Authoritarianism" or "the past tense" can be discussed more efficiently with words than with-out, although here, as elsewhere, illustrations often contribute. It is true that saintliness is defined by a man's life and beauty by a woman's face or a Greek temple. But few people have had extended contact with a saint's life, especially one that lived some centuries ago, and therefore they tend usually to learn about his saintliness inwords; and although a picture is incom-parably more effective than words in communicating how a Greek temple or a beautiful woman looks, still when one ab-stracts on the idea of beauty, talks about what it is that makes a Greek temple beautiful or how the builders tried to make it beautiful or for what purpose it was used, then the true effi-ciency of language becomes apparent.

Edward Sapir described nonverbal communication as "an elaborate code that is written nowhere, known by none, and understood by all." That suggests another characteristic of wordless human communication: It is extremely hard to codify or put into a dictionary. This is partly because it is often bound to a situation. A shrug of the shoulders in one situation may not mean precisely what it does in another. Downcast eyes in one situation may mean embarrassment; in another, boredom;

in still another, modesty. The same gesture in one culture will not necessarily mean what it means in another. Still another reason why we see no dictionaries of nonverbal communication is that it reflects what we have called the "endlessness" of meaning. It reaches down beyond the level of words into the abyss of feeling and emotion, and therefore does not readily yield itself to description in words.

Some signs are given, some are merely given *off*. John Goffman has pointed out that signs deliberately *given* usually convey specific information (for example, pointing to something); signs merely given off—that is, not purposefully made—are usually expressive or indicative, rather than communicative cues.[7] The information they provide, however, often has a great deal to do with the impressions people form of each other. For example, some information about a young man in the American culture today may be derived from the length of his hair. As we all know, this information may be differently interpreted by different age and value groups. Information of this kind, mostly unintentional, is being *given off* constantly by all of us. Our clothes, our way of walking and speaking, our way of looking at a person, our homes, our offices, the pictures on our walls—all are telling observers something about what kinds of people we are, what we care about and are interested in.

To a student of human communication, the nonverbal cues that are given off are rather more interesting than those given intentionally. Because the individual behaves as a total personality rather than a part of his personality and the communication act reflects the whole man, much of the information given through nonverbal cues comes from deep down and is hard to suppress. Ekman and Friesen in a 1969 experiment found that judges who were permitted to view feet and leg positions and movements were better able than judges viewing only heads and faces to perceive an effect that the person filmed was trying to conceal—the subjects were in better control of what their faces were saying than what other parts of their bodies were saying. The same experimenters in an earlier study found that they could tell from photographs alone what stage of a psychotherapy interview a patient was in at the time he was photographed.

Ekman found also that judges could match head or body photographs with verbal transcripts of speech recorded at the precise time when a photograph was taken. Obviously the people in these experiments were talking with their faces and bodies as well as their voices.[8]

Thus, nonverbal signs enter into human communication in a number of different ways. For one, they often carry information without any need whatsoever of words. A painting is a total communication, and in the case of many abstract paintings even a title is as likely to be counterproductive as to be helpful. A red light on the left wing of an airplane needs no accompanying words, nor do shaken fists in angry crowds. In the second place, nonverbal signs may reinforce or expand verbal information. This is what a gesture or a pause before the key word or emphasis in speaking or a "sincere look" does for a speaker and what an accompanying illustration does for a textbook or manual.

Again, the verbal and nonverbal channels may transmit apparently incongruent cues that nevertheless have a congruent meaning. An example is the kind of humor that requires the humorist to speak or write in a serious way while he relates hilarious events, or a clown to maintain a doleful face while doing funny things, or a satirist to lead his audience through a serious treatment of a subject until the final punch line reveals that he has been making fun of his subject all the time. When the newscaster Lowell Thomas was on television, he would sometimes wink at his audience as if to say, "Let's not get too serious about this serious news; let's look at the human side of things too." Still another function of nonverbal signs is to contradict the verbal communication. This is what happens, for example, when a confident voice is accompanied by trembling hands or a hostile voice conflicts with friendly words.

Needless to say, the combination of verbal and nonverbal tracks is a classic problem of television and film, and becomes a highly complicated problem especially when one tries to design a film or a broadcast for instruction. What part of the task should the words carry? How many examples or illustrations should be used, and how often should words draw attention to parts of the picture? To what extent must the verbal and nonverbal tracks be carrying the same information at the same time lest there be distraction? These questions are obvious enough, but what may be less obvious is that the same kind of problem exists in print (the relation of the verbal content to the appearance of the page and the illustrations on it) and, in a slightly different way, in radio (the relation of the words to the voice quality, the manner of speaking, and the sound effects if any).

We have said that it is difficult if not impossible to make a dictionary of nonverbal signs. On the other hand, understanding of some nonverbal "languages" is growing. The language of facial expression is rather hard to separate from its context. In general, a smile, a scowl, or a frown has a universal meaning. But the meaning of a frown may be dislike or disapproval or puzzlement or weariness or boredom. One smile may mean something far different from another smile: The emotion it expresses may be love, happiness, amusement, kindness, graciousness, or many other things. Yet the mobility and expressiveness of the human face is one of the remarkable things about human communication. John Gunther once wrote of President Franklin D. Roosevelt (in *Roosevelt in Retrospect*): "In twenty minutes Mr. Roosevelt's features had expressed amazement, curiosity, mock alarm, genuine interest, worry, rhetorical playing for suspense, sympathy, decision, playfulness, dignity, and surpassing charm. Yet he *said* almost nothing."[9] There is little doubt that FDR conveyed this information effectively. But the situation, and what was being said by whoever was talking, clearly were essential parts of the meaning.

Linda Johnson, a student of psychology at the University of Nevada, presented to a number of experimental subjects descriptions of two fictitious persons and then asked the subjects how these men would look.[10] The two descriptions were:

> Mr. A. This man is warmhearted and honest. He has a good sense of humor and is intelligent and unbiased in his opinion. He is responsible and self-confident with an air of refinement.
>
> Mr. B. This man is ruthless and brutal. He is extremely hostile, quick-tempered, and overbearing. He is well known for his boorish and vulgar manner and is a domineering and unsympathetic person.

So Mr. A was described very positively, Mr. B very negatively. How would they be expected to look? The subjects could answer readily the questions Miss Johnson asked, and were in close agreement. Here were some of the answers:

|  | Mr. A (Positive) | Mr. B (Negative) |
|---|---|---|
| Would he look directly at you? | Direct gaze | Averted gaze |
| Would he look mostly upward or downward? | Upward | Downward |
| Would his eyes be widened or narrowed? | Widened | Narrowed |
| Would his brow be knitted or smooth? | Smooth | Knitted |
| Would his nostrils be relaxed or distended? | Relaxed | Distended |
| Would the corners of his mouth curve upward or downward? | Upward | Downward |

What this experiment emphasizes is that people learn expectations of how a "good guy" and a "bad guy" will appear. This is interesting, not only because it indicates that nonverbal cues are coming through but also because it suggests how much potential danger lies in such a degree of simplification. Even in fiction a good-looking villain can often mislead the heroine!

Birdwhistell argues that "there is no body motion or gesture that can be regarded as a universal symbol."[11] By itself, perhaps not. Pointing must come close to universality, but the object pointed at will change from situation to situation, and therefore, in effect, additional information must be added to the gesture. When an orchestra conductor raises his right arm, a hush falls over the orchestra and the audience. His gesture might not have the same effect if he were to make it in a Japanese sumo ring or on the deck of a ship. The meanings of a hitchhiker's thumb, a traffic cop's palm, a V-sign given with two fingers, are quite clear in our culture today; yet we must point out that the traffic cop might not be understood where there were no automobiles or the hitchhiker where everyone walks, and the V-sign does not mean at present what it meant when Winston

Churchill used it in the early 1940s. Nevertheless, many observers feel that, second only to the face, the hands are the most expressive part of the body. William James was one of the first psychologists to point out that unconscious impulses suppressed from verbal behavior may often be read in the motions, positions, and tensions of the hands.

The Hawaiian hula tells a story through the dancer's hands, and there is a Hawaiian song that says, "Keep your eyes on the hands." This is not the case with the faster, hip-swinging Tahitian dance. A Tahitian girl once said to me, "If you keep your eyes on our hands, you miss the message." But in both of these Polynesian dances there is a message, and it is carried nonverbally.

Allport and Vernon found that for any given individual the patterns of physical movement in handwriting, walking, and sitting were relatively congruent and expressive of the personality.[12] I once asked a famous type designer how he could distinguish so many printing types so quickly and easily. He said, "I recognize them the same way that I recognize one of my friends when I see him walking along the hilltop. He *is* his walk. I don't have to look at every detail to know it is he. The same way with Garamond. Garamond *is* the type. I can look at the page and see it. Caxton *is* the type. I see the pattern without counting all the details. Caxton type is talking to me." This is what John Goffman was saying about human behavior when he wrote, "although an individual may stop talking, he cannot stop communicating through bodily idiom."[13]

Is there a language of eye contact? Simmel said that the mutual glance is "purest reciprocity" and perhaps the kind of communication in which humans come closest to engaging in simultaneously and jointly. "By the same act in which the observer seeks to know the observed, he surrenders himself to be understood," Simmel wrote. "The eye cannot take unless at the same time it gives."[14] Barnlund listed a number of messages communicated by glances: involvement, hostility, suspicion, absence of fear, command, and others. Mehrabian concludes that the more one likes a person, the more time one is likely to spend looking into his eyes.

Is there a language of posture? Deutsch said that every person has a characteristic basic posture at rest to which he returns whenever he has deviated from it.[16] Mehrabian says that the more a person leans toward the individual he is addressing, the more positively he feels about that person. If one's posture is very relaxed, this may mean (quoting Mehrabian again) that he dislikes the person he is talking to but is not threatened by him.[17] If he feels threatened, he is likely to be very tense; if he likes the person he is talking to, he is likely to be moderately relaxed. One relaxes most with a low-status person, less with a peer, and least with someone of higher status. Body relaxation is one of the physical communicative behaviors that have been measured fairly accurately. Mehrabian says that extreme relaxation is indicated by a reclining angle greater than 20 degrees and a sideways lean greater than 10 degrees. Least relaxation shows in muscular tension in the hands and rigidity of posture. Moderate relaxation is indicated, apparently, by a forward lean of about 20 degrees, a sidewise lean of less than 10 degrees, a curve back, and, for women, an open arm position. There have been a number of such efforts to identify specifically measurable physical or facial characteristics or behaviors that indicate an emotion, attitude, or intention. Fairly detailed codes have been worked out for facial expressions, for example, yet these are somewhat less than specific. One of the more interesting attempts to use nonverbal, visual cues to predict inner states was Maccoby's effort to predict from films of a class whether students were understanding what was being taught them. The predictions were somewhat better than chance and improved when the judges (who were schoolteachers) were given instruction, but the method did not prove very useful.[18]

The language of voice is relatively easy to understand. Actors have proved that they can read the same lines in such a way as to create many different emotional impressions through slight variations in inflection, volume, or timing. Fairbanks and Pronovost, for instance, had the actors read the same paragraph so as to convey (what they intended to be) anger, fear, grief, contempt, and indifference. Students listening to the readings on tape were able to identify these emotions readily.[19] Several researchers have tried to produce "content-free" speech by running a tape at such a speed as to make it impossible to understand the words. Even in this situation it was possible in many cases to detect different emotions—for example, love as distinguished from hatred. Other experimenters have instructed actors to emphasize different parts of a paragraph by means of whatever speech tactics they felt were appropriate—pauses, loudness, and so forth. As expected, the emphasized ideas or names were the ones most likely to be remembered by listeners. Therefore, the way one speaks, no less than what one says, communicates significant information.

There is a language of apparel. In a sense, all of us wear uniforms—whether work clothes, play clothes, formal dress, police, military, clerical—and these communicate something about us and our intentions, and sometimes our respect for the person whom we are going to visit or with whom we are going out. Such dress may encourage certain actions and inhibit others in the people who see us. As Fabun says "The kind of communication that is likely to take place between one man in bathing trunks and another in formal dress is likely to be different than the communication that would take place if both were dressed alike."[20] Roger Brown wrote of "People in Harvard Square" that "If a young man has a beard or a green book bag, he is from Harvard; if he is wearing an outdoor waist-length jacket he is a city boy. Girls in dark, heavy knee-length stocking are from Radcliffe."[21] McKeachie found that use of lipstick changed the personality ratings male interviewers gave female job applicants.[22] And for a long time we have known that a young person who wears glasses tends to be judged as more industrious and intelligent than one who does not.

Is there a language of color? Fabun sums up the general conclusion: "Warm" colors—yellow, orange, red—stimulate creativity and make people feel more outgoing, more responsive to others. "Cool" colors, it is thought, tend to "encourage meditation and deliberate thought processes," and may discourage conversation. It has been suggested, says Fabun, that people should do creative thinking in a red room and then proceed to a green one to carry out their ideas![23]

A language of odor? Very little research has been done on communication through odor, although sales of perfume, soaps, deodorants, and after-shave lotions indicate that some people think odors communicate messages. One thing on which both authors and scholars agree is that odors have a profound ability to call back memories out of one's past. Food smells remind one of his mother's cooking; flower smells, of springtime long ago, and the country where he grew up, and perhaps a girl he was fond of; train smoke or hot steam still rouses the old thrill of travel. Joost Meerlo wrote a lovely essay "A World of Smells," about a return to his old home in The Hague:

> It comes to me that I am still looking for a special old tree or a fountain, for a landmark where the miracle of something far away first began.
>
> And then, around the corner, a forgotten magic greets my nostrils, the old familiar sea breeze, the wind blowing in from the ocean and filled with salty delights. From that direction once came the storm-wind we used to battle in late autumn, while making our way through the dunes and struggling against the driving rain.
>
> As I walk along I pass my old school and another potpourri of smell memories washes over me . . . the scent of wooden floors intermingled with bathroom odors and children's moist clothes that seem to cling to all schools everywhere.
>
> Further on I find the little harbor with the pungent aromas of various mercantile products—coffee, cheese, and musty wheat flour, as well as the decaying flotsam floating in the water. Here in the park the flower buds open into blossoms and waft abroad their subtlest perfumes. There down a narrow street lives a wine merchant and always when passing I would try to sniff my fill of the intoxicating odors from his shop. The same thing happened when the baker brought his fresh bread out of the oven. It set my salivary juices flowing in great anticipation.[24]

All of us know there is a language of time. When one is invited to a party in the United States, it would ordinarily be impolite to arrive more than, say, half an hour late, and unexpected, if not impolite, to be on time. A business appointment is different. If you are an hour late, you are communicating something rather unpleasant, and you would probably be received in somewhat the same spirit. On the other hand, if you are in Sweden you had better be on time for either a party or an appointment. If you are in Latin America, you will find the time sense vague, and it is not at all a communication of disinterest or dislike to be an hour late. As Fabun says, each of us and each of our cultures has a unique cultural clock, which itself communicates something about us (for example, that we get up early and work hard, that we are punctual or not, and so forth.)

And how about the language of space? We know that a slight rearrangement of furniture may produce significant changes in communication flows and in the prejudgments people make of the person to whom the home or office belongs. For example, many physicians and psychiatrists have found that patients are more at ease when there is no desk between doctor and patient. Sommer observed that college students select different seats when they are expecting a casual and cooperative situation than when they expect a competing situation in a class; in the former case, they sit close or choose a corner; in the latter, they sit in the back or choose a place opposite the likely chief competitor.

Every individual seems to develop a sense of personal space, the distance at which he prefers to interact with others. Across cultures these differences are sometimes spectacular. For example, Latin Americans like to talk close together. Many North Americans like to maintain a considerable distance. Incidents have been reported in which visitors from the "close at hand" culture have jumped over a desk to be able to speak to their host at what seemed to them a proper distance, and hilarious stories have been told of a Latin American backing a North American the entire length of a long corridor, one party to the conversation trying to get closer, the other backing away to maintain what he considered proper distance.[25]

Man-made environment has two communication effects. In the first place, it communicates information about who has made it or who lives there. In the second place, it has an effect on the kind of human interaction that occurs within it. The architect Saarinen once said that he seldom feels indifferent about a room; either it dominates him or he dominates it. "The painter, Jackson Pollock is reported to have said that when he went into a house designed by Mies van der Rohe he " felt so taut" that he "couldn't say anything."[26] And Barnlund has written about the effects of dramatically different environments for human interaction. For example, he says, "the streets of Calcutta, the avenues of Brasilia, the Left Bank of Paris, the Gardens of Kyoto, the slums of Chicago, the canyons of lower Manhattan" provide different backgrounds for human interaction, and therefore both communication and other behavior are affected.[27]

Thus, a vast amount and variety of information comes to us through nonverbal signs, although they cannot readily be systematized into precise language codes. Now let us turn to verbal signs, where language codes are somewhat more definite.

# V.
# The Codes
# of Communication

In the first chapter of this book, and again in Chapter IV, we described how language probably developed and how children seem to learn a language. We suggested that the process was based on association and the rewarding of certain verbal responses. In order not to complicate the skein of ideas at those points, nothing was said about other possible explanations, and the impression may have been left that this behavioral model is universally accepted. That is not quite the case.

The liveliest linguistic controversy in a decade has raged around the head of Noam Chomsky, a linguist at MIT.[1] In 1957, when he was barely 30, Chomsky stated a theory of grammar that challenged the assumption on which the behavorial model of language had been built. His theory was at once very new and very old, for it sought to replace fifty years of increasingly scientific language study under the leadership of scholars like Sapir, Whorf, Jakobson, and Bloomfield, and returned to philosophical ideas that were enunciated in the seventeenth century be Descartes and have been relatively little used by behavioral scientists for many decades.

Chomsky might be described as a "mentalist"; that is, he appears to believe in the separation of mind and body (with language serving to help these entities interact in the human animal). In contrast to empiricist philosophers and behavioral psychologists, who think of the human mind as a *tabula rasa* at the beginning of life, to be filled in by experience, he believes that a child enters the world with certain innate ideas, including a mental representation of a universal grammar. This enables him to learn at a very early age a human language and by a series of transformations—Chomsky's theory is known as a "transformational" grammar—to generate an indefinite number of sentences in that language. But he could not learn, as a first language, either the language of another planet that was not constructed according to his built-in grammar or an artificial language made up on some basis other than the patterns implanted in his mind at birth.

These ideas are very different from the prevailing viewpoints in the field of linguistics. In contrast to structural linguists, who are interested primarily in classifying language behavior and establishing linguistic taxonomies, Chomsky and the other transformationists are chiefly interested in the philosophy of language. In contrast to psychologists and anthropologists, who are interested in language as a manifestation of culture and human behavior, they are scornful of behavioral research, preferring to "think out" the linguistic propositions they state. Asked by Ved Mehta in a recent interview whether he had ever studied children to find out how they acquired language, Chomsky answered, "No, I hate experiments." "We have a certain amount of evidence about the grammars that must be the output of an acquisition model," he said in 1966 at a scholarly debate in Boston. "This evidence shows clearly that knowledge of language cannot arise by application of step-by-step inductive operations (. . . association, conditioning, and so on) of any sort that have been developed or discussed within linguistics, psychology, or philosophy."[2]

Chomsky's insistence on a mentalist position brought him into conflict with empiricist philosophers. During a discussion with Chomsky on BBC's Third Programme, the conflicting positions were stated neatly by Stuart Hampshire, the Oxford philosopher:

We have a traditional philosophical claim—the claim of empiricist philosophy . . . from the eighteenth century onwards—that language is learnt by association of ideas and by reinforcing responses, that concepts are formed in this way by abstraction, and that our grammar is a cultural phenomenon that varies with different cultures, with no common underlying structure and no necessity to prefer one structure to another; and then one has a contrary philosophical tradition [the rationalist one], that there are predispositions to form certain ideas and to organize concepts in a certain order, and even more strongly, that these ideas can be stated in a propositional form. . . .

The empiricist tradition . . . has always denied that there was anything that could be called innate ideas, meaning by this substantive propositions, beliefs as opposed to predispositions to behave in certain ways. Supposing one found that there were preferences for certain sound orders or word orders that really were very general, this might seem a feature of human behavior which in no sense upsets the empiricist's picture—any more than it would if there were a predisposition to represent a scene on a piece of paper, given a pen, in a certain way. . . . I suppose that the contrast here, which empiricists would insist on, would be between knowledge in the sense of propositional knowledge, which is said [by Chomsky] to be innate, and features of behavior, such as the tendency to represent on paper a solid body in a certain way, which may greatly vary culturally.[3]

Many others, in addition to Hampshire, have argued this matter with Chomsky. Thanks to his formidable polemics and the striking quality of his ideas, he has come out of these encounters very well. His basic idea—that specific language-learning mechanisms are innate in a human being—is widely accepted among linguists, although there is by no means general agreement on the precise nature of the internal grammar.

The philosophical controversy over Chomsky (in contrast to the technical controversy over his transformational grammar) might be viewed as a part of the heredity-environment controversy and like other aspects of that argument is likely to be resolved by deciding that part of human language learning depends on genetic inheritance, part on behavioral experience and rewards. It does seem remarkable that a child can learn to distinguish the boundaries between sounds, and to indentify the contrasts in sounds that are crucial, and thus to master a double level of symbols—particular sounds combined into meaningful words —so very early in life. As we have remarked, this is truly one of the great intellectual achievements in every human career, and it occurs and develops with almost unbelievable speed during the years when, in every other respect, the learner is an infant dependent on adults. It is therefore not hard for anyone to believe that a child brings with him into the world certain qualities that make it easier for him than for other animals to learn a human language. The question at issue is really *what* is built into him: abilities or predispositions, or propositional knowledge such as an inherited basis for a particular grammar.

Furthermore, it is rather remarkable that so much similarity exists among the structures of various human languages. For example, there is a strong tendency to put the subject first in a sentence. If a language has developed or retained case endings, subject and object can be distinguished by their inflected endings and there is a tendency to place the verb last (as in German or Hindi). On the other hand, if most inflections have disappeared, as in English, it is usually necessary to place the verb where it can help distinguish object from subject. Greenberg has pointed out a number of apparent "universals" in language structures throughout the world.[4] This seems all the more significant when one considers how the linearity of human language contrasts with the lack of such order in perceptual experience, a point McLuhan makes again and again. Thus, human language is a human code imposed on experience, and it is perfectly reasonable to inquire whether there is not something inherited from the millenia of human experience that makes it easier for new members of the species to learn this artificial code.

Does the innateness hypothesis mean that there was one original human population and one original language? Hilary Putnam, a philosopher at Harvard, argues this strongly:

Suppose that language-using humans evolved *independently* in two or more places. Then, if Chomsky were right, there should be two or more types of human beings descended from the two or more original populations, and normal children of each type should fail to learn the languages used by the other types. Since we do not observe this . . . we have to conclude (if the Innateness Hypothesis is true) that language-using is an evolutionary "leap" that occurred but *once*. In that case it is overwhelmingly likely that all human languages are descended from a single original language.[5]

Thus, not only have Chomsky's theories had an enormous impact on the modern study of language, but they lead us back, so to speak, all the way past the Tower of Babel to the Garden of Eden.

The search for the aspects of language behavior that are innate and those that are learned will probably not be successful until we know more about human behavior itself. Chomsky has been compared to a man studying a computer from its output alone. From the output of the machine, he deduces propositions at a deeper and deeper level until he reconstructs the mechanism of the machine and the way it operates. Ultimately he is able to say what must have been the input to the machine. And although language behavior is indeed one of the most powerful devices we have by which to study the operation of the human central nervous system and other kinds of human behavior, this relationship is two-way: As we learn more about the process and origins of human behavior generally, we will be able to see more clearly into the depths of that sophisticated type of behavior we call language.

## Verbal Signs and Codes and the Whorf-Sapir Hypothesis

We usually think of language as a system of informational signs used in a generally uniform way by the members of a society. Thus, there are many kinds of languages. We usually think first of verbal languages, the kind we refer to, for example, as English, French, Chinese, or Swahili. But for some pages we were talking about nonverbal languages, some of which at least are systems of informational signs that are interpreted in about the same way by all members of a culture. It is possible to think also of a language of mathematics. For example, $a = \sqrt{b^2 + c^2}$

is systematic and meaningful, and is used in about the same way by all mathematicians. Signs like *e* and *m* have special meanings for mathematicians and physicists that they do not convey to the uninitiated. It might also be argued that there is a language of art or at least a grammar of art, although this is less obvious. And certainly there are special languages for special groups. Bookies, scientists, ghetto minorities, and even some families develop words of their own and ways of conveying meaning in a private manner that would be incomprehensible to non-members of the group.

The key word here is *group*. Just as meaning comes from experience in a widening circle of groups, so is language learning one of the first steps in socializing a child to be a member of a group. John Carroll, a psycholinguist remarked on this achievement in a recent paper:

> Children progress from diffuse babbling, to the babbling of recognizable consonant and vowel sounds, to the production of words, then two-word sentences, to the construction of simple grammatical sentences by the end of the third year. This is a remarkable feat considering that young children receive little direct language instruction and that linguists have yet to develop a theory of language structure that can generate the almost infinite possible constructions of which natural language is capable, even though children of all language communities learn to comprehend and produce such constructions.[6]

By a continuing process of social experience and social reinforcement, children accomplish the astonishing feat of actually learning a language before they achieve mastery of many simpler behavioral skills. Language is the first subtle tool of learning they possess. This raises one of the most important questions of human communication: Does not a person's language determine how he processes the information he gets from experience?

This is the so-called Whorf-Sapir hypothesis. Whorf argued that humans dissect nature along lines laid down by their native languages. Consequently, language serves not only as a channel of learning but as a filter for what is learned. Sapir said,

> Human beings . . . are very much at the mercy of the particular language which has become the medium of expression for their

society. It is quite an illusion to imagine that one adjusts to reality essentially without the use of language and that language is merely an incidental means of solving specific problems of communication or reflection. The fact of the matter is that the "real world" is to a large extent unconsciously built up on the language habits of the group. . . . We see and hear and otherwise experience very largely as we do because the language habits of our community predispose certain choices of interpretation.[7]

It seems only common sense that language should serve to some extent as a lens through which we view the world and a filing system for the meaning we abstract from sensory experience. Whorf gives as an example the Hopi language, which does not distinguish as English does between verbs and nouns. *Man, house, lightning, mountain* are nouns; *run, jump, hit, speak* are verbs. The Hopi people look at things differently: How long do they last? Words like *lightning, wave, flame, puff of smoke*, which are of short duration, cannot be anything but verbs. Nouns are longer-lasting things: *man, mountain, house.* Similarly, Hopi has a noun that covers everything that flies except birds, which are denoted by another noun. The Hopi actually call *airplane, aviator,* and *insect* by the same word and feel no difficulty about it. This Whorf sees as evidence that through their language they organize their world of experience differently from numerous other cultures

He points out that an Eskimo would find it almost impossible to limit his reference to snow to a single all-inclusive word. The Eskimo has different words for *falling snow, slushy snow,* and still other kinds and manifestations of *snow.* The Aztecs, on the other hand, represent *cold, ice,* and *snow* by the same word with different terminations. Someone else has pointed out that Arabic has about six thousand words related to "camel," words that for the most part are unknown to cultures where there are few camels and consequently represent different ways of coding human experience with camels.[8]

On the other hand, this concept of language as a determinant of one's knowledge of reality is by no means accepted by all linguists. It has proved a very difficult proposition to research, and much of the scientific evidence one would like to see is not yet in. But scholars like Brown and Lenneberg argue that the fact that English has only one word for *snow*, in contrast to the multiple words for *snow* in Eskimo, does not indicate that English speakers are unable to discriminate between these different manifestations of snow but rather that it is not so important to them as to the Eskimo and that consequently they have not felt the need of many different words for it. Similarly, the Aztecs have much less experience with snow than do either Eskimo or English-speakers and can get along with still fewer terms. Americans don't see camels very often and hardly need six thousand camel-related words of Arabic.

The question centers around causality. How much does language affect one's processing of information, and how much do one's needs to process information affect one's language? Is there, perhaps, an interaction? An Eskimo needs more words for snow and an Arab more words for camel-related topics in order to process a great amount of information about these two subjects efficiently. If Americans and Aztecs had such needs, might they also create multiple codings? Scientists have created a number of their own words, many at a very high level of abstraction, in order to handle efficiently the kinds of information they must process. A nonscientist entering a scientific meeting may feel that he too is hearing a strange language and that scientists must perceive the world differently from other men. Thus the need of any culture to process information from a given kind of experience must determine to some extent what linguistic forms are developed. And when these forms are in use, is it not possible that they will tend to guide the patterns of abstracting and even what information is coded? For example, will a scientist not tend a code in existing terms when possible rather than creating new ones?

Take, for example, the Hopi treatment of time to which we have already alluded. It is hard to say that this is not related to the relative lack of time pressure on the Hopi culture. But once given a set of categories such as the Hopi culture has developed for its language, would there not be certain difficulties in communicating with another culture about questions in which time was essential? Whorf has written interestingly about what kind of science might be developed out of Hopi categories and how scientists from that background might interact with scientists from a Western culture. "Hopi grammar," he says,

. . . makes it easy to distinguish between momentary, continued, and repeated occurrences, and to indicate the actual sequence of reported events. Thus the universe can be described without recourse to a concept of dimensional time. How would a physics constructed along these lines work, with no $T$ (time) in its equations? Perfectly, as far as I can see, though of course it would require different ideology and perhaps different mathematics. Of course $V$ (velocity) would have to go too. The Hopi language has no word really equivalent to our *speed* or *rapid*. What translates these terms is usually a word meaning *intense* or *very*, accompanying any verb of motion. Here is a clue to the nature of our new physics. We may have to introduce a new term $I$, intensity. Every thing and event will have an $I$, whether we regard the thing or event as moving or as just enduring or being. Perhaps the $I$ of an electric charge will turn out to be its voltage, or potential. We shall use clocks to measure some intensities, or, rather, some *relative* intensities, for the absolute intensity of anything will be meaningless. Our old friend acceleration will still be there but doubtless under a new name. We shall perhaps call it $V$, meaning not velocity but variation. Perhaps all growths and accumulations will be regarded as $V$'s. We should not have the concept of rate in the temporal sense, since, like velocity, rate introduces a mathematical and linguistic time. Of course we know that all measurements are ratios, but the measurements of intensities made by comparison with the standard intensity of a clock or a planet we do not treat as ratios, any more than we so treat a distance made by comparison with a yardstick.

A scientist from another culture that used time and velocity would have great difficulty in getting us to understand these concepts. We should talk about the intensity of a chemical reaction; he would speak of its velocity or its rate, which words we should at first think were simply words for intensity in his language. Likewise, he at first would think that intensity was simply our own word for velocity. At first we should agree, later we should begin to disagree, and it might dawn upon both sides that different systems of rationalization were being used. We would find it very hard to make us understand what he really meant by velocity of a chemical reaction. We should have no words that would fit. He would try to explain it by likening it to a running horse, to the difference between a good horse and a lazy horse. We should try to show him, with a superior laugh, that his analogy also was a matter of different intensities, aside from which there was little similarity between a horse and a chemical reaction in a beaker. We should point out that a running horse is moving relative to the ground, whereas the material in the beaker is at rest.[9]

It is not necessary at this moment to accept or reject absolutely the Whorf-Sapir hypothesis, certainly not to consider that it is proved or disproved—which it clearly is not, so far as research goes. What is necessary is to recognize the extraordinarily close relation of language to culture. Culture is to language as an individual's personality is to his communication. Cultural needs to process information determine, over a long period, what form a language takes. When one culture meets another, it often happens that new words, new linguistic forms, are borrowed by one culture from the other along with new ideas and concepts. An individual grows up in a culture speaking the language of that culture and consequently processing information in the terms and categories and relationships common to that culture. What this means essentially is not so much that his way of seeing reality is being affected by a language as that he is being socialized into a culture. He is growing up as a man of that culture, accepting its viewpoints and its customs and its world-view. These are very deep in a man. In every communication, therefore, he brings his culture along with him, and it is reflected in and through his language.

It is impossible to discuss language in any very deep way here or to suggest the analyses that have been made of it in recent decades by a group of really first-rate linguistic scholars. Readers who want to sample the literature could well start with the introduction to different linguistic viewpoints in the first chapter of Chomsky's 1968 book.[10] In the next few pages, however, we can at least suggest some of the problems that this flexible, sensitive tool of human communication poses for its users.

## Some Problems of Language

As Sassure has pointed out, human language really has two components: the one we usually call language, which is the unifying element of all the language behavior that goes on around it and a second component that Sassure and others have chosen to designate as *speaking*—the particular acts of using language *actes de parole*.

Language itself, in these terms, is a kind of social norm, a part of the codified culture, a system of agreed-upon signs that can be put into a dictionary and a grammar. Language behavior, on the other hand, is an individual act. It conforms to the practice of the language community and may vary considerably from the dictionary and grammar language. Language, in effect, is a kind of hypothetical construct put together by linguists and grammarians to account for the verbal communication that was going on long before language was systematically analyzed, the kind that every child learns before he learns to write a sentence or talk about sentence structure.

None of us speak a formal language; we speak the language we have heard, the sounds and patterns in the use of which we have been reinforced. When we learn to write, we come closer to using a formal language (in many cases too formal), but even here we vary from the norm. If enough of us vary, the norm changes, because formal language follows human communication rather than the reverse.

The picture of language behavior that a visitor from another planet would doubtless carry away with him (if he were given a grammar and a dictionary and then permitted to wander around a language community listening and talking) would be of a system of signs corresponding to what we might call in statistical terms a central tendency. This central tendency is the formal language. But as our interplanetary visitor moved from place to place, person to person, he would observe great variations around it.

Consider, for example, the varieties of English word-sounds he would listen to in the course of a brief motor tour through the shires of Britain, from London to York to Scotland. Consider how puzzled he might be at some of the contextual variations on verbal meanings. For example, "I love fish" might mean in an aquarium that someone is fond of the finny creatures swimming around in the tanks. In a restaurant, it might mean that someone thinks cooked fish are delicious. When he has mastered that difference, he hears someone called a "poor fish!" and wonders which aspect of fishiness that refers to. He then begins to meet usages like "I'd love to," "Love that tune," "My little love," and "I love you." There is a high probability that he would not translate the last of these phrases into, "I think you are delicious when cooked," but such contextual differences would hardly make communication between cultures and subcultures any easier. Our visiting Martian might need help in translating "Hudnathernex," heard on the New York subway system, into "Hundred and third street next." He might take a little while to grasp the distinction among "What are you doing?" "What *are* you doing" and "You are doing *what*?" And when he returns home he might write a learned article about the meaning or meanings of "you know," which occurs so often in the speech of today's younger generation. If he began with the formal language, therefore, he would spend much of his time finding his way outward from it.

Strangely enough, one of the greatest strengths of verbal language is also one of its greatest problems. This is its ability to work at so many levels of abstraction. On the one hand, different levels of abstraction make it possible to talk about the same topic (at a different rate) to a child and a Ph.D., to code as much information into a particular sign as one wishes to, and to bounce easily back and forth between reality and the philosophical question of what reality is. Some years ago, S. I. Hayakawa devised what he called a "ladder of abstraction" in order to illustrate the different levels at which human thought and discourse could operate. This is the way, he said, that "Bessie the cow" would be seen at different steps on the ladder:

1. The microscopic and submicroscopic cow known to science
2. The cow as we perceive it
3. Bessie—the name we use to identify the particular object we perceive

4. Cow—a sign we use to stand for the characteristics of "cowness" we have abstracted from Bessie and all the other cows we have perceived or learned about

5. Livestock—a still higher abstraction, standing for the characteristics cows have in common with pigs, chickens, sheep, etc.

6. Farm assets—a sign to represent what livestock has in common with other salable items on the farm

7. Asset—what farm assets have in common with other salable items

8. Wealth—a degree of assets, that may include the value of Bessie, but also a great deal more[11]

The farther one climbs on this ladder, the more the particular characteristics of Bessie are submerged in the total meaning. This is what gives human language its ability to code *different amounts* of information into a single sign. One can work at the most concrete or the most abstract level. One can talk about a particular cow (or a biological part of it). One can code that cow under a sign that lets one retrieve his picture of that particular cow, distinguished from other cows he may know (Helga, Jane, Empress Helena, or whatever *their* codes may be). Or he can go up the ladder and code more and more items and experiences together.

In one respect this is marvelously efficient because it greatly speeds up information processing. It is a great deal easier and quicker to say or think "farm assets" than to name Bessie the cow, Helga the cow, George the goat, 76 hens and 8 roosters, the tractor, the barn, and perhaps thousands of other things that the abstract term includes. But on the other hand, when you and someone else are standing beside Bessie and talking about her, there is relatively little doubt that both of you will be talking about the same thing, whereas an abstraction like *assets* may be interpreted variously—perhaps differently by the tax collector than by a prospective purchaser, and by little-educated people not understood at all. Thus, at the abstract end of the ladder one can handle information faster, but for fewer people and with greater risk of misunderstanding; at the other end, one can communicate with a wide range of people, but not very economically. Most scientific talk (scientists talking to other scientists) tends to be at a high level of abstraction; most practical, everyday talk tends to be at a low level of abstraction to make it easy for everyone to participate.

Talk about politics and values rapidly climbs into abstractions that make for misunderstanding and the introduction of emotionally loaded words. Wendell Johnson gave an example of how this happens:

> If your radio, your car, or your electric ironer does not function properly you consult a tradesman, a mechanic of some sort, and in the conversation that is carried on by you and the mechanic a language is used that is remarkable for its straightforward effectiveness, its expression of sheer sanity on the part of both of you, and especially on the part of the mechanic. You do not call a spark plug by forty different "respectable" names, and neither of you blushes when talking about the generator. Nor do you consider it a personal insult and become angry when the mechanic tells you that one of your tubes is dead. There is a minimum of identification of the words you use with the facts you are talking about, or of "self" with the realities to be dealt with.
>
> At any moment, however, all this can change appallingly. . . . The two of you might fall to talking about politics or religion, for example. The mature sanity which both of you had been exhibiting a moment before may well vanish like a startled dove. A kind of sparring attitude is likely to reveal itself in your conversation. And unless one, or preferably both, of you is very tactful, one, or probably both, of you is going to identify "yourself" with the remarks being made, and the remarks being made with that about which presumably they are being made. . . . You will be fortunate if one, or probably both, of you does not secretly or openly conclude that the other is a "red" or an "atheist."[12]

One secret of effective communication is the ability to keep one's language within the level of abstraction that the audience can handle and to vary the levels of abstraction within it so that the more abstract parts are built on a concrete base and the reader or listener can move easily from a simple and homely image to an abstract proposition or summary and back again if necessary. If you look carefully, you will perhaps be surprised at the high number of simple words and concrete images in the writing even of great poets and novelists, and of some of the greatest philosophers and historians. It is the stuffy writer, the self-conscious writer, unaware of his audience or trying to impress an audience of his peers who searches for the uncommon, the multisyllable word and the highly abstract formulation.

Finding appropriate levels and amounts of abstraction, then, is one of the problems we have in using our language. Another is what we might call the tendency toward "simplistics." When we are faced with complex ideas and highly abstract discourse, we tend to simplify our coding of these by any means possible. One of the devices we use, unfortunately—is what semanticists call the two-valued orientation. We tend to code concepts, ideas, and people as *either this or not-this*—good or bad, friend or enemy, a success or a failure—avoiding fine discriminations or the admission that something can be partly this or party not-this. We boast of our ability to consider *both* sides of a question, conveniently forgetting that a third side— or even a twenty-fifth side—may very possibly exist and be worth our attention. As Johnson says, viewed against what Karen Horney calls the "neurotic personality of our times," this is not a healthy symptom.[13] It makes for rigidity in person and in policy.

Another kind of simplistics is the creation of symbolic images to code parts of the torrent of information that flows past us. Kenneth Boulding noted in his book *The Image* that the human imagination can bear only a certain degree of complexity; when the complexity becomes intolerable it retreats into simplifying behavior such as symbolic images. A symbolic image, he says,

> is a kind of rough summation or index of a vast complexity of roles and structures. These symbolic images are of great importance in political life, and especially in international relations. We think of the United States, for instance, as Uncle Sam; of England, as John Bull; or of Russia as a performing bear. These symbolic

images are particularly important in the summation and presentation of value images. Value images do not usually consist of a long and detailed list of alternatives in a carefully compiled rank-order. They consist, rather, of a "posture" which in a sense summarizes an extremely complex network of alternatives and situations. In Christianity, for instance, the symbol of the Crucifix or of the Virgin has exercised an enormous evocative power through the centuries because of the way in which these symbols summarize a whole value system, a whole attitude toward life and the universe. Political images do the same thing at a different level. The creators of these symbolic images exercise quite extraordinary power over the imaginations of men and the course of events. Consider, for example, the image of the political party in the United States.

The Republican Party is conceived as an elephant, rather old, rather dignified, a little slow, not perhaps terribly bright, but with a good deal of wisdom, hard working, full of integrity, rather conservative, a little isolated from the world around him, patient, thick-skinned, but capable of occasional inarticulate squeals of rage. The Democratic Party is thought of as a donkey, active, agile, clever, a little unsure of himself, a bit of an upstart, quick, sensitive, a little vulgar, and cheerfully absurd. These images are reiterated by cartoons and have been of great importance in establishing the political climate.

In international relations, the symbolic image of the nation is of extraordinary importance. Indeed, it can be argued that it has developed to the point where it has become seriously pathological in its extreme form. The national symbol becomes the object of a kind of totem-worship. Cartoons and political speeches continually reinforce the image of roles of nations as "real" personalities—lions, bears, and eagles, loving, hating, embracing, rejecting, quarreling, fighting. By these symbols, the web of conflict is visualized not as a shifting, evanescent, unstable network of fine individual threads but as a simple tug-of-war between large opposing elements. This symbolic image is one of the major causes of international warfare and is the principal threat to the survival of our present world.[14]

It goes without saying that most of the leaders who would manipulate public opinion today are themselves expert, or have access to experts, in the creation of simplified images and slogans of the kind Boulding is talking about. And therefore one of the problems of public communication today is to be willing and able to look behind these stereotyped simplifications and measure them against the complexities of one's own experience with reality. Reality is complex. Simplistic language often makes it harder rather than easier to grasp reality. A productive communication relationship must therefore balance between the two extremes. It must be on levels of abstraction where the participants can comfortably work and must include enough examples and illustrations to anchor the abstractions.

Ultimately we ourselves are responsible for the kinds of pictures of reality we are able to store away to guide our behavior. We need rather special services from the mass media, the educational system, and other suppliers of our information, but we must *demand* it of them. This requires us to maintain a critical stance and a balanced response. Every writer on semantics remarks on how seldom one meets a person who listens patiently and attentively, and "asks questions as though he were really listening and not as though he were watching for an opening to take over the conversation." (The quotation is from Wendell Johnson.)[15] How often we suspend our critical faculties in the presence of resounding oratory, fine writing, an impressive television presence! "Some people," says Hayakawa, stop listening "to *what* is being said," and seem to be interested "only in what might be called the gentle inward message that the *sound* of words gives them. Just as cats and dogs like to be stroked, so do some humans like to be verbally stroked at fairly regular intervals. . . . Because listeners of this kind are numerous, intellectual shortcomings are rarely a barrier to a successful career in public life, on the stage or radio, on the lecture platform, or in the ministry."[16] One thing we can do is to discriminate between the different ways that something is *said* to be true. Hayakawa gives these examples:

> Some mushrooms are poisonous (a statement that has been scientifically verified)
> Sally is the sweetest girl in the world (at least that's what someone thinks)

All men are created equal (this is a directive which we think should be obeyed)

$(x + y)^2 = x^2 + 2xy + y^2$ (means that this statement is consistent with the system of statements that can be made in algebra)[17]

To which we might add:

This is the party of the people (means that election time is coming around again, not any particular difference in parties)

To err is human. We cannot expect perfection of ourselves. And yet human frailty is more responsible than deficiencies in language for the imperfect lens we turn on the world around us. Let us conclude with one more example of how some of our human characteristics keep us from using language to perceive a balanced picture of reality. Some years ago a funny-bitter few minutes on BBC's "Brains Trust" program poked fun at the way many people build their pictures of the world around themselves. Bertrand Russell "conjugated" what he called an "irregular verb." It went like this:

> I am firm.
> You are obstinate.
> He is a pig-headed fool.

Later the *New Statesman* and *Nation* ran a contest for similar "irregular verbs." Here are some entries they received:

> I am sparkling.
> You are unusually talkative.
> He is drunk.

> I am righteously indignant.
> You are annoyed.
> He is making a fuss about nothing.[18]

Let it not be thought, however, that we too are "making a fuss about nothing" in making so much of problems of human language behavior. Language is a beautifully engineered instrument. But even a Ferrari or a Mercedes has to be driven and sometimes tuned up. In fact, the finer the instrument the greater the invitation to skill. Human language asks the same of its users.

# vi.
# The Pathways
# of Communication:
# Who Talks to Whom

Try sometime to make a list of all the people you would be able to call by name if you saw them. You will find that the list will be a kind of map of your life. Everywhere you have lived or studied or worked you have left a trail of acquaintances. Names will cluster around the places where you have spent the most time, around the relationships that are most important and necessary to you, and the list will thin out with distance and time.

But when you have written down the hundreds of names on your list, you will have only begun to make a map of your communication. There are hundreds or thousands of persons with whom you have communicated but whose names you have forgotten. There are countless persons whom you have met, and in some cases come to know well, through books and other mass media. There are organizations and individuals whom you have met less personally through such forms of communication as STOP signs, advertising, income tax forms, or such culture cues as the way a lawn is mowed or the statues carved above a cathedral door. There are many communications you have overheard, such as a song drifting up from the beach or a quarrel in the next apartment. And finally there is the silent talking all of us do to ourselves, which we sometimes dignify by calling it *thinking* and which uses the same signs one would use in talking with someone else. As a matter of fact, this last communication activity probably fills more time in our experience than any of the others.

This, then, is what the map of any individual's communication looks like:

1. A great deal of internal communication—talking to oneself, thinking things out, remembering, deciding, dreaming
2. Communication with people socially close to one—family, friends, neighbors
3. Communication within one's work group
4. What might be called "maintenance" communication required by the way one lives and the society one lives in—with tradesmen and service people; with doctor, dentist, lawyer; with barber, filling station operator, taxi driver; with government people such as the tax collectors, the Department of Motor Vehicles, the police and fire departments (fortunately seldom)
5. Communication with casual acquaintances, business and social
6. Communication with (mostly *from*) personalities known chiefly through books and the mass media
7. Finally, a great mass of information from anonymous sources in the media, reference books, and all the miscellaneous cues of the culture through which one moves every day.

Of course the pattern varies with the individual. Some will have more communication with friends and neighbors; some will be reclusive. Some will communicate as a result of wider experience over longer pathways. Some will read the great books; others will simply watch television.

## The Wide-Angle Lens

So much for the individual map. Now, what would we see if we could view human communication with sufficient perspective to see it as a society-wide network of connected individuals and institutions—if we could look at it, for example, as we might a telephone network or a computer system, with lights indicating what circuits are in use?

We would see communication flowing over an almost infinite number of circuits. For any individual most circuits, the most-used ones, lead to other individuals near him. But there are some very long hookups: postal service, telephone, telegraph, and travel. Throughout the system are placed what in an electronic network we might call amplifiers. These are the mass media organizations—the schools, the libraries, the wire services, and other institutions and organizations—into which many circuits flow and which have the function of filtering out the input and producing a very large output of relatively few messages that go to many receiving points. Each of these institutions has its own internal communication network. On these networks and along the interpersonal chains of communication, we see smaller amplifiers: individuals who serve special functions in passing on communication—teachers, reporters, broadcasters, preachers, public information men, authors, advertising specialists, travelers, gossips, and many others.

Observing this network as a whole, we should be able to identify patterns. There is the casual everyday flow of information—the greetings, the social invitations, the traffic lights, the names read on office doors, the uniforms on policemen, the telephone books and street maps that help make it easy to live in modern society. There is also a long-range flow of news and interpretation that comes often to the wire services and the mass media, and lights up for a time the channels of most individuals each day. There are institutions like the schools that also light up a number of information circuits regularly. This pattern of flow corresponds to the basic brain waves that pass through an oscilloscope when an individual is in a state of activity sufficient to maintain the organism rather than meet any special challenges.

But one would also observe, in addition to the even and measured flow of everyday communication, that from time to time circuits light up like a Christmas tree in one part of the network or another, and these may trigger some special activity elsewhere. What is happening in those cases?

A neighbor falls ill. The doctor is called, perhaps an ambulance. Concerned inquiries and offers of help flow to the family. If the case is serious enough, there may be some emergency activity at a hospital or a clinic. Medicine is ordered from a pharmacy. Possibly some of the neighbors are impressed enough to go to their own doctors for a checkup.

A house catches fire. A frantic call goes to the fire department. Spectators gather. There are messages of sympathy and offers of help. A newspaper reporter interviews the fire chief, the owner, the person who first saw the flames. The insurance man is called in. The incident is discussed in many places. The owner seeks estimates and advice: Should he rebuild or repair? Where should he live in the meantime?

An election is called. The newspapers speculate about candidates. The political parties gather, first in leadership groups, then in larger assemblies, to talk about candidates and issues. Candidates offer themselves, speak at meetings and on radio and television. Primary elections and nominating conventions are held so that party members can speak their wishes. Communication boils for a few months around personalities and issues. The candidates visit, speak, are interviewed, get their pictures on posters and in the media, and become well known. Public opinion polls are conducted to try to predict the result. The media report what is happening, what is said, argue the issues back and forth. Doorbells are rung, materials handed out, promises sought. Persuasive materials go through the mail. Housewives organize "coffee hours." People discuss. And then finally the election day arrives and the voters, who have been spoken to so much for so long, now speak for themselves.

Communication flows where it is needed in society. It warns of dangers and tells of opportunities. It assembles the resources of society to meet emergencies. It aids in decision making. It informs, educates, entertains as needed. Some of these needs require little variation in the everyday flow over the network. Some are larger. Some are so large that they nearly take over the network. A San Francisco earthquake requires more from the network than does a single house afire. If an astronaut actually returned with an incurable "Andromeda strain," that information would take over the network in a way that one sick man could not. When gold was discovered in California, that must have commandeered the network to a degree that a sale at the local department store never would. And no one in the United States who was old enough to realize what was happening will ever forget the impact of a brief news bulletin interpolated into the radio broadcast of the New York Philharmonic Orchestra on the afternoon of December 7, 1941, and how the entire network of social communication lit up, jerked Americans away from their Sunday afternoons, their comfortable plans, and their confidence in their national security, took over most of the news, most of the conversation, and most of the private thoughts, and focused attention inexorably on the implications of an event in Pearl Harbor, Hawaii.

## Some Patterns of Communication Pathways

So there are at least two patterns of communication flow through society: the kind necessary to maintain the social organism at its ordinary level of functioning and the kind necessary to meet challenges to and serious problems of the organism. What other characteristics of the flow through the network would be noticeable?

For one, we might notice that there are dark places in the network where circuits connecting large masses of people are seldom used. One of these dark places, until recently, was between the United States and China. We might observe a number of points in the network whare circuits are little used between groups of people representing different social classes—for example, ghettoes and suburbs, central governments and villagars, rich landowners and tenant farmers.

We should also notice, probably, that most communication tends to flow horizontally in society but vertical communication flows downward more than upward. This is somewhat different in the case of status derived from expertise or authority. An expert is as likely to communicate up as down, depending on where his skills are chiefly needed. The man with authority, on the other hand, is likely to communicate downward, and more information will probably go downward from him than upward to him. More information flows from government to any citizen than from any citizen to government. In fact, if we could ob-

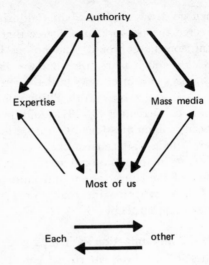

**Figure 1** An impressionistic representation of the flow of social communication.

serve the communication networks of the world in the way I have suggested, we might be able to distinguish the more democratic from the more authoritarian states by the number of messages that flow upward to government.

An army would furnish an extreme example of hierarchical communication: commands flowing from upper levels downward; the ordinary soldiers, the noncoms, and the commissioned officers all patronizing their own clubs and socializing at their own level; and even within the top group the general officers somewhat removed from the officers of company or lower field grade. Or consider the communication patterns in an industry. By far the greatest amount of communication takes place among people who work together and share common problems. The workmen talk together, the foremen and supervisors talk together, the middle-level and top management talk together—all have their own sets of tasks and interests, and a large share of their information channels to people at their own level. When serious problems occur they are reported upward in the hierarchy as far as necessary for the requisite decisions to be made. Sometimes a grievance committee or a strike is required to accomplish this. It is much easier for communication to move down the ladder, for management to pass down orders to the supervisors and supervisors to give orders to the people working for them.

Research literature contains interesting findings about the effects of different communication patterns. Let us take the example of work groups, which are small enough to make it possible to study their communication in detail. Leavitt has found, and others have confirmed, that groups in which everyone can communicate freely with every other member have higher morale than groups in which there is any restriction on communication.[1] For example, the so-called "star" is usually a happier organization than the so-called "wheel" group:

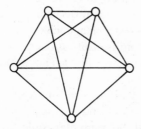 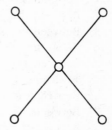

On the other hand, there are several findings that the wheel group, where one member is in charge and all communication goes to and from him, may be somewhat more efficient in solving problems. The kind of problem seems to make a difference. Time is saved by the wheel organization if the problems require a great deal of different information to be combined in one place. However, Shaw found that whereas the wheel group was quicker at solving simple problems, the star group did better with more difficult problems for which a maximum number of ideas and inputs was needed.[2]

A different series of studies by Thibaut and others revealed that the ability to communicate upward in the hierarchy often substitutes in a man's mind for his inability to *move* upward.[3] And still other experiments (for example, by Leavitt) showed that the further a member of a group was placed from the center of communication and decision—for example, the individuals at positions A and E in this kind of group organization:

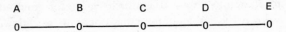

—the less satisfactory he finds the task. So it does make a difference, often a considerable difference, where the paths of communication reach.

Professor S. C. Dube, a distinguished Indian sociologist, has described the communication pathways that had to be cleared before India could launch out efficiently on its own as an independent nation. It was found, he said, that effective communication had to be established between these segments at least:

1. Between the political sector and the bureaucracy
2. Between the planner and the political decision-maker
3. Between the planner and the research agencies
4. Between the planner and the units of production
5. Between the different departments and agencies of the government
6. Between the different levels of administration
7. Between the general administrator and the technician
8. Between the modernizers and the common people
9. Between aid-giving and aid-receiving countries
10. Between overseas consultants/advisers and their native counterparts.[4]

You may ask whether these channels were not already in existence. The answer is that some of them were, but even in those cases considerable revisions in role patterns and practice had to be accomplished before the channels worked effectively. For example, the bureaucracy (the old civil service of colonial days) and the political sector (made up of the freedom fighters who had led the revolution and then moved into elective and high appointive places in government) had a difficult time learning to work together. The politicians were annoyed by the bureaucrats' emphasis on routine and fixed procedures; the bureaucrats were annoyed by the politicians' impatience and lack of administrative skills. Ultimately both roles had to be modified.

The meaning of this is what we have said before: that when we are studying communication we are studying human behavior. When we study pathways of information, we are studying the relationships of people at different ends of the path. The network we have been talking about is really far different from a telephone circuit board or from anything electronic or mechanical. It is *people* who are relating to each other, influencing each other, sharing information for some common purpose. That is what social communication is.

## Why These Pathways?

Man thus lives in a sea of communication the way he lives in a sea of air, and just as naturally. He does not often feel overburdened by the weight of the ocean because he adjusts to it; he takes what he wants from what comes to his attention, makes such use of it as he wishes to and can, and contributes to the ocean as he feels the need to do. Just as he feels discomfort when the air moves too strongly in a windstorm, so does he sometimes become uncomfortable when communication flows in too great quantities—when there are too many telephone calls, too many documents to read, too many letters to write (though he discovers after a while that if he postpones answering letters many of them will never need answering). Just as he feels uncomfortable when the supply of air is thin, so does he when the supply of communication is short—for instance, when someone he loves does not write to him or he cannot find out what is really happening in Indochina. But in this case, too, he usually finds a way to fill the gap or adjust to it; the ability of humans to adjust to their environment and society is phenomenal. For most people at most times, therefore, the supply of communication seems adequate in the sense that Mark Twain described the most appropriate length of a man's legs: long enough to reach from the man to the ground.

Now the question is, what determines which pathways will be well worn and which ones little used? Why are certain roads marked on the map with heavy lines and others not so marked?

It is partly a matter of need, partly of convenience and habit and chance. If I want another cup of coffee after dinner, I ask someone for it rather than writing a letter to the newspaper.

If I want to hear a symphony, I am more likely to turn on the stereo than the television receiver. If I want to hear the late news while I am driving, I turn on the car radio. I have a neighbor who always reads the morning San Francisco *Chronicle* on the 8 A.M. commuter train and another who takes along the San Francisco *Examiner* from the previous evening because, he says, he cannot stand the *Chronicle.*

Therefore, if we ask whether a person selects a pathway of communication on the basis of the medium or the message, we must answer that he selects both. He selects the one that will meet the need most adequately and, other things being equal, most conveniently and quickly.

When the needs are personalized, pathways are pretty well determined. When I asked a certain girl to marry me, I needed an answer from *her*, and the obvious pathway was face-to-face communication under the most favorable conditions possible. When I am ill I need a channel that will bring me information from a doctor, preferably my own doctor, although I suppose I could get some advice from a medical book. But if all I need to know is the name of the capital of Liechtenstein, I have a choice among many channels: atlas, encyclopedia, the *New York Times Encyclopedic Almanac,* the library reference desk, the fellow in the next office. In this case, availability is likely to determine which channel I use.

Availability of channels depends on where we grow up, what we can afford, what constraints are placed on us by our culture. For example, if I had grown up in a thatched hut in Africa instead of a clapboard house in the United States, I would certainly have had different pathways of information. There would probably have been no newspapers and no *Book of Knowledge*, but I might have learned to understand talking drums, and instead of my doctor I might have been consulting a witch doctor. If I had grown up in another part of the world, I would probably have been asking that question of a different girl or, very possibly, of her father rather than the girl herself.

Culture and environment thus enter into individual choices of information pathways in several respects. They require, or at least encourage, us to seek certain kinds of information rather than others. Reacting partly to these needs for information, they encourage the growth of institutions and media of communication. And they reinforce patterns of using certain channels and talking to certain people rather than others.

Let us say something about the "fraction of selection," which I suggested nearly twenty years ago as a rule-of-thumb approach to help explain the probability of any given communication being selected by any given individual.[5] It was stated this way:

$$\frac{\text{Promise of reward}}{\text{Effort required}} = \text{Probability of selection}$$

At the time this was formulated, I was probably influenced by George K. Zipf's "Principle of Least Effort,"[6] which helps explain the wording of the bottom term. I could just as easily have said something about availability. But like Zipf I was impressed by the tendency of human behavior, other things being equal, to flow into a path of minimum effort. But of course other things are not always equal. Consequently, one can raise the probability of selection of a given communication *either* by decreasing the lower term (the expected difficulty) or by increasing the upper term (expected reward). These are individual assessments. The potential reward of asking Miss X to marry Mr. Y or Mr. Z may be estimated quite differently by these two gentlemen. And an outside observer may estimate either the reward or the difficulty quite otherwise than do the actual participants. For example, I recently suggested to a student who has a problem in a course that he talk it over with his teacher. "Oh, I can't talk to him about that," the student said in obvious distress, although to me it seemed a relatively easy thing to do.

If we consider the fraction of selection in terms of the selection of channels and pathways, I think we can say that the upper term—promise of reward—has chiefly to do with the content and how likely it is to satisfy needs as they are felt at a given time. The lower term, on the other hand, has to do mostly with the availability and ease of using pathways. Habits tend to develop out of experience with these two estimates. For example, one finds satisfactory reading in the morning paper, and soon that journal appears each day at the breakfast table. One finds that the 9 o'clock program on television helps him unwind after a hard day, and one begins to tune to it regularly. Or one finds that a particular author has a pleasant soporific effect, and this author's books begin to appear on the bedside table.

To the test of introspection and nonrigorous observation, the fraction of selection stands up well. Countless audience studies have shown that people select easily available entertainment from their television tube in preference—other things being equal—to going out for equally promising entertainment. Yet when the reward of peer group company is added in, we see teen-agers go to the movies or even the public library. Then, when those teen-agers marry and grow into adulthood and settle into their own homes, the rewards of going out seem to be reduced, and before long they are watching the TV movies and the TV professional football. When College Board examinations draw near, students are likely to perceive greater reward in their books than in the movies or TV, and they even, occasionally, turn off their radios. By the same token, our choice of interpersonal pathways reflects both our needs and easy availability. Most of such communication goes to and from people nearest at hand, the people one spends most time with.

On the other hand all of us have seen that at *some* times, in *some* situations, some particular kind of information is suddenly so important to us that it is worth almost any kind of effort. Even then we tend to choose the most readily available channel or the one we feel most confident and comfortable about using. But for rewards of sufficient size we are willing to spend years studying to get a Ph.D. or spend $22 billion to go to the moon.

The operation of the fraction of selection is hidden in the black box, and the proposition itself is so general that psychological research on it is not easy. Research has concentrated on one aspect of the proposition: whether people select information that supports their beliefs and values and consequently reduces their sense of cognitive dissonance. Freedman and Sears reviewed the literature on selective exposure[7] and concluded that exposure to communication really is selective and that people tend to expose themselves to information with which they agree. "Republican rallies are mainly attended by Republicans," they point out. "Baptist services are attended mainly by Baptists, the readers of the *New Republic* are mostly liberals and those of the *National Review* mostly conservatives. AMA journals are read primarily by doctors, and APA journals primarily by psychologists. The audiences for most mass communications are disproportionately made up of those with initial sympathy for the viewpoints expressed." They could not find, however, any very convincing proof of a general *psychological* tendency to prefer supportive information. They decided that there must be other reasons—possibly the usefulness of the information (of medical journals to medical practitioners, psychological journals to psychologists, and so forth), friendships, social roles and customs, and others—behind such selective exposure.

Selective exposure is not really in doubt, but its causes are. There must be a variety of causes and combinations of causes, some operative at one time, some at another, but all affecting the judgment we make on the question of reward as opposed to effort.

## Summary and Questions

So man walks through life, doing what comes naturally with communication, using his skills and directing his attention where he feels it will be most rewarding, sometimes following along the easiest communication pathways but on other occasions making great efforts to take paths that are not easy to use. Sometimes he communicates merely to pass the time of day; sometimes out of a sense of great urgency or crisis; sometimes in a node where little information flows; sometimes in a great tidal wave through society, as happens, for example, in a period of rapid social change. His map of communication is a map of life, and the map of communication in the society around him is a better map of that society than most cartographers can draw.

That is the larger picture that emerges of man communicating. As we ask the smaller question, Why does one certain communication circuit tend to light up rather than another? we turn back to the fraction of selection. People make judgments about the promise of reward as against the need of effort, and if we want to think of that in even simpler terms, we can consider why a person selects one form of communication rather than another from all that are available around him. And then we ask questions like these:

**How readily available is the communication?** Political pros like to *saturate* a broadcasting station with spot announcements concerning their candidate. Advertisers know that large ads are more likely to be seen than are small ads. Both politicians and advertisers try to rent the billboards where many people pass. And all of us know that we are more likely, of an evening, to pick up the magazine beside our chair than go out for another one, unless that other one contains an article we very much want to read.

**How much does it stand out?** Do the message signs contrast with the field around them? Are they bigger, louder, more pervasive, different from the colors and patterns surrounding them? All of us have had our attention jerked to a sudden change in our perceived environment: a swift movement in a still forest; a baby's wail in the night; a few seconds of silence in the midst of a noisy party; a falling star against the sky; a spot of orange against the blue of the sea. And if we are parents, we know we must sometimes raise our voices if we want our children to "pay attention" while they are playing.

**How appealing is the content?** This depends partly on the characteristics of the selector; consequently, a great part of all audience research deals with the question of what people select what kinds of material from the media. For example, we know that the more education a person has, the more likely he is to select print over television, public affairs content over westerns or whodunits. We know that men read or view more sports than do women. We know that children's tastes in mass media change considerably as they grow up to adulthood.

Some years ago, working along this line, I factor-analyzed the news choices of a number of readers and found that they could be described to a great extent in three clusters. One of them was how *near* the news seemed to the reader. Not necessarily physically near, but how likely to affect him or his neighbors. A story of an epidemic of measles would seem nearer to a woman with young children than to an elderly man with no grandchildren. A story about a crime wave in San Francisco would seem nearer to a San Francisco reader than a Bostonian, and nearest of all to a reader in whose neighborhood the crimes were most frequent. There seemed to be a considerable difference among readers, however, in their ability to perceive a story as potentially affecting *them*; for example, a person with higher education or cosmopolitan interests might consider a story of rising tension in the Middle East as near and potentially significant to him, whereas another reader might pass it by and turn to local politics or the grocery ads.

A second determinant was how *big* the story seemed to the reader—that is, how significant, how exciting, how important. There was a close interaction between bigness and nearness. The election of a mayor in Gary, Indiana, seemed bigger to residents of Gary than to residents of Phoenix, Arizona. But among individuals there seemed to be a considerable difference in willingness to read the "big" news of the day. Some, for personality reasons, seemed actually to avoid it or to prefer to take it in the form of headlines or a news summary. Others concentrated on the "big" stories.

In the third place, there was the question of how *serious* or *entertaining* the news appeared to be. In this respect also, there was a considerable difference among people in their preference for public affairs or feature news, which is to say for potentially challenging and disturbing news as against news intended to make them chuckle or say "I'll be darned!" and settle back comfortably in their chairs.

This kind of study, of course, describes rather than explains. The underlying process must be inferred or otherwise derived.

**What is the individual looking for?** A person comes to any communication supermarket with a certain shopping list. We call it a "set." A fisherman is set to look for fish rather than wildflowers beside the stream. A student goes to class prepared to look for cues different from those he seeks in the cafeteria. At any given time an individual may be seeking information on how to pass a test, whether to take an umbrella with him, what quotation to use in a talk, why his child is sulking.

**What communication habits has he learned?** Some sources have proved over time to have utility for certain purposes and not for others. A student who has been in class long enough knows pretty well what he must pay attention to and how much attention. When a commuter settles down into his seat with a familiar newspaper, he has learned to look at certain parts of that paper, probably in a preferred order.

**What communication skills has he?** Reading skills, to take one example, are obviously related to preference for the print media. Skill in listening, skill in viewing—things we still know too little about —are related to the use of the electronic media.

These are simple and practical questions. They are asked every day by advertisers and other professional communicators. But what underlies the kind of behavior these questions are designed to identify? For example, what determines a person's judgment of what is rewarding and what requires too much effort? What determines how appealing certain content is to him, or what his set is at a given time, or what communication habits or skills he brings with him? Some of this is time-bound of course: One doesn't usually apologize or offer to fight unless something has just happened to bring that about. Some of it is relatively timeless: the habit of acknowledging a greeting, smiling at a pretty girl, or communicating in a way that will help one obtain food when one grows hungry. Much of it depends on what one has been and what one has experienced, the kind of family and community one has grown up in, and the education one has had.

# vii.
# The Media
# of Communication:
# Mass and Personal

Media, as we have been taught by Marshall McLuhan, are extensions of man.[1] Like so many of McLuhan's utterances, this provokes thought. One's hands are media. So are the wheels one rides on, says McLuhan. Television and radio, newspapers and magazines and film are media: They extend one's senses. An individual has at least three kinds of media at his command—one that carries his own messages (for example, voice and gestures), one that brings messages (television, newspaper), and one that does both (the telephone). The hands must qualify as two-way media because they carry messages through contact and bring back messages through the sense of touch. Are the senses themselves media because they extend the ability of the central nervous system to receive messages?

Whether or not we go as far as McLuhan's definition would seem to take us, it is evident that the concept of media is not so simple as it has sometimes seemed. For one thing, clearly there were media before there were *mass* media. But even if we do not think of hands and voice and other parts of man as media, we still have to classify as media such pre-mass media devices as the talking drum, the smoke signal, and even the town crier and the bazaar, because they all extend beyond man his ability to communicate. The town crier is a formal role, and the talking drum might be called a machine, interposed in the communication process much as the newscaster and radio are today.

The late Paul Deutschmann suggested a way of classifying communication situations so as to throw light on the relation of channels to pathways.[2]

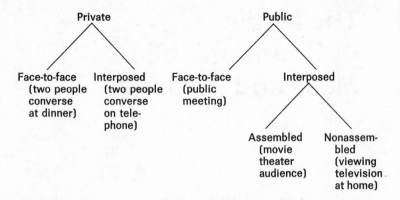

It is helpful to use his scheme (with our examples added) to indicate how arbitrary the distinction is between the mass and interpersonal channels of communication. "Private" communication is not quite the same when it is face-to-face as it is by telephone or by letter. Private or public face-to-face communication is different alone or on an interview show, in a group of two, a group large enough to fill a living room, a group large enough to fill a hall, an acting crowd, or a mob. Public communication through a mass medium is different when it is received in a group situation (a movie theater or a Radio Rural Forum) or in a living room and, if in a living room, by one person or several. Indeed, it could be argued that many qualities of an inflammatory face-to-face speech to a mob are less personal, more mass, than a singer crooning through a radio into the ear of a teen-ager alone in her room.

Thus, although from the viewpoints of production and delivery there are clear distinctions between communication through a mass medium and communication otherwise, from the viewpoint of an audience—whether one person or millions—the distinction is not always that sharp.

When we speak of a mass medium, we usually mean a channel of communication in which a machine (to duplicate and distribute the information signs) and a communicating organization (like the staff of a newspaper or broadcasting station) has been interposed. When we speak of an interpersonal channel, we mean a channel that reaches from person to person without such things interposed. As we have seen, the distinction blurs: For example, on which side of the fence does the telephone fit?

Let us first try to sum up some of the things we think we know about the differences between mass and interpersonal channels, then talk about one of the most famous scholarly hypotheses relating mass media to interpersonal channels (the "two-step flow"), and finally consider McLuhan's much-discussed approach to communication media.

## The Naive Psychology of Channels

It must be confessed that our state of knowledge concerning the effect and effectiveness of these two different kinds of channel is still not far from the level of "naive psychology," by which psychologists mean something for which they do not have much research evidence but still think is worth saying. However, consider some of the fairly obvious differences in the two kinds of channels:

1. **The senses they stimulate.** As we have said, man communicates as a total person. In face-to-face communication it is possible to stimulate all the senses and for the communication partner to relate to this whole-person communication. When anything is interposed, some restriction is put on the use of the senses. Thus radio and telephone reach only the ear and print only the eye (although we must not underestimate the tactile pleasure of handling a beautifully made book). Television and sound movies reach both eye and ear, and McLuhan claims (without evidence) that television stimulates also the tactile sense. It seems reasonable, therefore, that a face-to-face situation, other things being equal, should make it possible to communicate *more* and *more complete* information. It seems also that there would be an advantage in being able to communicate at the same time to as many senses as possible,

and thus the audiovisual media would have some advantage over the merely audio or the merely visual in communicating a certain amount of information on a given topic.

However, against the apparent advantage of face-to-face whole-person communication one must weigh the advantage of skillful production and programming on the media. Against the advantage of communicating to several senses at once one must weigh that of being able to concentrate attention on *one* sense —for example, on listening to a telephone call (especially if one must listen very hard in order to hear) or on the act of reading (especially if the text is difficult enough to demand close attention). Against the advantage of being able to communicate to both the audio and visual senses, one must weigh the theory of Broadbent, Travers, and others that human perception operates through one channel only.[3] In other words, the path from the sense organs to the brain is a one-lane road, and either audio or visual information can pass over it but not at the same instant. One part of the total message must wait in a short-term memory for its turn, and therefore an individual can by no means expect to process twice as much information from a two-sense communication as from a single-sense one. Furthermore, there is evidence that interference sometimes occurs between the information on a sound track and that on a visual track so that far from being twice as effective, in some cases an audiovisual channel may be *less* effective than a single-sense channel.

Among single-sense channels there is reason to suspect differences also, because good evidence exists that the eye can absorb information more rapidly than the ear, and the sense of smell has a remarkable ability to call up old memories associated with odors.

2. **The opportunity for feedback.** In a face-to-face situation, there is maximum opportunity for quick exchange of information. Two-way communication is easy. Consequently, there is continuing opportunity to assess the effect of the signs one puts out, to correct, to explain, to amplify, to answer objections. As the face-to-face group grows larger, the leader can pay careful attention to fewer members, and the talking time must be divided into smaller fractions. When anything is interposed, the feedback is attenuated. Thus, a telephone restricts not the

speed but the amount of feedback, because it will not carry—unless it is a picture phone—any of the information that might be communicated visually. Interposing a mass medium restricts both the speed and the amount of feedback, and the distance and impersonality of the media discourage it. When media organizations feel that feedback is very important—as, for example, in advertising or in making an instructional television program like "Sesame Street"—they pretest materials, put audiences in studios, and make arrangements to obtain quick reports from the classroom or the markets.

**3. Control of the pace.** In face-to-face communication a person can ask questions, help steer the conversation, and exert some control over its pace. A person reading can set his own pace, pause to think over a point, repeat a passage when necessary and desirable to do so. A teacher can do the same thing for a class, though he must average out the feedback cues he receives in order to know how best to meet the class's needs. A listener to radio, a viewer of films or television, however, has no such control. To be sure, he can turn off the receiver, leave the theater, or allow his attention to wander, but he cannot control the pace or cause the flow of information to pause while he thinks about it. This is one of the reasons why advertising on television has drawn more complaints than advertising in newspapers and printed texts have proved so effective for individual study.

Traditionally people have believed that sender control makes for more effective persuasion, receiver control for more effective learning. In the past decade technology has moved to try to satisfy both—to provide more efficient circulation of information centrally controlled (as for instance, via satellites) and to provide more opportunity for control by the receiver (for instance, with recording and playback devices, and computerized methods of individualizing instruction). The problem is how to combine the cost efficiency of central distribution and control with the efficient fit to individual differences that individual control makes possible.

**4. Message codes.** In face-to-face communication a high proportion of all the available information is nonverbal. This is slightly less true of television and sound movies, still less of silent movies and radio, and least of print. Therefore, the silent language of culture, the language of gesture and emphasis and body movement, is more readily codable in some delivery systems than in others. A high proportion of printed communication is coded in orthographic signs as compared to a very low proportion of television and movies, and almost none of painting, sculpture, music, or dance. Thus, it is possible in printed media to abstract easily; in the audiovisual media, to concretize.

5. **The multiplicative power.** Face-to-face communication can be multiplied only with great effort. Even a meeting of a hundred thousand people, such as Nehru sometimes addressed, was not really multiplying face-to-face communication, because information had necessarily to flow mostly in one direction only. Mass media, on the other hand, have an enormous ability to multiply one-way communication and make it available in many places. They can overcome distance and time. The audiovisual media can also overleap the barriers of illiteracy in developing regions. Therefore, the advantages of this multiplicative power must be weighed against the advantages of the kind of feedback provided by face-to-face communication.

A considerable amount of attention has been given in recent years to combinations of the two in an effort to salvage some of the best of each: for example, the Radio Rural Forum, in which groups meet face-to-face to hear and discuss broadcasts made especially for them, and the combination of television teaching with related activities, face-to-face, in the classroom. Attention has also been attracted to the effects of face-to-face communication in very large meetings and the use of interpersonal networks. For example, when huge crowds come together at a sports event or a political rally, the crowd effects are themselves an element of great importance in the communication, and when a message must be spread person to person, the personal networks may sometimes be spectacularly effective, as they were when the news that "Gandhi-ji is dead!" spread by word of mouth over India. On the other hand, a network message may be easily distorted—as Allport and Postman, Festinger and Thibaut, and other students of rumor have discovered.[4]

6. **The power to preserve a message.** Face-to-face communication is gone in a second. So, except when recorded, are

the electronic media. It is difficult, therefore, for a person to relive a motion picture experience or enjoy a television program again, except in memory. The printed media have a great advantage in being able to perserve facts, ideas, or pictures. Not until a way was found to record meaningful visual symbols was it possible to preserve human records, except in the memories of old men and women. The importance of libraries, archives and encylopedias testifies to the continuing need to preserve messages today. Now that there is such a glut of information, new electronic retrieval systems are being designed to supplement the storage of information and the wish to preserve audiovisual materials is creating a market for simple recording machines, low-priced cassettes and tapes, and video recorders.

7. **The power to overcome selectivity.** It is easy to change the television channel, hard to tune out face-to-face communication without being rude. It is easier to doze in a large class than in a small discussion group. It is easier to turn off the radio than to make oneself walk out of a movie theater. It is probably easier to avoid reading a news item or an advertisement in a newspaper than to avoid a news item or a commercial on the radio or television, although if the audience can seek out what it wants it may be more receptive. And all of us know that it is easier to command and monopolize attention through face-to-face communication than through media channels—other things being equal. But again, they are *not* equal. If one of your friends is telling you an old story for the third time, face-to-face, your attention is still likely to stray and if your radio is broadcasting a bulletin on the assassination of a President, your attention is very likely to be riveted to it.

8. **The power to meet specialized needs.** The mass media have an unequalled power to serve *common* needs of society quickly and efficiently. For example, the weather forecast, the day's chief news bulletins, the Saturday football scores, the announcements of sales and sale prices, a policy address by the President of the United States—all can be circulated much more efficiently by mass channels than person to person. On the other hand, radio, television, films and newspapers are very inefficient channels for meeting needs that are felt by different

people at different times and by only a few people at any given time. What is the capital of Liechtenstein? What is the name of the red-haired girl down the street? How can I change the spark plugs in my car? Questions like these one asks an informed individual or studies a sheet of directions or looks it up in a handbook. If he finds the information he wants, when he wants it, on television, it will truly be a miracle. For most such specialized information another person is the best source, a bit of print that can be kept around for emergencies is next best, and the electronic media are least effective. The time may come when video cassettes will be so cheap and plentiful that we can afford to keep some information on them rather than in print, but not yet.

Do not think, however, of interpersonal and mediated communication as opposed or mutually exclusive. Actually, as we have tried to point out, the distinctions and boundaries are much less clear than that. Most campaigns aimed at teaching or persuading try to combine media and personal channels so that one will reinforce and supplement the other. Political campaigners use all the media but still arrange door-to-door visits and public meetings. Family planning, agricultural, and health campaigns maintain field staffs but support them with all the media they can afford. And one concept of the supplementary functioning of media and interpersonal communication has been put forward as the "two-step flow" theory, which now warrants our attention.

## The Two-Step Flow Theory

The idea of the two-step flow of communication came out of a study in Erie County, Ohio, of the 1940 U.S. Presidential election, under the direction of Paul Lazarsfeld and some of his colleagues from the Department of Sociology and the Bureau of Applied Social Research at Columbia University.[5] The researchers expected to find that the mass media, at that time chiefly radio and press, had a great influence on the election. However, very few people reported being influenced by the media. In the cases where voting decisions were influenced, it was usually by personal contacts and face-to-face persuasion. To explain these findings, the researchers advanced for the first time the two-step flow hypothesis: "that ideas often flow from radio and print to opinion leaders and from these to the less active sections of the population."

Incomplete and ultimately unsatisfactory as it was, this theory turned out to be a very fruitful one for communication study and research. For one thing, it was hard thereafter to think of "faceless masses" or of audiences consisting of individuals disconnected from each other but connected to the mass channels. Gradually it came to be seen that individuals were connected to each other. Instead of being faceless or passive, they were extremely active. An enormous amount of discussion and persuasion and informing went on within the audience.

Moreover, the two-step flow theory set in motion a number of studies of audience behavior, especially in relation to campaigns and to the media. Merton and some of his colleagues studied opinion leadership in a suburban community, which they called Rovere. Consumer decisions were studied in Decatur, Illinois. The 1948 election campaign was studied in Elmira, New York. The diffusion of information on medicinal drugs among physicians was studied in an eastern city.

The research by the Columbia scholars was supplemented by others. The Presidential elections from 1952 on have been researched by the Survey Research Center at Michigan.[6] Diffusion of news was studied by Deutschmann and Danielson, and later by Greenberg.[7] Rural sociologists found that their diffusion model would contribute to understanding of the two-step flow.[8] Trohldahl and others at Michigan State and Wisconsin looked in more detail at the seeking as well as the giving of advice in electoral campaigns.[9] The spread of information and ideas at the time of the assassination of President Kennedy were subjects for research in several parts of the country. All this research was stimulated or shaped in part by the two-step flow hypothesis. And even though every study pointed out deficiencies in the theory until finally there was not much left of the original conception, today much is known about the flow of information and ideas that was not known before the two-step flow concept was proposed. This is the function of a good theoretical hypothesis: It leads toward better theory.

What have we found wrong with the original two-step

flow formulation? Simply that it doesn't explain fully enough what actually happens.

In the first place, it neglects the fact that a great amount of information flows directly from the media to users of the media rather than through a middleman. Deutschmann and Danielson, for example, found that most news was so received. Greenberg demonstrated ingeniously (Figure 2) that only the *most* and the *least* widely important news is carried to any extent by word of mouth.[10] Thus, about half the American people learned of the death of President Kennedy by word of mouth rather than from the media, and most local events unimportant enough for newspaper or broadcast coverage are carried from person to person. However, the bulk of the news, which is important enough to cover but not so shocking that it must be passed on at once to others, comes to people mainly through the press and newscasts. In recent political campaigns the bulk

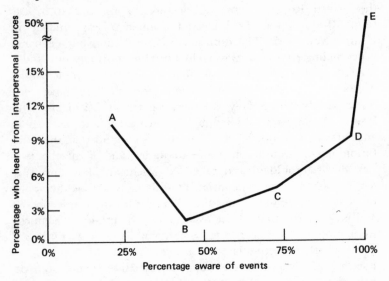

**Figure 2**  A through E are news items that came to the attention of different percentages of the American public. Word of mouth played an important part in carrying the first news of only the least and the most widely interesting items. (W. Schramm in B. S. Greenberg and E. B. Parker (eds.), *The Kennedy assassination and the American public*. Stanford, Calif.: Stanford University Press, 1965, p. 17)

of information and persuasion has been piped directly to individuals through the media. This includes press conferences, political addresses, conventions, meetings, and political advertisements. We are by no means saying that personal influence is not exerted in political campaigns, merely that much information and persuasion still comes directly rather than through an "opinion leader" or another kind of intermediary.

In the second place, the concept of a society divided into leaders and followers, or active and passive participants, has not held up. Trohldahl found in Detroit that relatively few voters ever sought any advice at all, whether from "opinion leaders" or anyone else.[11] On the other hand, there is no very convincing evidence that "opinion leaders" are typically active forces in social persuasion. Apparently they are just as likely to be passive as to be active and to wait for someone to ask their advice rather than trying to persuade.

The concept of opinion leaders receiving information from the media and passing it on also proved to be too simple. Actually, opinion leaders, when they can be identified, have many sources of information. They go to meetings, try things out, and—most important—talk to other people who serve as *their* sources. In other words, opinion leaders also have opinion leaders.

Therefore, the theory of a *two*-step flow is not a realistic description of what happens. There may be one step, two steps, or many steps. The chain of influence and information may be of considerable length, with the true origin in doubt.

In the third place, rural sociologists have demonstrated that a potential adopter of a new idea or innovation is more likely to seek or accept information from the mass media very early in the process, when he is still canvassing what is available, and to seek information from informed and respected people later in the process of adoption, when he has become interested and wants to know more about it, especially about other users' experience with it.[12] Again, after he has committed himself he may try to reduce his dissonance by seeking reinforcement from the media. Thus, the two-step flow more often applies at the stage of information and decision than earlier or later.

Finally, the "opinion leader" concept itself has proved to be far too simple. As Rogers, one of the leading students of diffusion, has justly pointed out, opinion leadership is really a continuous variable.[13] There are all shades and levels of opinion leaders. Some are strong and widely accepted "leaders," others not. From the time of the Decatur study, we have known that advice is usually sought with respect to a particular topic; *generalized* opinion-leadership status is scarce. Futhermore, such leaders appear at all levels of society and at different ages, according to what knowledge they are expected to have. For information about the new movies or the new dances, for example, one would not ordinarily ask an elderly bank president. But the point is that even in their separate specialties people are not neatly divided into leaders and followers. A person who is asked for advice because of his special knowledge or expertise may well ask someone else's advice in the same specialty. A person who has sought some special information may pass it on. There are people—gossips, for example, or people who work in places like barber or beauty shops, where they see and talk with many people—who serve to multiply information without having any special expertise. Thus, there are so many levels and forms of information multiplication and influence that to think of a single social role designated "opinion leader" is an unsatisfactory way of trying to understand what is going on.

What is really going on? Perhaps the best way to say it, in the present state of knowledge, is that there is a continuing flow of information and ideas through society. The mass media greatly influence—directly or indirectly—what flows through these channels. Certain individuals also influence it, either by sharing their special knowledge, expertise, or conviction on a certain topic or by being articulate and talkative. As a matter of fact, all people, at some time or other, in some relationship or other, on some subject or other, by seeking or by giving, probably influence the flow. Some influence it more than others. But there are not two classes, the leaders and the led, nor is there in most cases a two-step flow from media to leader to follower. You can think of it as a multistep flow. Better, think of it as a systemic flow with information moving continuously through a social system, following the constraints and the needs of the system, shaped by the roles and sped by the institutions within the system.

## The McLuhan Approach

Marshall McLuhan's ideas concerning communication channels and media have probably received more public attention during recent years than the combined total of all other scholarly approaches to the subject. Now the vogue of McLuhan seems to have waned, but it seems appropriate to sketch in his approach here.

He does not make this easy. Doubtless because he distrusts the linear, logical presentation typical of printed media (which he holds responsible for many of the undesirable trends of the last five centuries), he chooses to write in a disconnected fashion that has been described as resembling Roman candles aimed in all directions. He seldom develops an idea fully and disdains research evidence because he feels that research is biased toward print and incapable of dealing with the new electronic media. His device, as he describes it, is the "probe" —a statement that penetrates the intellectual stereotypes of his audiences and causes them to rethink old positions. These "probes" are often cryptic statements worded so as to shock or puzzle, perhaps deliberately left incomplete or unqualified (as in "The medium is the massage"). Therefore his scholarly stance is somewhat oracular; like the priests of Delphi he produces messages that can be interpreted in different ways but do stimulate thought and in many cases have a considerable impact on the people who consult the oracle.

McLuhan, like his mentor Harold Innis,[14] is a technological determinist. Like Innis he interprets the recent history of the West as "the history of a bias of communication and a monopoly of knowledge founded on print."[15] The quotation is actually from a paper by James Carey; because of McLuhan's style of writing, it is sometimes more satisfactory to quote his interpreters.

By the "bias of communication" (which is the title of one of Innis's books) is meant the dominance of print. Both Innis and McLuhan regard this as an undesirable development. The swift growth of printed communication since the fifteenth century, Innis argues, has killed the oral tradition, replaced the temporal organization of Western society with a spatial organization, transformed religion, privatized a large portion of man's communication activities, brought about a relatively of values, shifted the locus of authority from church to state, and encouraged rampant nationalism. These are interesting and challenging insights, although most scholars would not credit so much effect exclusively to the development of print technology. Other technologies had some effect, too—fast transportation, new power sources, machinery, electronics, and with these the Revival of Learning, the growth of democracy, the rise of a middle class, the division of labor, and the stirring of a new social idealism. Granted that print had something to do with all of these, they had something to do with print, too. However, the replacement of the oral society clearly has made fundamental changes in man's whole orientation to his environment; it has transferred power from those who can remember the past and the holy writ to those who know about faraway places and different ways of doing things and it has made possible the formation and sometimes the collision of large social groups under central leadership. The changes from an oral to a media society are visible today in dozens of developing countries.

So far, these ideas are Innis's accepted by McLuhan. McLuhan's approach to them, however, is psychological rather than institutional. It is in fact reminiscent of the Sapir-Whorf hypothesis, although McLuhan is interested in how media rather than languages influence a person's view of the world and the way he thinks. His central idea (to quote Carey again) is that "media of communication . . . are vast social metaphors that not only transmit information but tell us what kind of world exists; that not only excite and delight our senses but, by altering the ratio of sensory equipment that we use, actually change our character."[16] McLuhan is not the first to say that "the things on which words were written down count more than the words themselves," but his way of saying it is the one most often quoted: The medium is the massage.

Perhaps the most interesting of McLuhan's additions to Innis is his analysis of how print has its supposed effect. He contends that communication through print imposes a "particular logic on the organization of visual experience." It breaks down reality into discrete units, logically and causally related, perceived linearly across a page, abstracted from the wholeness and disorder and multisensory quality of life. Above all, it causes an imbalance in man's relation to environment by emphasizing the kind of information received through the eye rather than the kind received in personal communication from all of the senses. Because reading and writing are essentially private activities and deal with abstracted experience, they "detribalize" man, take him out of a tightly knit oral culture and put him into a private situation far from the reality with which his communication deals. And of course the development of print tends to standardize the vernacular, improve distant communication, and therefore replace the village with the city and the city-state with the nation-state.

McLuhan is, therefore, attacking not only the linearity but also the abstraction of printed language, which, as we have said, is both its greatest strength and the source of many of our problems with it. In place of the ability to abstract, he is concerned with the ability to imagine. This is behind his other most-quoted concept, the distinction between "hot" and "cool" media.

A "hot" medium at one time seems to be one that does not maintain a sensory balance, at another one that comes with the meaning relatively prefabricated and requiring as little imaginative effort as possible to leap from signs to a picture of reality. A "cool" medium, on the other hand, is one that has sensory balance and requires considerable imagination. McLuhan himself has not been entirely consistent in classifying the media but considers print and radio to be "hot" media, using one sense each and (according to McLuhan) requiring relatively little imagination, whereas sound films to a certain degree and television above all are "cool media," which, McLuhan says, demand a maximum degree of imaginative effort on the part of their viewers. Strangely enough, for his conclusions concerning imagination McLuhan does not rely chiefly on the need to organize and abstract on the great amount of concrete experience furnished by television, but rather on a perceptual argument: that the television screen presents a large number of small dots of light, which the sensory and central nervous systems must organize into pictures of reality.

It is almost futile to check McLuhan's ideas against research evidence because he seldom states them in testable form and because he and his chief followers are scornful of scientific research, arguing that it is biased in the direction of print, linearity, and logic, and unable to deal with the concepts of electronic communication. A more fruitful activity is to take those insights of McLuhan's that seem promising and follow them out in one's own thinking until one comes to a point at which testable and usable propositions can be formed. And it hardly needs saying that the effects of an age of print, of the transition from oral to media culture, and of the acts of imagination required in communication are well worth conceptualizing and studying—indeed on a much broader basis than that on which McLuhan has examined them.

However, one cannot leave McLuhan entirely in one world and all scientific scholarship in another. Perhaps the oracular quality of his writing and speaking is responsible for some of the extreme nature of his statements, but these have been picked up by amateurs with the same rigidity. Therefore, it is well to point out that whereas McLuhan's emphasis on the effect of the medium itself is salutary, still researchers have found a much larger portion of the variation in the effects of a communication within the message than within the medium. The message is the message, and the medium is the medium, and one affects the other but not to the exclusion of either. For example, could anyone argue that the effect of the news of President Kennedy's death was determined chiefly by whether it came via television, radio, print, or word of mouth? Or that the different effects of the Kennedy news and a domestic serial can be attributed chiefly to the fact that someone received the news by print and the serial by television?

Similarly, there is no evidence that the perception and combination of the points of light on a television screen are responsible for any essential difference in effect. If this were so, we should expect the perception of halftones in a newspaper to have the same effect and the perception of type from the dots of a halftone to have an essentially different effect from that of print reproduced by offset or letterpress. Indeed, the whole question of imagination required by a given form of communication is in need of post-McLuhan rethinking, a need for which we must give McLuhan full credit. May it not be that the act of imagination necessary to translate print into a picture of reality could be greater than that required of a television viewer? Or that the absence of a sound track on silent films may actually be an invitation to imagination greater than that in sound films?

On the other hand, McLuhan's emphasis on the effect of the medium itself is useful, and his suggestion of the effect of a balance or imbalance of sensory channels and of linear print on the logic of thinking are worth further study. But chiefly his impact seems to have come from what he has said about television.

For McLuhan and Innis both, the growth of print has seemed disastrous. McLuhan, however, looks beyond the age of print to a new age of television. Television, he thinks, will restore the healthful balance of the senses. It will de-privatize, "re-tribalize" man, lead him back to the communal experiences of an oral culture. It will encourage participation rather than withdrawal, action rather than meditation, peaceful relations rather than nationalism. This vision of a salutary effect of television—while other people are worrying about the effects of its materialistic and violent content—was more than anything else responsible for McLuhan's vogue. And to make a judgment on it we must wait a while on history.

McLuhan's own history in the mass media is illustrative of one way in which the mass media feed the other channels of information. For the media have a fashion of creating instant heroes and then forgetting them, although the waves from the first splash keep on rolling outward through society. But while the intense light of the media rests on an individual, the effect is remarkable indeed. I remember one cartoon that appeared at the height of McLuhan's vogue. It showed two workmen carrying a television set—apparently repossessed for lack of payment—out of a house. The irate house-holder was shouting, "McLuhan won't like this!"

## Conclusion

These approaches seem to throw brief bright flashes, rather than a clear light, on the media of communication. Understanding the differences between forms of communication is obviously not a simple matter. It is easier to examine the mass media as institutions and organizations, which we shall do in the next chapter, and ultimately more useful to think of channels and pathways in terms of a continuing flow of information through society. Some of the flow is short-range—person to person. Some of it is long-range, carried by a wire or a postal service or a mass medium. Some of it reaches a single individual, some an assembled group, some a number of widely dispersed individuals or groups. Each of these ways of circulating information has its own strengths and weaknesses, its own advantages and disadvantages for any particular purpose at a given time. At various points in the system, there are people or working groups, with or without communicating machines, that multiply and distribute and put their own stamps on the flow of information.

But there is a danger in thinking of these acts of information sharing as single acts. In the wide-angle lens they are related. The flow of information does not often stop with any receiver. In one form or another it is likely to move on. And the sum of all these short and long, wide and narrow, personal and mediated relationships is the continuing surge of information that keeps society alive.

# viii.
# The Structure of
# Mass Communication

One afternoon in the late 1940s, in a sunny village of southern France, I heard a drum being beaten vigorously, not to say enthusiastically. In fact, someone was beating the stuffing out of the drum. People began hurrying out of houses, shops, even the church. I followed them to a tall young man, a block or two away, who was indeed beating his drum as though he wanted the world to know. When enough of us had gathered, he began to speak in a wonderfully resonant and carrying voice. He had three or four things to tell us. There was to be a meeting in a nearby town to greet General de Gaulle. There had been a fire. The National Assembly had taken an action of local importance about taxes. And a farmer had a bull for sale.

It took me a minute to realize that I was listening to a town crier. In the era of *Figaro* and *Le Monde*, communication patterns had suddenly rolled back a thousand years, and I was hearing news as people had heard it when the earliest medieval cathedrals were just being built. And—*la plus ça change, la plus que même*—it was in the form of a newscast with a commercial!

I would call the town crier one of the authentic communication media. And that brings us back to the question raised in Chapter I: How old are the media?

If we think of media as machines interposed in the communication process to multiply and extend the delivery of information, the first mass medium was printing from movable metal type, and the great age of media development has been the period from the Industrial Revolution to the present.

However, if we think of a communication medium simply as a social institution designed to speed and extend the exchange of information, the "mass" media were late comers to this group.

The town crier was by no means the first of the communication institutions. The school is so ancient that no one knows when a tribe first thought of gathering a group of children to be taught by a knowledgeable elder rather than by their own mothers and fathers. The church, ever since its ancient origin, has been conveying information directly and indirectly to masses of people. Libraries are at least as ancient as the clay tablets of Babylon and the stones and papyri of Alexandria. Bazaars, markets, fairs have for many thousands of years brought people together to exchange news and ideas and pleasantries. When markets or public events or circuses have not been readily available, people have developed their own ways of assembling to exchange information. Even today, in many villages of Asia the clothes-washing hour is as much a time for social communication as it is a work period. In Africa the *palaver* has long made it possible for tribal people to talk over their problems with the chief. The forums of the Mediterranean world were gathering places where people could meet, information passed, new laws promulgated, and decisions taken in public view. In many parts of the world, traveling players, puppet shows, dance troupes, and ballad singers went—and still go—from community to community, entertaining and carrying information. In the Middle East the coffeehouse has long been a center for discourse as well as relaxation. And in addition to all these places where people could come to talk and be talked to and informed, there is a long tradition of "silent media": statues communicating the greatness of the gods of the ancient world, buildings and monuments communicating the achievements of a kingdom or a ruler, memorials like the Taj Mahal and the Pyramids, and remarkable conceptions like the cathedral, which not only brought together a community and communicated a way of life but also taught the history of man and what he could expect in a life to come.

These face-to-face media, like their print and electronic successors, existed to facilitate social communication. They were institutionalized around that function and organized with rules, goal expectations, professional roles, and support. Like modern media, even the most serious of them included a considerable admixture of entertainment. And the fact that most of them are still in use today is testimony to their effectiveness.

When the machine-interposed media came in, they made changes in many of the face-to-face media. The printed book made it possible in some countries to extend education to nearly all children. The newspaper added a new function to the coffee-house. The mail-order catalog made possible a different type of bazaar, and advertising made large stores a continuous market-place. Films and television formalized the traveling players.

Thus the modern mass media are not really something new in the world, except with respect to how far and how fast they can disperse information. They are simply the latest of a long series of efforts to gather and exchange information more efficiently. And even in content they are not so new and different. As they have to some extent remodeled the face-to-face media, so have the face-to-face media taken over the newer ones. The forum is in the press; the town crier and the ballad singer on radio; the circus, the dance troupe, and the players on television; the palaver in the broadcast press conference or interview show.

The personal channels are still active and effective side by side with the media. In Asia community development programs rely more than anyone would expect on puppet shows and traveling players. The Chinese opera has been revised to carry a political message. When Ghandi was killed, when Indian and Chinese troops fought on the roof of the world, it was word of mouth that carried the news to most of the Indian people. But that is a developing country, you say. In the United States, where there are five radios for every household, where daily newspapers and television receivers are available in almost every home, could such a situation exist? But what happened when President Kennedy was assassinated? As we noted in the preceding chapter, almost exactly half the people heard the news first by word of mouth. And how does one explain the enormous gatherings of young people in America in recent years—the rock festival at Woodstock, for example, and the political demonstrations that have drawn a hundred thousand people or more? Granted that they were stimulated and abetted by the mass media, still they were clearly a throwback to the old patterns of mass communication before machines were interposed.

## The Knowledge Industry

If the mass media were not the first media, neither are they the only communication institutions. Indeed, one thing the machine-interposed media, particularly the electronic media, have done is to help create an enormous knowledge industry in the world that had no parallel before their time. Fritz Machlup, a Princeton economist, summed up this development in admirable fashion a decade ago in a volume he titled *The Knowledge Industry*.[1] His analysis still stands, although it is necessary now to supply some new figures.

The knowledge industry is organized along these lines:

Multipliers of messages: the mass media—newspapers, magazines, books, films, radio, television

Carriers of messages: telephone, telegraph, postal services, satellite systems, and so forth

Providers of information for individual needs: libraries, abstract services, computer services, data banks, and the like

Manufacturers and maintainers: printing organizations, makers of electronic and printing equipment, technicians to install and service the machines interposed in the media, and so forth

Special services contributing to content: news agencies, studios to make programs, writers, performers, artists, designers of educational materials, makers of computer programs, and so forth

Economic support agencies: advertising agencies and departments, distribution and sales agencies, and others

Administrative support agencies: legal counsel and guidance, publicity and public relations, financial and accounting services, administrative consultants, and the like

Personnel support: unions and trade associations, organizations for in-service and pre-service training of personnel, talent agencies, and so forth

Data-gathering services: general research and development, field and audience research, intelligence-gathering services, opinion research, censuses and other major suppliers of statistics, and so forth

Education: schools and colleges, universities, home-study opportunities, special schools for industry, for the military, for government, and so forth

It goes without saying that these activities represent a substantial part of the national expenditure. Exactly how much could only be determined by a detailed and careful analysis such as Machlup made in the 1950s, eliminating the overlaps in figures and assigning to the knowledge sector what properly belongs there rather than elsewhere. Even a quick scan, however, shows that the United States is spending on these communication activities over $150 billion annually, and the total is probably near $200 billion, or somewhere in the neighborhood of 20 percent of the gross national product.

Is this an uncommon allocation of national resources for communication in today's world? The dollar figures in the United States are higher than for any other country, but proportionally they are not out of line. For example, the typical Latin American country is now spending about 30 percent of its national budget, perhaps 10 percent of its national income, for education alone.

In his fascinating recent book *The Information Machines*,[2] Ben Bagdikian calculates the annual consumer expenditures of an average American home for communication services, excluding education, as $688 a year. This is divided as follows:

| telephone | $225 |
| newspapers | 120 |
| postal service | 116 |
| television | 102 |
| periodicals | 44 |
| books | 42 |
| radio | 26 |
| disks and tapes | 13 |

Bagdikian arrived at those figures by dividing total expenditures in the separate categories by the number of households in the United States. Since total expenditures on education for 1969 and later years have averaged about $1000 per household (the total was $61.4 billion in 1969 and an estimated $65.8 billion for 1970), another $1000 should be added to that $688.

In addition to that, public libraries alone (excluding private and special libraries) cost $304 million in 1965. Research costs are a legitimate part of the bill for the knowledge sector, as are the costs of computing and office machinery, communication equipment, photographic equipment and supplies, and research costs. These figures are impressive; here are annual expenditures for the most recent year available in the *Statistical Abstract of the United States*. The figures are in millions of dollars.

| | |
|---|---|
| Education | $75,300 (estimated for 1971); $61,200 was for public education |
| Postal service | $ 7,983 (1970) |
| Telephone | $19,831 (1969); $17,369 for Bell companies |
| Telegraph | $571 (1969); $154 for overseas cables |
| Research and development | $27,850 (estimated for 1971) |
| Printing and publishing | $25,068 (1969); includes printing of newspapers, books, and periodicals. The bill for business forms alone was $1,167, for greeting cards $613 |
| Paper mills, excluding building paper | $ 5,620 (1969) |
| Office and computing machinery | $ 7,397 (1969) |
| Communication equipment | $12,974 (1969) |
| Photographic equipment and supplies | $ 4,317 (1969) |
| Advertising (all kinds) | $25,565 (estimated for 1970) |

What do the mass media themselves cost?

We do not have a recent and reliable figure for films or for non-daily newspapers. Books and periodicals each have been grossing in the neighborhood of $2.5 billion per year. Television's total time sales for 1970 were reported by the FCC at $3.2 billion and radio's at $1.3 billion. Daily newspapers are estimated by the American Newspaper Publishers Association to have grossed $8.498 billion in 1970. In other words, the mass media are something like a $20 billion industry, even excluding related expenses for items such as receiving sets and maintenance.

The number of skilled workers involved in the knowledge industry can be suggested from the fact that there are about 3 million teachers in schools and colleges, over 700,000 postal employees, almost 900,000 telephone employees, and 370,000 newspaper employees. Add to these the numbers engaged in printing, in the manufacture and maintenance of all kinds of communication equipment, in the broadcast and film media, in publishing other than daily newspapers, in libraries and research and advertising, and it is apparent that the knowledge industry employs a substantial part of the American labor force and that these employees include a very large proportion of the nation's professional or highly trained workers.

The main thrust of the figures we have given is not merely that the knowledge industry is a very large one intimately connected to all other industry or that it is responsible for 15 percent or more of the country's gross national product or even that it absorbs a substantial part of household expenditures, but rather how intimately it touches the life of every home.

The average family in America

has one young person in school or college
has one television receiver (the actual figure is nearly 1.5 receivers per average home)
has several radios
receives a daily newspaper
receives one or two magazines
has a small shelf of books

makes seven telephone calls a day and calls long distance every other day

indirectly supports over $300 worth of advertising per year

is the recipient of whatever comes out of about $60 per year spent on basic research and an additional amount, very hard to estimate, on developmental research

Of course, not many homes are likely to fit this description exactly. Many homes have no children in schools; many others have several schoolchildren. Some homes receive several newspapers, and a few receive none. Similarly, one household may actually be spending thousands of dollars on communication activities and services (particularly when the children are in college), while another is spending only a few hundred. But the knowledge industry is in the life pattern of modern society alongside food, housing, automobiles, and the other services that are omnipresent in our everyday lives.

## The Structure and Function of the Mass Media

The mass media are thus only one part of a very large industry that provides and circulates knowledge. In fact they are not even the largest part; that distinction belongs to education. But an interplanetary visitor would probably find them the most spectacular part.

The way the media are organized tells us a great deal about how they must necessarily operate and the problems they have.

Their function is to make information widely, readily, speedily available. In system terms they are chiefly filters and amplifiers. They select, from all the information available to them in society, the items they wish to circulate. They process and amplify these for a very large audience.

The act of selection is probably the most important part of their operation. Instead of referring to them as filters, let us use the term *gatekeeper*, which the late Kurt Lewin contributed to social psychology. The mass media are among the chief gatekeepers of the flow of information through society.

Gatekeepers are placed throughout the information network. They include the reporter deciding what facts to put down about a court trial or an accident or a political demonstration, the editor deciding what to print and what to discard from the wire news, the author deciding what kinds of people and events to write about and what view of life to present, the publisher's editor deciding what authors to publish and what to cut out of their manuscripts, the television or film producer deciding where to point his camera, the film editor deciding what to edit out and leave on the cutting-room floor, the librarian deciding what books to purchase, the teacher deciding what textbooks or teaching films to use, the briefing officer deciding what facts to tell his superiors, and even the husband at the dinner table deciding what to tell his wife about the day's events at the office.

How this function affects the product can be illustrated from any medium, but perhaps nowhere as spectacularly as in the case of news. For example, recall how long it took the news of Mylai to reach the American people through a series of gates or what happens to the news from distant places as it passes one gatekeeper after another. On the following page is a visual example, based on material from Scott Cutlip, of what happens to the wire news as it moves toward readers of a newspaper in the central United States. This shows that only 1 or 2 percent of the news that was considered important enough to go on the wire in the first place actually got to the reader. And what originally went on the wire may have been only 1 percent of what was considered significant at the point of origin!

The study of how a gatekeeper works, how the decision is made, what to pass on, what to change, and what to refuse passage is therefore one of the truly significant topics in communication research. David Manning White made a very interesting study of a newspaper gatekeeper twenty years ago in Illinois—a wire editor who frankly admitted his prejudices and hoped that because he recognized them he could still decide as objectively as possible.[3] The Lang study of the MacArthur parade in Chicago showed how much more exciting television made the event appear than it seemed to people who were present.[4] The studies of what happens to rumors as they pass from person to person and the investigation by Tannenbaum

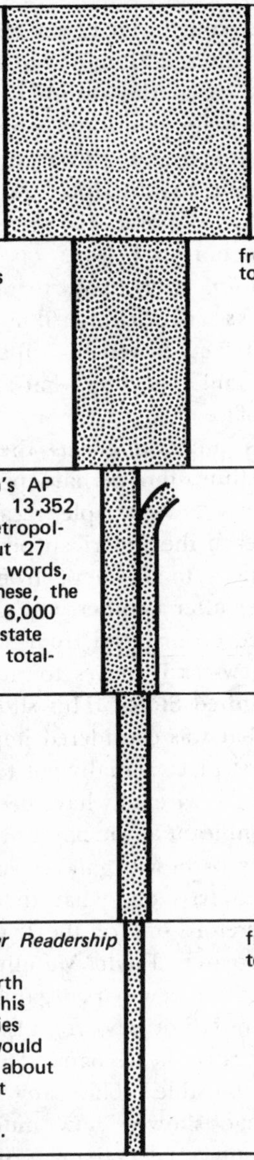

An estimated 100,000 to 125,000 words of news copy flows into the AP from various sources, each news cycle. The exact amount of copy is not known.

News flows into the AP, then goes

From this copy, the AP editors select and transmit about 283 items totaling nearly 57,000 words. This volume of news rolls across the United States each news cycle, on the several AP wires.

from AP bureaus to trunk wires

From the mass of news, Wisconsin's AP Bureau selects about 77 items and 13,352 words for retransmission to nonmetropolitan Wisconsin dailies. This is about 27 per cent of items, 24 per cent of words, received on the trunk wires. To these, the Bureau adds about 45 stories and 6,000 words of Wisconsin news. To the state wire, therefore, it sent 122 items, totaling 19,423 words.

from trunk wires to state TTS wire

From the state wire, four typical Wisconsin dailies select and use about 74 items and 12,848 words. This is about 61 per cent of items, 66 per cent of words available on the state wire.

from state TTS wire to daily newspapers

The *Continuing Study of Newspaper Readership* and other readership studies show that the average reader reads a fourth to a fifth of the stories printed in his paper. Of the total number of stories reprinted from the state wire, he would therefore read about 15 stories, or about 2,800 words. Of the 283 items that started out on the trunk wire, he would probably read about nine.

from newspapers to readers

**Figure 3** Flow of Associated Press news from agency home offices to four Wisconsin nonmetropolitan daily newspapers. (Adapted from S. C. Cutlip, "Content and flow of AP news." *Journalism Quarterly*, 31, 1954, 434–446)

and Gerbner as to why journals use the material they do on mental health and illness have been gatekeeper studies. Research of this kind is valuable in two ways: By showing how the gatekeeping is done, it gives the audience a better idea of how to evaluate what comes through the gate; in addition, it challenges a gatekeeper to evaluate his reasons for selecting and rejecting.[5]

The speed with which the mass media operate is one of the factors that make their gatekeeping so difficult. A book publisher has several months, if necessary, to decide on a manuscript, and then he has additional months in which to edit and improve it if he decides to publish. A news editor on a daily newspaper has an entirely different problem. An afternoon paper may receive 400,000 words, or 2,500 items, of regional and national news alone, of which it can use about 10 percent— 40,000 words, 300 items—and they must be chosen in the course of a working day. Bagdikian reports an observation study of one news editor on a suburban evening paper. Between 6 A.M. and 1 P.M. this gatekeeper processed 110,000 words of news, including 5,000 words of local news that took special attention. He decided to use about 20,000 words. He inspected 96 wirephotos and selected 16.[6] He went through a number of press releases, approving or discarding. He made and remade the dummies of the news pages. He was responsive to updates and rewrites. He talked to reporters and others. All this was done in the seven hours of the editing day. Perhaps the figure on which to focus our attention is the 110,000 words of copy that passed over this editor's desk in the course of the day. This is the size of a slightly larger than average book.

Move one step farther along the scale of speed, and consider what happens in a television studio where a news event is being reported. A gatekeeper, the program director, sits with his eyes on three or four monitors. Two of them may have different camera angles on the scene being broadcast; a third may have a feed from another location; a fourth may hold a visual intended to explain something that is going on or expected to go on. This gatekeeper has to point at one of the monitors or flip a switch to determine what the viewer is going to see on his screen in the next second. He doesn't have a year or a few hours; he must decide in a split second. He doesn't have time to think it over or research it or ask advice. As Walter Cronkite said in his book *Challengers of Change*, this is truly a new form of editing and a new skill in the world of news.[7]

What gets past the gatekeeper must then be handed over to a different group of people to be amplified and distributed. In the case of a newspaper, it goes to the printers and the circulation department. In radio or television it goes to the studio and transmitter engineers.

This is one of the peculiar characteristics of the media. The creative and production people, the writers and editors and skilled studio technicians, are responsible for the product on the basis of which audiences buy or do not buy, tune in or tune out. But their work on the product is completed as soon as it leaves their hands. Thereafter it must be turned over to technical and business people. The technical people are responsible for the quality of the picture that reaches the picture tubes or the appearance of the copy that comes to the reading tables of the media audience. The sales people are responsible for the advertising, subscriptions, and copy sales that keep the medium in business. One division of the business staff is responsible for delivering copies of the printed media. And management is responsible for keeping these complex and very different components of the medium working together.

The mass media—in a bigger, more professional way and with incomparably more audience—do exactly what an individual does in the network of social communication. He too decides what information to select, how to process it, what to pass on. The medium is, in effect, a communal sensory apparatus, central nervous system, and communicating musculatures. This is what makes the operation of a newspaper or a broadcasting station seem to anyone who views it closely a "slight miracle." Management, backed by role prescriptions, training, and tradition, has the task of coordinating the work of hundreds of individuals so that they function like one communicating person.

Because each component of the organization is really serving as part of this single communicating person, each has an influence on the product. The part played by the content staff

—writers, editors, performers, producers, and so forth—is, of course, basic. But some of the decisions on what the medium will carry are essentially technical ones: Is it "television"—meaning, is there a significant visual component? Will the scene photograph well? Can the sound be made good enough? In the print media, how much copy can be set in time for the edition? Will there be time or machines to reset a story to include new developments? How many stories should be on an attractive front page? Can we get a camera to the scene of the news?

There are other decisions that depend largely on salespeople. One of the most important for a newspaper is, How many columns of news will the day's advertising justify? For television or radio, Can enough local advertising be sold to pay for a particular program that comes without network support? What kinds of programs will attract advertising, and what kinds will not? If a public service program draws a small audience and the audience of the following commercial program is correspondingly reduced, will the advertising sponsors cancel out?

Management obviously has an influence on the product, too. The publisher or station manager represents the owner. The organization works for the owner. He has the right to say what kind of medium he wants it to be. Most management stays close to editorial policy but has little directly to do with the content of news or local programs or features. Even so, the viewpoints and preferences of management are often communicated subtly and silently to writers, editors, and producers. An illuminating study of the newspaper was Warren Breed's "Social Control in the News Room," which grew out of a long period of participant observation and demonstrated quite conclusively that the news staff learned readily what management wanted simply by noting what behavior was rewarded, although this was never overtly stated.[8]

The "slight miracle" is the welding of all of these viewpoints and activities and sometimes divergent and conflicting interests, all of these individual communicators and their networks of communication within the organization, into a single efficiently operating unit that submerges individual personalities in an organizational personality.

Figure 4 illustrates a good way to look at the structure and function of the mass media.

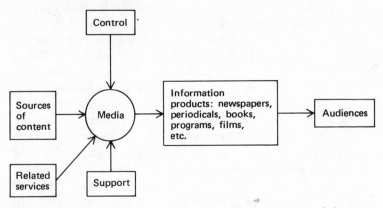

**Figure 4** A diagrammatic view of the structure and function of the mass media.

It may be helpful to fill out the diagram for one set of media, the broadcast organizations, in order to show what kinds of supporting services tend to gather around the media (Figure 5).

The same kinds of related services cluster around the printed and filmed media also. In fact, the structures of all of the media in the United States are much the same: (1) an organizational unit with creative, production, technical, sales, and management components, (2) in most cases privately owned, (3) with a minimum of government regulation, (4) aided by a variety of related services, (5) operating as gatekeeper, processor, and amplifier of information to (6) produce informational and entertainment products for (7) large audiences.[9]

So far we have suggested the size of the media industry only in terms of annual costs. Here is a summary of the media units in the United States alone:

927 television stations (700 commercial: 510 VHF, 190 UHF; 227 noncommercial: 92 VHF, 135 UHF)
7,131 radio stations (4,354 AM; 2,777 FM, including 478 noncommercial FM)
2,883 cable television systems

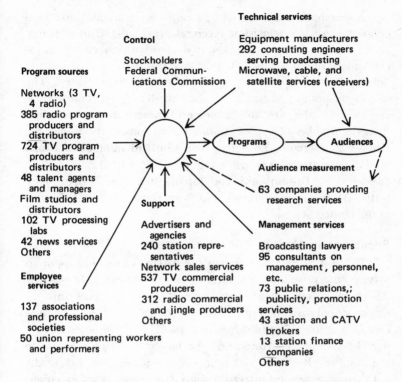

**Program sources**

Networks (3 TV,
4 radio)
385 radio program
producers and
distributors
724 TV program
producers and
distributors
48 talent agents
and managers
Film studios and
distributors
102 TV processing
labs
42 news services
Others

**Employee
services**

137 associations
and professional
societies
50 union representing workers
and performers

**Control**

Stockholders
Federal Commun-
ications Commission

**Support**

Advertisers and
agencies
240 station repre-
sentatives
Network sales services
537 TV commercial
producers
312 radio commercial
and jingle producers
Others

**Technical services**

Equipment manufacturers
292 consulting engineers
serving broadcasting
Microwave, cable, and
satellite services (receivers)

Programs

Audiences

**Audience measurement**

63 companies providing
research services

**Management services**

Broadcasting lawyers
95 consultants on
management, personnel,
etc.
73 public relations,;
publicity, promotion
services
43 station and CATV
brokers
13 station finance
companies
Others

**Figure 5** Applying the general scheme of Figure 4 to a specific media.

1,749 daily newspapers (334 publishing in the morning, 1,429
in the evening, and 586 on Sunday)

about 9,000 weekly newspapers

about 8,000 magazines (600 of which are of general circulation, 2,500 special business and trade journals, 1,500 religious, and 800 agricultural; in addition to these, there
are no longer tied to studios, and there is considerable
industry)

about 900 book publishers (of whom 300 issue 90 percent of
the books)

about 1,500 film-making organizations (film organizations
are no longer tied to studios, and there is considerable
overlap between film and television film making)

about 13,00 indoor and 4,500 outdoor film theaters

About half of all the world's radio receivers and one-third of all the world's television receivers are in the United States. More than half the world's annual consumption of newsprint takes place in the United States. Only Japan has a broadcasting development comparable to that of the United States. The enormous amount of newsprint used in the United States, however, reflects the size and number of American papers rather than the number of copies. Among the nations of the world, the United States stands no better than ninth in number of copies of daily newspaper per thousand people (with 312, as against Sweden's 501, Britain's 488, and Japan's 465; New Zealand, Australia, Denmark, Switzerland, and West Germany are also ahead of the United States).

## Support of the Media

In the United States system the pattern of media support is private enterprise with a minimum of government intervention. There are a few broadcasting stations owned by state universities or school systems. Both state and federal agencies carry on a certain amount of publishing, and the U.S. Government Printing Office might be considered the largest publishing house in the country. But the government does nothing or practically nothing with general-interest material or news. This is chiefly the province of private ownership and enterprise.

This pattern of support and ownership is by no means typical of patterns of support throughout the world. No less than 69 percent of the world's radio broadcasting systems are operated either by government or a public corporation created by government, and 17 percent of the remaining systems are partly government, partly private. In television, 57 percent of the systems are operated by a government agency or a public corporation, and 16 percent are partly government, partly private. Only 13 percent of the radio systems and 21 percent of the television systems are wholly privately owned, and these are mostly in the Americas. There is a somewhat larger proportion of private ownership in the world press than in broadcasting, but in the socialist countries the press is thoroughly integrated into the political system, as it is in many of the less developed countries, where the governments feel that national stability may be threatened by private media.

The nature of support differs among the privately owned American media. Television and radio, of course, receive their money wholly from the sale of advertising; there are no tickets to buy, no admission charge except the need to have a receiving set in working order. On the other hand, books are financed entirely by the sale of copies, and films (except those that appear on television) predominantly by the sale of admissions to theaters, although a small fraction of the exhibitor's income comes from theater advertising. Newspapers and magazines, on the other hand, depend both on subscriptions and on advertising, with advertising the senior partner. Between 60 and 75 percent of the cost of a newspaper or a magazine is likely to come from advertising; the subscription price that you and I pay typically covers less than one-third of the total cost of producing and delivering the journal or periodical to us. Thus, the major media are spread along this kind of support spectrum:

| ADVERTISING | | AUDIENCE PURCHASE |
|---|---|---|
| Television Radio | Newspapers Magazines | Films Books |

One end of the spectrum might better be called *indirect* and the other *direct* public support. Although there are no tickets to buy and no subscriptions to pay for television, still the average American home, as we have pointed out, contributes over $300 a year indirectly to the cost of advertising.[10] In countries where broadcasting is a part of government or under a public corporation, users pay through general taxes or a tax on receiving sets.

These differences in patterns of support help us understand two parallel currents that seem to be flowing in our mass media. On the one hand there is a strong trend toward reducing competitive ownership in large city newspapers and toward the formation of both newspaper and broadcasting chains owned by the same individuals or companies. In 1910, when there were 1200 cities in the United States with daily newspapers, 57 percent of these had competing managements; today, when 1589 cities have dailies, only 3 percent of them (in a total of 45 cities in the whole country) have competing managements. And as Bagdikian notes, fewer than a dozen cities have competing papers issued at the same hour of the day—that is, two morning or two evening papers under different management.[11]

The figures on newspaper chains tell the same story. In 1910, when newspaper titans like Hearst and Scripps were active, only 3 percent of the dailies in the country were owned by chains; today the figure is about 47 percent. The largest 35 chains in the country (such as Thompson, Gannett, Scripps, and Newhouse) publish 63 percent of all the newspapers in the United States.

In thirty years the percentage of AM radio stations owned by chains has increased from 14 percent to 31 percent. Although the FCC forbids any owner to have more than seven television stations, of which only five can be UHF, still the number of individuals and corporations owning three or more stations increased from 34 to 84 between 1956 and 1967. In the top 50 markets of the country, where 75 percent of the American people live, the three major networks—NBC, CBS, ABC—have 94 percent of the measured cumulative audience, which means that three programming organizations furnish well over 75 percent of all the television viewed in America.

Still another example of the trend toward concentration is the growth of cross-media ownership. Bagdikian has summed up the record on this: In 25 television markets serving more than half the U.S. population, newspapers own 35 percent of all the television stations. Newspapers also own 8 percent of the AM radio stations, and these are mostly in the very large and rich markets.[12]

So on the one hand there is a powerful trend toward concentration of ownership and less competition. On the other hand there is what looks like an opposite trend. Some of the largest magazines in the country have gone out of business in recent years, whereas smaller and specialized magazines are flourishing. Despite the concentration in television and AM radio, there has been a very large growth in small radio stations (largely FM) and a considerable growth in UHF television. Moreover, as large city newspapers have diminished, suburban papers have increased in number and affluence, and there has been an interesting development of "underground" newspapers with viewpoints geared to left-wing political movements.

In part, the latter trend is an artifact of the FCC requirement that all new television sets receive UHF signals. UHF has therefore looked to some people like a potentially good long-term investment, although it has not proved very profitable over the short term. Furthermore, the growth in number of FM receivers and the possibility of establishing FM radio stations with low capital cost and very low program cost inasmuch as they could broadcast mostly recorded music, has made it more tempting to enter that field. But that is only part of it.

The tradition of American media has been a highly competitive one, as might be expected of private ownership. This competition has been partly in ideas and service but even more, of late, for audience and the resultant income. It is hardly conceivable that American commercial networks would establish something like the BBC's Third Programme, which was designed deliberately to appeal to highly educated listeners and a highly rarefied atmosphere of taste—and consequently reaches a very small audience. In a system like ours the rewards have come with large audiences because that is where the advertising goes.

In the printed media the bulk of the cost comes in making and delivering the physical product. The larger the circulation, the greater the proportion of the cost that goes into printing and delivery. For example, as Bagdikian points out in his usual incisive way, a small paper that grosses $4 million a year will spend half of it on printing and circulation, a medium-sized paper with a $14 million gross will spend $8 million on the post-editorial functions, and a large paper with a $60 million annual gross will spend $40 million of it for newsprint, production, and distribution.[13] This comes out to about $100 for every subscriber, who will probably pay less than half that amount in subscription fees.

The costs of printing and newsprint have been rising

rapidly. This means that there is some point at which bigness ceases to be more profitable than smallness. Advertising charges for large magazines can only be raised so far, lest advertisers turn to competitive media like television. Therefore, a very large general magazine comes to a point of growth at which income no longer rises with circulation. The subscriber pays perhaps 20 percent of the cost of the copy he buys. If advertising does not pay the rest of it, the periodical is in trouble. This is why it has proved more profitable in recent years to operate magazines at a middle level of circulation rather than a very high level.

What does this mean for newspapers? If two newspapers in a large market can merge, the total advertising income of both can be concentrated in one at higher rates. If two newspapers with separate managements can combine their printing and distribution departments, they can handle these at lower unit costs, and there may also be some advantage in offering advertisers a combined rate for using the two papers. Consequently, there have beeen a number of mergers in recent years.

What does it mean for broadcasting? In the case of broadcasting stations, there is little cost increase with increasing audience. Once the basic expenses of studio and transmitter have been met, the operation is no more expensive for an audience of a million people than for one of twenty thousand. The chief cost variable is programming. In the case of even a medium-sized station, about a third of the budget goes to programming and only about 10 or 15 percent to technical operation. (The remainder is sales and management.) It is the ability of programs to attract large audiences that makes the difference in the attractiveness of the station to advertisers. The primary requisite of commercial broadcasting, therefore, is programs that attract large general audiences. This is why high-cost entertainment programs from the three networks are so important in determining how the viewing audience is distributed among stations.

In the long view, however, not all of these developments can be explained in economic terms. The magazines that are comparatively most profitable now are specialized ones serving particular interests and needs rather than general tastes. There has been a great trend toward specialization in radio—news stations, talk stations, music stations of different kinds, even "underground" and "overground" rock music stations. There has been a reaction against the pattern of the successful metropolitan newspaper, which now consists typically of general news plus a great many entertaining features. The attraction of serving local interests, as in the suburban communities, has been rediscovered. Some publishers have gone back 150 years and resurrected the pattern of the underground special-interest newspaper. In television, attractive alternatives to the large general-interest network programs have been discovered by some independent stations, presenting movies, reruns, sports, and syndicated nonnetwork programs. A number of these have done well. And the noncommercial "public" stations, supported by community organizations and offering a local and high-taste alternative to commercial programming, have noticeably increased their audiences.

Theoretically, then, it would seem that there are both economic and taste correctives limiting the tendency of a private enterprise system to concentrate ownership in one place and as much of the audience as possible on a single set of general programs that please most and offend none. For magazines, at least, there seems to be a point of growth beyond which few enterprises can operate profitably. For both broadcasting and print there seems to be a limit to the attractiveness of bland, self-imitating, general-audience programming and content. Beyond this, the way forward seems to be to pay attention to special audience interests and needs.

# ix.
# Social Control and the Future of Mass Communication

Concentration of ownership and proliferation of general-audience entertainment in a system like ours raises questions of control and national policy. Every nation promises its people freedom of expression, yet each one controls its mass media to greater or less extent as, indeed, it controls all its social institutions.

The first amendment to the United States Constitution specifies that "Congress shall make no law . . . abridging the freedom of speech, or of the press," and the Fourteenth Amendment forbids any state to "make or enforce any law which shall abridge the privileges or immunities of citizens of the United States." Article 125 of the Constitution of the Soviet Union states that "the citizēns of the U.S.S.R. are guaranteed by law (a) freedom of speech; (b) freedom of the press." Article 12 of the Spanish Charter of July 13, 1945 proclaims that "all Spaniards may freely express their ideas."[1]

It is evident that different societies are defining freedom differently. The United States is concerned with political freedom, freedom from the hand of government. The Soviet Union is concerned with freedom from certain economic and social class controls, and freedom *within* a set body of doctrine. When a Soviet spokesman says that the United States media are not free, he is thinking of the fact that they are owned by capitalists. When a United States spokesman says that the Soviet media are not free, he is thinking of the fact that they operate under the Minister of Culture and under the constant surveillance of party and government bodies. The United States would say that its media are free to compete for audience and for profit without government interference; the Soviet Union would say that its media are free to serve the people under the guidance of representatives of the people, free from a capitalistic bias.

It may be helpful to sketch briefly some of the history of controls on mass media. When printing came into existence in western Europe, it was under authoritarian governments that were already concerned about revolutionary tendencies and justifiably worried about how much further printed matter might rouse the people. When printing moved out of the shops of a few specialists and began to produce tracts and news sheets, governments took pains to control the new medium. They gave licenses to publish only to people they considered politically "safe." In the seventeenth century they established precensorship—approval of books and periodicals in the areas of politics and religion before publication—and later postcensorship—fines and jail terms for publications that they considered treason or "seditious libel" (a term meaning a lower level of dissent).

These controls were not a new idea. They grew out of a long tradition of authoritarian thought. Plato thought the state was safe only under the guidance of its wise men. Hobbes considered the power to maintain order to be sovereign and not subject to individual objection. Hegel said that "the State, being an end in itself, is provided with the maximum of rights over and against the individual citizen, whose highest duty it is to be members of the State." This line of thinking led to a policy of "caretaking" on the part of the government, which excused the restriction of individual freedom on the ground that it was done for the greater good of the whole state.

But revolutions took place anyway, and the policies of the new governments were built on the philosophy of the Enlightenment, including belief in the innate rights of man and confidence that man, given a fair chance, can rationally distinguish truth from error. John Milton and John Stuart Mill gave voice to these doctrines in words we still quote. Milton said, "Let her [Truth] and Falsehood grapple: whoever knew Truth put to the worse in a free and open encounter?"[2] Mill wrote in his treatise *On Liberty*, "If all mankind minus one, were of one opinion, and only one person were of the contrary opinion, mankind would be no more justified in silencing that one person, than he, if he had the power, would be justified in silencing mankind."[3] This was the intellectual atmosphere in which American mass media came into being.

Out of these doctrines grew a private-enterprise press, relatively free from government control in order to keep watch on and criticize the government, and supposed to operate in a "free marketplace of ideas" from which readers could select what they felt to be right and true.

By the late nineteenth and twentieth centuries, this unlimited libertarianism had been modified in practice. Psychology cast doubt on the ability of "rational man" to sort out truth from error, given the ability of one side to say more and say it better. Concentration of ownership in the media raised the question of whether a truly free "marketplace of ideas" existed and whether all viewpoints, popular or unpopular, would be represented. Film and broadcast media, because they were supposed to have a heavy influence on morals and beliefs, and because channels had to be allocated to avoid interference, invited a higher degree of control by official bodies. Consequently, in the twentieth century the media were asked to assume more responsibility for their own performance than merely to present their own ideas and observations freely, and government undertook, even in the most libertarian societies, more acts of control.

Since 1917 a new type of mass media system has developed in some of the socialist countries that is not at all like the libertarian system of the nineteenth-century West and not quite like the old authoritarianism. This new authoritarianism appeared first in the Soviet Union, grounded in the thinking of Hegel, Marx, Lenin, and others and beginning with the proposition that private ownership is incompatible with freedom of the press. "Only when the resources necessary for the control of the press are *public* property do the people enjoy effective freedom of the press," said a Soviet delegate to the United Nations Economic and Social Council. What is the press to be free to do? "Not to trade in news," said a Soviet spokesman, "but to educate the great mass of the workers and to organize them, under the sole guidance of the Party, to achieve clearly definable aims." Out of this thinking grew a mass media system integrated fully into the government and the party, a planned and systematic press that discusses the controversial events of the world with a unanimity of opinion and interpretation that would be startling to a Western reader.

Beside the transformed libertarian systems of Western Europe and North America, and the communized systems of Eastern Europe and China, lineal descendants of the authoritarian systems of the sixteenth and seventeenth centuries still exist in countries like Spain and Portugal, and many of the emerging and somewhat unstable nations.

In fact, there is much greater variation among systems than we have suggested with these three patterns. Terrou and Solal say that all media systems today can be classified as either "subordinate" or "nonsubordinate" to government. This is doubtless true, but it fails to describe the more subtle and distinctive differences within each group.[4]

This is especially true of the differences in broadcasting systems. At one end of the spectrum would be the many countries where broadcasting is actually a part of the government and its content is closely watched or the socialist countries in which it is integrated into the political machinery and under careful surveillance of the party. At the other end would be a country like Sweden, where television functions as a private company under the direction of a board of eleven members, of whom the chairman and five others are appointed by the government, or a country like the United States where stations are privately owned and the government is most wary about interfering with their handling of content.

Between these limits are many different patterns. For example:

British Broadcasting Corporation (BBC)—a nonprofit corporate body set up by a royal charter, with a board of governors appointed by the sovereign and granted almost complete freedom with its programs

NHK (Japan)—a public juridical person free in large part from government control but regulated by a government agency

German broadcasting—under chartered corporations in the several provinces, which are neither governmental agencies nor private companies but are intended to be as free as possible from government controls

Radiodiffusion-Télévision Francaise (France)—a public organization under the joint supervision of the Minister of Information and the Minister of Finance of Economic Affairs, who frequently exert rather close control over news and political broadcasts

In any broadcast system one can expect control, at least to the extent of allocating frequencies, and laws to protect audiences against libelous or obscene material, owners of material against violation of copyright, and governments against seditious broadcasts. With the exception of frequency allocation, newspapers are subject to these same controls whatever the system. All systems, that is to say, must regulate and control their media to some extent.

However, beyond these basic controls the different systems go about communications in very different ways. We have mentioned the almost complete integration of the Soviet type of system into the operation of party and government, and the layers of controls that are placed on the media in authoritarian countries. In countries with libertarian traditions the government is most loath to step in, but it does. The United Kingdom is an example. British media have been as "free" as any on earth, and British news is known worldwide for its credibility and absence of government control. Yet all British broadcasting has been under a public corporation until recent years, when private-enterprise television, supported by advertising, has been permitted to come in beside the BBC. The press has been called to account for its performance by an occasional Royal Commission whose wisdom and balanced decisions have provided a model for all media councils and investigations. There have also been censorship bodies to review new films. So there have been controls, though very light ones indeed.

In the United States, governmental agencies have picked their way among the problems of controlling the media as though they were walking on eggs. The easiest problems to handle have been those related to the "free marketplace" philosophy of the founding fathers. As the amount of competitive ownership and management in the cities decreased almost to zero, the Department of Justice became concerned about the number of mergers and the tendency of newspapers to use the same printing and circulation organizations and to offer joint advertising rates. A few cases of this kind are being tested in the courts under the antitrust laws. In broadcasting, the FCC has refused some transfers of broadcasting licenses to newspapers in the same city on the principle that this would unduly limit the free marketplace. They have expressed general distrust of cross-media ownership and, as noted, have placed limits on the number of stations any individual or corporation may own.

But the really troublesome problem is what control, if any, to exert over content. Newspapers in the United States have been free from such controls except under the laws of libel, sedition, and copyright. Films have not been subject to national censorship, although there are some state and city censorship boards. It has proved almost impossible to get a court to decide that a film or book is legally obscene. Broadcasting content is the most sensitive area. Here the FCC has moved very slowly— too slowly for most of its critics. The Commission has established a "fairness" doctrine under which any person or organization that has been attacked on the air has the right of reply on the air. This is generally honored, and when a station has refused to do so (for example, in the *Red Lion* case,[5] when a station in Pennsylvania would not grant a newsman the right to reply to an attack by the Rev. Billie James Hargis) the courts have been ready to step in and enforce the right of reply. The only real questions about this doctrine have been what constitutes an attack and who has the right to reply. For example, when the President of the United States broadcasts, inasmuch as he is a political as well as an official figure, does the opposition party or a senator whose position he is opposing have the right to free reply on the networks? When a network, with all its skill and resources, attacks an individual, how can he assemble the resources to reply as effectively as he has been attacked?

The crunch comes because of the way in which frequency allocations are given out by the FCC. If there is but a single application for a frequency, the Commission has to determine only that the applicant is financially, technically, and legally qualified ("legally" in this case means chiefly citizenship). However, if there is more than one qualified applicant, the Commission must take into account what kind of public service the applicant promises. "Public service," insofar as it differentiates applications, means chiefly the amount of local programming, the amount of news, and coverage of public problems. When one applicant is chosen, he is given a license for three years, at the end of which he must apply for renewal.

This is where the Commission and the broadcasters have not seen eye to eye. The broadcasters have made a large capital investment in their stations, but the value of their property depends on the frequency on which the station operates. For example, a VHF channel in a city like Los Angeles may be worth $40 million as against a capital investment of $2 to $5 million. Therefore, the frequency has seemed to the broadcasters to be a property right of great value that should not be taken from them any more than the land should be pulled out from under their stations.

As long as there have been no competitive applications at the time of renewal, this has caused no difficulty, and in truth most renewals have been granted fairly automatically. But in recent years there have been an increasing number of new applicants for existing allocations at renewal time, and many of these have been community groups concerned about the way their station is or is not serving the "public interest, convenience, and necessity" as the Federal Communications Act says it should. So the Commission has been handed a very hot potato. The original allocation was made, in most cases, on the basis of a promise by an applicant to provide certain public services in his programming. At the time of renewal, especially if there is a competing applicant, should not the Commission examine the record of the successful applicant to see whether he has kept his promise? This, however, would require it to become concerned with the programming of the station and, to that extent, to "control" programming.

The Commission has been sharply divided on this question ever since the famous Blue Book of 1948 (*Broadcast Responsibilities of Public Service Licensees*[6]) raised the possibility of reviewing a station's performance at time of renewal. Needless to say, the commercial broadcasters have bitterly fought any such review by the FCC on the ground that it represents government control of content, in conflict with the First Amendment. The Commission itself had moved only twice (although it handles 2500 renewal applications a year) to take away a station's license because of its performance, each time in response to prodding of the courts, until in 1970 it vacated the license of a Boston commercial station and turned the frequency over to a competing group. To say that American station owners were aghast is to put it mildly.

The significance of this question, which we have had to present so briefly but is discussed at much greater length in readily available sources, is simply how to ensure responsible public service in the mass media. We talk mostly about "freedom" of the media. Soviet theorists talk mostly about the "responsibility" of their media. But in our system we too want responsible performance in covering the events of the world, appealing to different levels of taste and interest, providing fair access to competing opinions, and the like. With our traditional aversion to any government control of content—so that the news media can be free to report to the people on the performance of their government—we have placed our bets on *voluntary* "responsible" performance by the media. For this reason we have encouraged professional training, professional associations, and inter- and intramedia criticism (of which, unfortunately, there has been very little except in book reviewing). We have counted on responsible news coverage in the press, responsible program service in broadcasting.

The Commission on Freedom of the Press, chaired by Robert Maynard Hutchins, said in its 1947 report (which was given a disapproving cold shoulder by the media) that if media owners and operators did not perform responsibly something would have to be done about it.[7] This commission called for the formation of a council or board to review and criticize media performance. But behind all this was clearly the threat that the government would have to do something about performance.

Even the Hutchins Commission was loath to suggest that the government have anything to do with programming. And yet, what if it is determined that the media are *not* acting responsibly in some way or failing to serve the public interest? What if it is suspected that the people are *not* being given a "real choice" in taste, that opposing viewpoints do *not* have adequate access to media visibility, that the media are *not* being provided in every respect with an adequate coverage of events? This is the problem with which the American mass media system is now wrestling. When the vice president of the United States scolds the media, what he says is frightening to them because it raises the specter of increased government control. This has not happened, and even the bitterest critics of the media are not anxious for it to happen. But the debate that has centered on the question of responsibility and control illustrates how a social system founded on the ideas of Milton and Mill, and the politics of Jefferson and Adams, struggles with the problems of mass communication.

Marxist and Maoist critics would say that the argument is beside the point, that the real controls on American media come from their ownership by rich men and large corporations. And it is impossible to argue that the ideas of this social and economic class have not dominated the editorial pages of the nation and to some extent (see the study by Breed previously mentioned) news coverage. Yet the same Republican party that has been supported editorially for two decades by 60 to 80 percent of all newspapers has continually complained that news correspondents have been overwhelmingly opposed to that party's policies and candidates.

Another viewpoint, more often expressed by broadcasters than others, is that the public itself, through audience ratings and circulation figures, and resulting advertising support, controls the media and in general gets what it wants. Carried to its logical conclusion, this implies that audience size is a test of public service and seems to encourage a system in which all programs reach the largest possible number of people rather than serving different needs and tastes, and in which all newspapers maximize circulation by feature and entertainment materials rather than serious coverage of public affairs. Working along this line, network broadcasters frequently cancel programs that are only one rating point behind their competition, but this has been done for the advertiser rather than for the public. When newspapers engage in a circulation war, the weapons are usually feature materials rather than news or analysis, and this too is aimed at taking over a market and collecting advertising income rather than any very enlightened view of public service. Critics ask, therefore, whether the attempt to serve maximum audiences is motivated by economic interest or the public interest and whether a public vote of the kind expressed by circulation or small differences in audience ratings is very significant if there is no real choice available—if there is only one newspaper, or only one kind of programming.

Therefore, economic controls on American mass media are far more potent than government controls. But the system as a whole is struggling with a definition of what constitutes responsible performance in the media and how to attain it—recognizing, on the one hand, that free media must be economically secure, and on the other, that the basic goal is to maintain the free marketplace of ideas on which the system is built.

The basic principle is that the controls any society places on its communication institutions grow out of the society and represent its beliefs and values. The Soviet system integrates them into its entire political system so that they are controlled like any other political institution. The noncommunist authoritarian system controls through government restriction and supervision and often by government ownership, assuming a "caretaker" point of view. The social system in the United States exercises a bare minimum of political and government control, and though private ownership permits a great deal of economic control. How questions of public control come to be decided in this or any other country will obviously have much to do with the future of the mass media.

## The Control Problem in Practical Terms

In Los Angeles a housemaid found a 7-year-old boy sprinkling ground glass into the family's food in order to find out (so he said) whether it would work as well as it did on television. In Brooklyn the 6-year-old son of a policeman asked for real bullets because his little sister did not "die for real when I shoot her like they do when Hopalong Cassidy kills 'em."[8] In 1971 television showed a crime program built around the placing in a passenger airplane of a bomb that would be triggered by air pressure when the plane descended to a certain altitude; within a month, more than half a million dollars was extorted from Qantas Airlines in Australia by the same threat, and soon after that the trick was tried also in the United States.

This is the kind of effect of the mass media that most bothers parents and law enforcement officers: the moral effect, especially the kind of effect that leads to asocial behavior. True, we have worried about our children and about crime in our society since time immemorial. The mass media have merely provided a new reason for worrying. And concern about the mass media began long before television.

I once knew a man who ran away from Buttercup Academy in an East Coast city to make a career riding the range in the Far West, influenced by the dime novels he had read. At least that was what his parents believed; others felt that the same result might have come about without the novels, and the man himself said in his old age that no red-blooded American boy could have submitted to being sent to Buttercup Academy! My own parents were concerned about the language they feared their children were learning from the comics and the probability that movies were undermining our characters. But now television, because it has many of the same characteristics as the movies and the comics but dominates a child's time in a way that films and comics never have, has become the chief source of concern among the media influences on children and young people.

Not parents alone but also child specialists, psychiatrists, and social and psychological researchers of many kinds share this concern. The chief question is whether televison is teaching undesirable social behavior and in particular whether violence on the air leads to violence in human life. The argument has been heated, with representatives of the broadcasters arrayed against specialists and concerned laymen.

There has been a great deal of research on the problem. Research on children, of course, is limited by different ethics from those applied to laboratory animals or inert materials. We cannot experiment on children in ways that have been used to study causality elsewhere; we cannot, for example, try different ways of bringing about overaggressiveness, delinquency, or crime in order to identify the truly active and dangerous combinations of causes. Therefore, it has been much harder to demonstrate direct causal effects in the extremely complex relationship of children to television than, say, to find out the effects of heat on a metal or the result of infecting a laboratory animal with a certain virus. Nevertheless, a great deal has been found out.

The most important finding is the enormous amount children learn from the mass media—especially from television, which absorbs so much of their time. They learn facts, they learn attitudes, they learn how people act and what is expected of them in many social situations. They model no small part of their behavior on what they see on the tube. They learn both directly and indirectly: Indeed, they pick up a startling amount of incidental information from media content that is intended to entertain rather than inform. For many children entertainment media (especially television) provide a kind of social map. They learn what the distant world is like, who and what is worth looking at, what kind of behavior is valued. And this map is extremely vivid because children give themselves to entertainment media. The media attract them, excite them, arouse them.[9]

Many laboratory studies have demonstrated that children can learn violent behavior from television or films and be made more aggressive by viewing violence.[10] To be sure, this has been demonstrated in the laboratory, where the relation of television to behavior can be kept free of other influences; the doubt concerning such laboratory findings, of course, is whether they would work in real life. And it is evident that the relationship between viewing and behavior in society is nowhere near as simple and direct as in the laboratory. Social restraints, social norms against violent behavior, are so strong that they will inhibit most tendencies toward violence. The research conclusion is that violent television is likely to have a "contributory effect" on real-life violence. As Leonard Berkowitz, one of the chief students of human aggression, summed it up, viewing televison violence "heightens the probability" that someone in real life will commit a violent act.[11]

We have lived with that uneasy conclusion for a number of years. Expressions of concern, demands on the media to present less violent entertainment have risen and fallen like a sine wave. An attempt to derive clearer directives from research has been made in the past two years by the Surgeon General of the United States. Acting on the instruction of Congress, his office has supported 23 related research studies, at a cost of more than a million dollars to try to answer, once and for all so far as research can answer it, the question of whether TV violence is harmful to children.

The results of these studies are now out—in five volumes.[12] The battle about interpretation of the evidence began, however, even before the research. The television industry was permitted to blackball from the supervisory commission seven scholars whose attitudes toward television violence the industry regarded as negative. On the other hand, two employees and three former employees or frequent consultants of the networks were appointed to the commission. The report of the commission itself was so full of qualifications that it hardly provided a clear directive, and early and incautious newspaper reports actually presented it as concluding that television violence is not harmful. But the results of the 23 studies, as contrasted with sections of the commission report, were convincing enough that the Surgeon General went before the Senate Commerce Subcommittee, which had sponsored the investigation, and said:

My professional response today [March 21, 1972] is that the broadcasters should be put on notice. The overwhelming consensus and the unanimous scientific advisory committee's report indicates that televised violence, indeed, does have an adverse effect on certain members of our society. . . .

It is clear to me that a causal relationship between televised violence and anti-social behavior is sufficient to warrant appropriate and immediate remedial action. The data in social phenomena such as television and violence and/or aggressive behavior will never be clear enough for all social scientists to agree on the formulation of a succinct statement of causality. But there comes a time when the data are sufficient to justify action. That time has come.[13]

Senator Pastore, chairman of the subcommittee, reflecting on the meaning of the Surgeon General's statement that televised violence has an adverse effect on "some members of our society," noted that if only one child a year were led into "unfeeling violent attitudes" and if that child affected only one other, in 20 years there would be 1,048,575 violence-prone people in our midst.[14]

Now, what do we do about a problem like this?

In a more authoritarian system it would be less of a problem. In the Soviet Union the mass media have been used, in all good conscience, to help produce a "new Soviet man," the kind of citizen considered desirable. In China all the forces and elements of public communication have similarly been focused on teaching the attitudes, values, aspirations, and behaviors the nation's leaders have considered desirable. In both countries, incidentally, the amount of violence on television has been greatly restricted.

But in our system things do not work that way. We expect our government to keep its hands off the media and our media to act responsibly without being forced into it. Consequently, we have besought our media industries to police themselves, and we have advised parents to keep their children away from violent programs or to provide a corrective to media violence by means of alternative experiences.

One can but sympathize with parents who read advice like that, because it asks them to add further to child rearing burdens that are already beyond their powers to cope with.

They are already faced with the problems of drugs, rebellion in sex mores and politics, and a spreading distrust of the older generation. And individual parents do not feel that they should be blamed for the example of a whole society. The daily news has been full of violence in Southeast Asia, in the cities, and in movements that often aim at the highest moral objectives. How, then, can one expect parents to convince their children that violence is not an acceptable way of life? Yet what they can do they must do. And a family in which respect and affection are a way of life, in which the two generations talk together and sometimes play together, provides a certain amount of insurance against undesirable character effects, whether from the media or other sources.

But the media, particularly commercial television, are in a position to do something directly about the problem. Will they do so? Is it not possible for the skilled and creative people in the mass media to make programs that will attract children without attracting them to violence? Is it not possible to treat violence not as a shooting-gallery experience but as it looks in real life, ugly and resulting in suffering and sorrow? If we want children to learn alternatives to violence, we must present models whom the child admires and identifies with, behaving in nonviolent ways. The gripping scene in "To Kill a Mocking-bird" in which Atticus walks away from a fight despite the fact that he has already proved himself the best shot in town, despite the fact that a "no-goodnik" had spat in his face, despite the fact that his son Jem was watching, hoping his father would thrash the other man—the fact that he could walk away from that situation and still keep the respect of his son and of the audience is the kind of dramatic alternative to violence we need. A few more like it, rather than simplistic violent solutions, would make a difference.

Similarly, if we do not want to have film or television violence imitated, we can avoid putting it in a situation or setting where a child is likely to find himself. We can avoid directing it toward a target for which the child might later easily find a counterpart, avoid using tools on which a child might easily get his hands in an aggressive moment.

These are things it would seem we have a right to expect

of the media on which a child spends more time during his first 16 years of life than he spends in school or on any other activity except sleeping. Is it tolerable that anything less should be acceptable? Apparently it *is* tolerable. We are unwilling to interfere with the content of our media, set up watchdogs over them, or prescribe what they shall present because of our dislike of censorship and our overriding concern that we not weaken a free marketplace of political ideas.

This is one example of the control problem as it looks in real life. It is something of a test case and will be worth watching. Will the government move more vigorously than it has before? Will public anger rise to a point at which the media will have to do something about violence? Or will the media, despite their economic constraints and their insistence on freedom of action, themselves take significant action? How these questions are answered will be most significant in pointing the way ahead for the media in a free system.

## What Next in the Media?

One difficulty with emphasizing the medium over the message is that we sometimes lose sight of real changes in the content of the media and the social functions they perform for their audiences. In the relatively short history of mass media, no medium has gone out of existence. The electronic media have not done away with print. Television has not done away with radio or film. And yet both film and radio are vastly different media than they were before television, and newspapers are different than they were before the electronic and photographic media began to compete with them.

Whereas one medium never replaces another *in toto*, it displaces whatever functions of the older medium it can handle more effectively. Radio replaced the newspaper "extra." Television displaced radio as a center of family entertainment, and radio became a specialized medium for music, news bulletins, automobile listening, and background music for other tasks.

We can expect the same general trend of development in the next few decades. The present media are unlikely to go out of existence, but certain technologies within the present system are likely to displace some of the functions of present technology. Already on the horizon is the possibility of a combination of technologies and functions that may come close to being a new medium. Let us look at some of the trends.

One important trend is simply the enormous growth of speed and coverage in producing and delivering information. Take the example of the oldest of the mass media, printing. Type could, and still can, be set by hand at the rate of about one line a minute. The linotype was capable of a speed of nearly 5 (newspaper) lines a minute. When the teletypesetter came into use, it could set about 6 lines a minute from tape and the addition of a computer to the system in 1960 made it possible to set 14 lines a minute. Then the real breakthrough came with the introduction of phototypesetting for offset printing. In 1964 an early phototypesetter, the photon, proved its ability to set 80 lines a minute. An RCA typesetting device raised the record to 1,800 lines in 1966. And in 1967 a special CBS-Mergenthaler Linotron phototypesetter was installed in the U.S. Government Printing Office, with the astounding capability of setting 15,000 lines a minute! In other words, thanks to a photographic process and computer control, the speed of setting type has been increased by four orders of magnitude in ten years.

The same trend of development has been seen in the computer, which may well be the dominant communicating machine of the next quarter century. Bagdikian, using Rand figures, has compared the state of computers in 1955 with the expected development by 1975. A 1975 computer, he says, will be about one ten-thousandth the size of the 1955 computer and able to do comparable work. The same problem that took the 1955 computer 11 hours to solve will probably take the 1975 computer 1 second. A computation that cost $200,000 on the 1955 computer will probably cost about $1 in 1975.[15]

A similar evolution has taken place in communication satellites. In 1965, Early Bird had the capacity for 240 telephone circuits, and the cost per circuit of building and launching the satellite was $15,300. In 1968, Intelsat III had 1200 telephone circuits and cost only $1450 per circuit. Intelsat IV handles the equivalent of 6,000 telephone circuits at a cost per circuit of about $500. The costs of using the satellites have not come down proportionately, but this development undoubtedly will be reflected both in costs of use and in much wider use of the instrument for data transmission and television as well as for telephone communication.

A most promising technological development is the growth of cable systems. In the United States these systems number more than 3,000. They were installed at first to provide reliable television reception. Now, however, it has become possible to send into the home, office, or school by coaxial cable as many as 40 channels, and most cables now being installed have 10 more channels. Therefore, the prospect is not merely for more reliable TV reception by cable but also a considerable addition to the number and kind of services that can be offered to the public by cable.

Still another technological development of real promise is the ready availability of audio cassettes and the imminent coming into use of videocassettes. The cassette itself—a small housing for magnetic tape that eliminates the need to wind, unwind, or thread the tape once it is placed inside the cassette—is a great stimulus to tape use by the amateur, and consequently to home recording and the use of audiotapes for instruction. The videocassette, playing through a television receiver, will probably become the television phonograph of the future, both for purchased cassettes and ultimately for home or school recordings.

Together with these technological developments we must also consider a trend in the use of new communication technologies. The most spectacular development in recent years have been ones that speeded up or expanded the flow of information. Satellites, television, high-speed phototypesetting, and the general trend of developments around them have all had the effect of greatly increasing the amount of information available to an audience. This has presented problems. The printed output is so large that scientists cannot keep up with their fields. The news flow is so great that there is far more than any reader can handle, yet readers have the greatest trouble finding out in sufficient detail about an event or problem in which they have a special interest. That is to say, the typical pattern of news presentation today is the short item and topics likely to appeal to a maximum of readers. Entertainment material is available in much greater quantity than before, but still the viewers whose tastes do not fit those of the mass have difficulty getting the kind of program they want when they can look at it.

In other words, most of the great technological developments of the last several decades have had the effect of putting more control over the flow of information in the hands of the senders and proportionately less in the hands of the receivers. The currently developing trend is to resist and reverse this ratio. It is reasonable to expect that as the system develops the need of the receiver will bulk larger.

In this situation the development of the cassette, cable, and computer are of considerable importance, because each of these, in a way, can be used to give the receiver more control over his part of the system so that he has a greater chance of getting what he wants when he wants it.

Two examples, One of the greatest difficulties with making effective use of instructional television is that it has two conflicting needs. For one thing, it needs higher-quality programs. The best way of obtaining these is to have more central production, at higher cost, with more research and pretesting—in other words, the same order of care and support put behind all programs as was put behind "Sesame Street." But it also needs more control in the hands of the teacher or the learner. A teacher needs to be able to present a television program when the class is ready for it. He needs to be able to repeat part or all of the program if necessary, and at any appropriate time to stop the program and discuss with the students what has just been seen. If a student is studying individually, he requires even more flexibility in making maximum use of his learning device.

But now consider how these two needs are in conflict. The more we centralize high-cost production, the more it becomes economically necessary to broadcast such programs over large areas at the same time. This keeps the control in the hands of the sender rather than the teacher or the learner. If we want to keep maximum control of broadcast ITV programs in the hands of users, that implies locally made materials. But these are not likely to be of high quality.

A possible solution is a nerve center in most school systems, in which instructional television (ITV) can be recorded as received from central distributors and then redistributed by cable or by the 2500 mc instructional television fixed service (ITFS) band to classrooms or study carrels at such times as the teacher or the learner needs them. A further possible development would be to place videocassette players in classrooms or study places, where the programs could be made available on cassettes at such time and for such repetition or study use as the situation requires. This would do a great deal to put the receiver in charge and let him use technology as he finds it will serve him best.

But these are only a few of the existing possibilities. A much more dramatic possibility arises from the introduction of large cable services into the home. This is the development that really has the potential of becoming "the next medium," because it could furnish a complete or nearly complete home information service in a way that no other medium now does.

At the time of this writing, a home that subscribes to a cable television system in upper Manhattan has available to it three network channels, three local independent channels, one public broadcasting station, one New York city station, one channel that carries the Associated Press wire 24 hours a day, one channel divided between the Board of Education station and the stock exchange ticker tapes, one channel that carries the program schedules for all the others, and still another channel that intersperses background music with weather and time reports and public announcements, and originates its own programs between noon and 8 P.M. daily.

But even this 12-channel service is primitive compared to what it might be. The capacity of large cables makes it possible to send information outward from the home as well as inward. Therefore, in theory a user could call on a computer to search a library, a reference service, or a data bank for particular information needed at a particular time and, if necessary, to deliver printed material on a screen, a facsimile printer, or a Xerox-like machine. A user could thus have such material printed out in his home if he wished. He could order within limits, news, films, or recorded entertainment to meet his individual interests.

Several channels would be used for home study to support the kind of lifelong learning that is becoming increasingly necessary; much of this could be in the form of computer-assisted instruction delivered by cable. It may well be that channels would be distinguished by content rather than network—for example, a channel for news, one for drama, one for movies, one for music, one for sports, and so forth. There should be no special difficulty in recording programs for later use if they come at an inconvenient time. Some shopping might well be done by cable, and the purchaser could see what he or she was ordering. Meetings—anything from small conferences to conventions—could be held without leaving one's own city.

This is not fantasy. Most of it is within the present state of the art. It would be expensive. To maintain a "home information center" like this might at present prices cost some thousands of dollars a year—perhaps as much as a new car annually. Until a technical or organizational breakthrough comes about, the economic obstacles will be very difficult to overcome. In particular, it will prove difficult to remodel existing media systems— such as open-circuit broadcasting—without undue loss to owners and operators. But something much like this home information center very likely will come into being. When it does, it will have profound social effects. Such a clustering of services around the cable to the home, meeting a wider diversity of needs and interests than any present medium can possibly service, will have the effect of actually making more knowledge available in the home than in the school. If so, it is likely to speed the process of "de-schooling" education written about so eloquently by Ivan Illich and begun by such educational innovations as Open Universities and Schools without Walls. It is likely also to contribute in a fundamental way to patterns of leisure use as our leisure time expands during the next decades. Indeed, if it develops up to its promise it may become the supermedium of the 1980s and 1990s.

# X.
# The Audiences of Mass Communication

On any weekday evening, 75 million Americans are likely to be watching television. On any weekday, over 60 million daily papers will be bought and read by 90 million people. Three media—television, radio, and newspapers—reach more than 100 million people in the United States each week. The approximately 75 percent of American adults who read newspapers regularly spend an average of 35 minutes a day on them; the approximately 40 percent of Americans who read magazines regularly spend an average of 33 minutes per day on them; the one-third of Americans who read books regularly spend an average of 47 minutes a day on them.[1] The television receiver in an average American home (if there *is* an average home) is turned on more than 6 hours a day during the winter months, and all the media together absorb more than 5 hours per day of an average American's time (if there *is* an average American)— more than he allocates to anything else except work and sleep.

It is no news that mass media audiences are very large in the United States, and indeed in most other countries where media are widely available. Of greater interest to us is the pattern we can discern in this impressive amount of media use.

## Patterns Through Life

An American child born in the 1960s or 1970s will become acquainted, even in his first year, with the activity on the picture tube whether or not he understands what is going on. He may find that television is occasionally his surrogate baby sitter. He will hear the radio. He will have stories read to him and will be shown printed pictures. After a while he will find these pictures himself and probably ask for the television to be turned on. The electronic media will dominate his experience until he learns to read. At that time there will be an enormous expansion of interests and ability to understand new concepts, and the wonders of print will begin to compete with the marvels of the picture tube.

The amount of exposure to media in the early years is startling to anyone who has not recently observed children. Yet it was already the prevailing pattern in the early years of television, as Table 1 shows.

**Table 1** Cumulative Percentage of Children Who Have Begun to Use Given Media by a Given Age (San Francisco, 1958, $n = 754$)

| | | | | | | Books | | Newspapers | |
| | | | Maga- | Comic | | Read to | They | Read to | They |
| Age | TV | Radio | zines | books | Movies | them | read | them | read |
|---|---|---|---|---|---|---|---|---|---|
| 2 | 14 | 11 | 3 | 1 | 0 | 38 | 0 | 0 | 0 |
| 3 | 37 | 20 | 11 | 6 | 8 | 58 | 0 | 0 | 0 |
| 4 | 65 | 27 | 20 | 17 | 21 | 72 | 2 | 4 | 0 |
| 5 | 82 | 40 | 33 | 35 | 39 | 74 | 9 | 9 | 0 |
| 6 | 91 | 47 | 41 | 50 | 60 | 75 | 40 | 12 | 9 |
| 7 | 94 | 53 | 53 | 61 | 70 | 75 | 73 | 12 | 44 |
| 8 | 95 | 62 | 59 | 68 | 76 | 75 | 86 | 12 | 59 |

Source: W. Schramm, J. Lyle, and E. B. Parker. *Television in the lives of our children*. Stanford, Calif.: Stanford University Press, 1961, p. 218.

These results are almost 15 years old. The amount of exposure to television is greater now than it was then. We have figures from Japanese studies made in 1962 and 1969. In both cases they are higher than the American figures; in the 1969 study they are spectacularly higher (Table 2).

**Table 2** Proportion of Children Who Have Already Begun to Use Television

| Age (years) | U.S., 1959 | Japan, 1969 (Viewing TV) | Japan, 1969 (Viewing specific programs) |
|---|---|---|---|
| 1 | — | 12% | 1% |
| 1½ | — | 29 | 7 |
| 2 | 14% | 55 | 24 |
| 2½ | — | 68 | 36 |
| 3 | 37 | 86 | 61 |
| 3½ | — | 92 | 73 |
| 4 | 65 | 100 | 100 |

Source: Shizuoka study, published in the *Bunken Geppo*, Tokyo, 1970, 10, 1–33.

In 1962, the Japanese children were about a year ahead of American children (in 1959) in beginning to use television; in 1969, about two years ahead. New small-sample studies from the Surgeon General's research also show considerably more use of television at an early age in the United States.[2]

In the first eight or ten years of life, family patterns of media use have most influence on the time a child spends and the content he seeks in the media. In the next ten years, his media behavior reflects the development of his reading skill, the broadening of his knowledge and interests, the influence of school and peer groups, the demands and uncertainties of teen-age roles as he searches for his own identity and his place in life, and the maturing of his tastes and needs toward adulthood. At first his media choices are mostly for entertainment; comics, entertainment programs on television, popular music. As he experiments with teen-age roles, he finds it socially attractive to go out for entertainment and information to movies and the public library. Beginning in the early teens, he brings schoolwork to do at home. He often studies to the background of rock music on his transistor radio but has less time for television. As his interests broaden, his tastes broaden also. He reads fewer comics, more about hobbies or careers. He begins to read some public affairs news in the newspaper. Some children even discover the editorials. As the younger children turn toward slapstick and fantasy, the teen-agers consult advice columns.

Here is another table (Table 3) that shows the general pattern:

**Table 3** Use of Different Media by Children and Young People in the Fourth Through the Twelfth Grades (San Francisco, 1958–1959)

| Medium | Grade | | | | |
|---|---|---|---|---|---|
| | 4 | 6 | 8 | 10 | 12 |
| Television (median hours per day) | 2.2 | 2.5 | 3.2 | 2.9 | 2.4 |
| Radio (median hours per day) | 1.1 | 1.3 | 1.4 | 2.0 | 1.9 |
| Movies (median number in last month) | | 1.4 | 1.8 | 1.4 | 1.2 |
| Newspapers (percent who read every day) | | | 47.6 | 55.3 | 66.2 |
| Books (median number per month nonschool use) | 1.8 | 2.1 | 1.6 | 1.0 | 0.9 |
| Magazines (median number read per month) | | | 4.1 | 3.9 | 2.8 |
| Comic books (median number read per month) | 1.3 | 2.4 | 3.9 | 2.2 | 0.8* |
| | $n =$ (263) | (262) | (219) | (201) | (232) |

Source: W. Schramm, J. Lyle, and E. B. Parker. *Television in the lives of our children.* Stanford, Calif.: Stanford University Press, 1961, pp. 219–266.

As in the case of Table 1, it is necessary to warn that changes have probably come about in the intervening years. For example, present Nielsen figures for time spent by children and teen-agers on television are higher than these. Nevertheless, the trends in the table are supported by such recent evidence as we have. In the second ten years of life there appears to be a maturing of tastes, a reflection of new social roles, and a reduction in time given to mass media after the middle teens, when the demands of school and social life compete seriously with the media for time.

In the adult years television, newspapers, and radio are almost universal media. Television receivers are in about 95 percent of American homes, radios in about 98 percent (as well as in 75 million automobiles and 10 million public places). Newspapers come into about 85 percent of all homes. Moreover the use of television and newspapers (no directly comparable figures are now available for radio) rises or remains fairly stable at a high level during adulthood. Newspaper reading falls off slightly from a peak in the 40s, possibly because of vision changes, whereas television is actually used more in the years after 55. One of the remarkable findings of audience research is the amount of use given the mass media by people in their 60s and 70s, when the media may be serving to combat loneliness and alienation from the central activities of society. Table 4 presents some figures on newspaper and radio use:

**Table 4** Teen-age and Adult Use of Television and Newspapers, by Age

|  | Teens | 20–35 | 35–49 | 50 and over |
|---|---|---|---|---|
| Mean daily television viewing time (Nielsen, January 1965) | M 3:14<br>F 2:52 | 3:00<br>4:08 | 2:58<br>3:53 | 3:58<br>4:49 |

|  | 15–16 | 17–19 | 20–29 | 30–49 | 50 and over |
|---|---|---|---|---|---|
| Read newspaper within last 6 days (Canadian Newspaper Publishers national study, 1962, $n = 3,222$) | 72% | 78 | 80 | 82 | 82 |

|  | 15–17 | 18–20 | 21–29 | 30–39 | 40–54 | 55 and over |
|---|---|---|---|---|---|---|
| Read daily newspaper in U.S. (Newsprint Information Committee, national study, 1961, $n = 2,449$) | 69.4% | 74.9 | 74.2 | 81.9 | 83.0 | 77.8 |

|  | 10–19 | 20–29 | 30–39 | 40–49 | 50–59 | 60 and over |
|---|---|---|---|---|---|---|
| Proportion of news read in daily paper (Schramm and White, 1949, $n = 746$) | 9.3% | 18.3 | 21.8 | 21.2 | 21.4 | 19.4[*] |

Source: Nielsen figures for 1965; *Newspaper reading.* Toronto: Canadian Newspaper Publishers Association, 1962; *Reading of daily newspapers.* New York: Newsprint Information Committee, 1961; W. Schramm and D. M. White. Age, education, and economic status as factors in newspaper reading. *Journalism Quarterly, 26,* 1949, 149–159.

Newspapers, television, and radio, as we have said, can be considered universal media. They reach into almost all homes, have cumulative reading audiences of 90 to 120 million people a week, and record spectacular records for individual audiences.

For example, according to Nielsen figures the average network evening program is viewed in 18.9 percent of all television homes, where an average of 2.16 people per home are watching. This means that perhaps 25 million people are concentrating on this single program, which is by no means the most popular of the week's programs. The Television Information Office reports that network evening news goes into 78 percent of American homes during the winter months, making its coverage nearly comparable to that of all newspapers and larger than the coverage of evening newspapers. What about magazines and movies? There is no recent study of periodicals that can be used for comparison, but the best estimate seems to be that magazines reach about three-fourths of American homes. Theater movie attendance is between 25 and 35 million, 50 percent or more below pre-television levels. To be fair to that industry, however, we should also count the audiences of movie reruns on television, where so much film viewing now takes place.

What information do we have about media use by time of day? The early hours of the day belong to radio; the later ones to television. Nielsen reports that the use of television doubles at night and that the daytime audience is largely women and children, although even in the evening hours women make up a larger part of the audience than do men, as Table 5 shows:

**Table 5** U.S. TV-Viewing Audience

|  | Men | Women | Teen-Agers | Children |
|---|---|---|---|---|
| Monday-Friday |  |  |  |  |
| 10 A.M.–1 P.M. | 16% | 52% | 5% | 27% |
| 1 P.M.–5 P.M. | 15 | 56 | 7 | 22 |
| All nights |  |  |  |  |
| 7:30 P.M.–11 P.M. | 31 | 40 | 11 | 18 |

Source: Nielsen figures for 1969.

## Patterns of Taste

We can get an idea of television tastes from the following figures compiled by Nielsen after a study in March and April of 1969. The rather surprising thing about it is how little variation there is by type. The real variation, of course, comes in the "serious" programs carried by public television stations. An extraordinary BBC program on the history of art, Kenneth Clark's "Civilisation," may draw a rating of 5 to 7 and a local news program in depth may go into 3 percent of homes on public television. This latter figure compares to 20 or so for the most popular, but by no means "in depth," network news programs. In Table 6 we have Nielsen figures on prime-time commercial programs by type:

**Table 6** Nielsen Audience Ratings for Different Kinds of Prime-Time Network Programs (March–April 1971)

|  | Number of programs | Percent of evening hours | Average rating |
|---|---|---|---|
| General drama | 8 | 10 | 16.6 |
| Variety | 16 | 21 | 17.4 |
| Western drama | 5 | 7 | 20.8 |
| Situation comedy | 27 | 35 | 20.8 |
| Quiz and audience participation | 3 | 4 | 15.6 |
| Mystery and suspense drama | 9 | 12 | 19.9 |
| Feature films | 8 | 10 | 18.5 |
| *All programs* | 77 | 100 | 18.2 |

Source: Nielsen figures for 1971, in *Broadcasting Yearbook, 1972.*

Taste differences and changes are worthy of much more study than they have received. One of the most significant trends in the currently available evidence is the overall pattern of change in taste through life. As people grow older and begin to value knowledge and wisdom more and physical accomplishment less, they turn more toward serious public affairs content in the media. This can be illustrated, for example, by Steiner's 1963 study of the television audience (Table 7).

Schramm and White found a steady increase in the amount of public affairs news, as compared with features, read in newspapers throughout six ten-year groupings beginning with the teens. The same study found that the reading of editorials increased steadily through age 60, while the reading of comics declined, sports reading fell after the 20s, and reading of crime and disaster news decreased after the 30s.[3] Handel found some-

**Table 7** Proportion of Information Programs Compared to Entertainment Programs Selected by Different Age Groups (1960 national survey, total, $n = 2427$)

| Age | Percentage information vs. entertainment | Ave. number information programs per viewer per week |
|---|---|---|
| Under 25 | .20% | 5.2 |
| 25–34 | 33 | 8.9 |
| 35–44 | 31 | 8.8 |
| 45–54 | 35 | 11.2 |
| 55–64 | 44 | 16.4 |
| 65 and over | 48 | 22.4 |

Source: G. Steiner. *The people look at television.* New York: Knopf, 1963, p. 178.

what similar changes in tastes in his early study of the movie audience. (Table 8)

This seems to be a very general trend. The question is, What lies behind it? In order to answer the question, we must consider what effect education has on media behavior.

## Education and Media Use

Most scholars find that education correlates more closely than any other variable with patterns of information intake, and

**Table 8** Changing Likes and Dislikes for Different Types of Motion Picture Stories, by Age (1942 survey in 45 cities and towns, $n = 2000$)

| Age | Slapstick | Mystery, horror | History, biography | Serious drama |
|---|---|---|---|---|
| 12–16 | | | | |
| Like | 4.0% | 8.5% | 3.8% | 5.1% |
| Dislike | 4.4 | 7.6 | 8.7 | 6.4 |
| 17–29 | | | | |
| Like | 2.4 | 5.4 | 5.8 | 10.3 |
| Dislike | 10.8 | 8.3 | 7.3 | 3.9 |
| 30–44 | | | | |
| Like | 2.9 | 4.5 | 6.3 | 10.8 |
| Dislike | 11.0 | 10.4 | 4.5 | 2.9 |
| 45 and over | | | | |
| Like | 1.1 | 5.3 | 7.1 | 12.2 |
| Dislike | 12.6 | 11.3 | 3.7 | 5.3 |

Source: L. A. Handel. *Hollywood looks at its audience.* Urbana: University of Illinois Press, 1950, p. 125.

age and education together account for a high proportion of the variance in media habits. For example, the choice of "serious" media content increases with both age and education. This can be illustrated by another of Steiner's tables (Table 9).

**Table 9** Percentages of Different Kinds of Television Programs Chosen by Persons of Different Age and Education (1960 national survey, $n = 2428$)

| Age | High school or less | | | |
|---|---|---|---|---|
| | Light Entertainment | Heavy | News | Information and public affairs |
| Under 35 | 76% | 3% | 22% | 2% |
| 35–54 | 66 | 3 | 27 | 4 |
| 55 and over | 56 | 3 | 34 | 7 |
| | College or beyond | | | |
| Under 35 | 53 | 9 | 33 | 5 |
| 35–54 | 59 | 7 | 28 | 6 |
| 55 and over | 38 | 2 | 47 | 13 |

Source: G. Steiner. *The people look at television.* New York: Knopf, 1963, p. 177.

This table shows a fairly strong positive relationship of both age and education to the choice of television news and public affairs material, and a negative relationship to the choice of entertainment. Lazarsfeld and Kendall found a strong relationship between education and the reading of books and magazines but a weaker one between age and reading.[4] Link and Hopf, in a study made when radio was still dominant and television was just beginning to come in, found that time of use and percentage of readers making use of print both increased with education, but radio and movies were used less by college-educated people than by those with less education.[5] Lazarsfeld and Kendall also found that radio listening decreased with education.[6] Handel found that movie attendance definitely fell off (in the heyday of theater movies) among older people in highly educated groups.[7] Steiner, too, discovered that the more education people had, the fewer television programs they were likely to see a week: An average of 40 programs a week were watched by people who had not gone past the eighth grade, 32 by people who had finished high school but gone no farther, 27 by people who had finished college, and 25 people who had gone on to graduate study.[8]

But the amount of leisure time available to different people must be taken into account. More highly educated people are likely to go out to meetings and concerts, have more memberships and civic responsibilities, and have more money to seek entertainment outside their homes. And they become busier as they grow older. Consequently, they have less time for the media. This argument is made cogently by Samuelson, Carter, and Ruggels. By statistically manipulating the media-use reports of a sample of San Francisco adult males so as to allow for the amount of available leisure, they were able to obtain small but positive correlations between education and the use of radio and television, and strong and positive correlations between education and the use of printed media (somewhat weaker for newspapers than for books and magazines).[9] It is reasonable, therefore, to suppose that, within the limits of free time, human appetite for *all* the mass media rises with education.

To say only this, however, is to miss the point that when highly educated people have to decide how to distribute their available time, they are more likely to reduce the time allocated to the electronic media than that allocated to print. This must reflect the priorities they put on kinds of content. Recall also Steiner's finding that appetite for public affairs and news on television rises with education and age, but appetite for entertainment does not, and Schramm and White's conclusion that the more highly educated a person the more likely he is to read public affairs news, editorials, serious columns, and letters to the editor. Public television, which offers very little entertainment and emphasizes public affairs and "educational" programs, has an audience strongly skewed to viewers with college and postcollege education.

Now, what must be going on in the growth of human personality to explain patterns like these? Let us begin with the idea of the "life space." As we said in an earlier chapter, Kurt Lewin used this concept to represent the stored and funded experience of an individual—the ideas and concepts he had run up against, the meaningful contacts he had had with his environment, all of which had been processed in some way and the usable residue stored as a basis for the "pictures in his head" and guides for his social behavior.

All of a man's experience contributes to filling his life space. Therefore, other things being equal, the older a person is, the more his life space should contain. But the intensive period of filling it in, the most systematic experience he has in organizing it, is during his school years. The school years make another contribution that is significant in terms of an individual's media behavior: They develop his reading skill. Some day our curricula may make a parallel contribution to using the audiovisual media, but not now. At present the basic skill, basic to the other basic skills taught in school, is reading. And one's reading skill continues to improve as one continues one's education because one reads more and more difficult subject matter.

Enlarging one's life space, whether in or out of school, expands one's range of interests and needs for information. It does not especially expand the need for entertainment. Indeed, entertainment, fantasy, "escape" may well seem to compete with the serious business of seeking current information. Therefore, with greater age and education there is a tendency, as we have seen, to select increasing amounts of informative material. More interests and a broader distribution of interests within one's life space are calling for information and understanding.

When time pinches, highly educated people tend to seek their information in the printed media, where they can often find it more easily and quickly. *They* are in charge of the selection and the pace when they use print. And their highly developed skill of reading leads them to print. This, rather than rejection of the audiovisual media for entertainment, seems to explain the considerable preference of more highly educated people (relative to less educated people) for print over electronic media.

The strong and steady use of the newspaper throughout the life cycle can be explained in terms of its success in meeting the need for current information. The heavy use of television throughout life can be better explained in terms of its power to furnish entertainment, and only secondarily by its informational services. The increased use of books and magazines with education can be explained in terms of the demands of the life space. The decreasing use of books, magazines, and movies during adult life must be explained by other variables such as the principle of least effort, which makes it increasingly easier for adults to enjoy the media close at hand than to go out, to use what is in the living room (radio and television) and what comes in every day (the newspaper) rather than making special purchases or going out to borrow. In addition, the changing pattern of roles throughout life—the new responsibilities that fall on the shoulders of the teen-ager, the young mother, the young man trying to make a career, the couple putting down

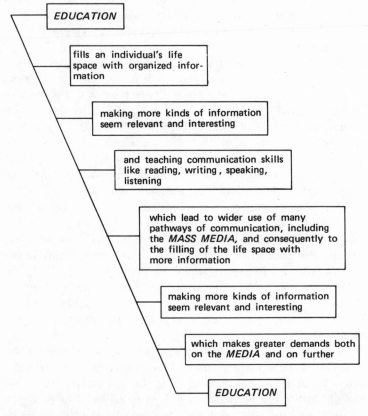

**Figure 6** Relation of education, mass media, and information seeking in the life of an individual.

roots in a new social setting, and finally the retired person—all these must enter into the patterns of media choice.

This model, despite all the things we have put into it, leaves out personality and individual differences, which obviously have much to do with what and how much use a man makes of a given medium or a given kind of content. But if we begin with the human life space, the contribution to it made by education and other experience, and the relationship of media content to the kinds of information and interests represented in one's life space, we are in a position to understand a great deal of what audience research discovers. Figure 6 is a good starting place.

## Education, Mass Media, and Knowledge

The Survey Research Center of the University of Michigan made national studies during the Presidential elections of 1952, 1956, 1960, and 1964. Among other things, it tried to find out how much use people had made of different mass media during the campaign. The researchers asked how much the respondents had read newspaper articles, viewed television programs, and so forth, for information about the election campaign. The possible answers were "regularly," "often," "from time to time," or "just once in a while." Then they asked from which medium the respondents felt they had obtained the most information about the election.[10]

Television came out with a very good report card. There were differences, as expected, in the use of printed media by people with different amounts of education, but the trend was definitely toward television as the chief source of election information. Dependence on newspapers remained remarkably steady during the 12 years from 1952 to 1964, magazines remained the "most used" source for a small but educated minority, and radio as a chief source lost ground almost as a reciprocal of television's gain. Television proved more likely to be the main source of election information for people with little education, for females, nonwhites, and farm and blue-collar workers, than for others, whereas print was likely to serve as the major source for highly educated groups, whites, males, professional, managerial, and white-collar workers, as well as high-income groups. But these differences are relative. The fact remains that television stood out as the chief source of political information during campaigns for the majority of the public.

We must be careful not to equate the results of these election campaign surveys with the media preferences for public affairs information in general. Six Roper surveys, made between campaigns for the Television Information Office, have also found an advantage for television in answer to the question, "Where do you generally get most of your news about what is going on in the world today?"[11] Television took the lead over newspapers in the third survey and has widened it since. Other Roper studies in 1964 and 1968 found that during election campaigns television is the chief source of information on the candidates for national office but not for local offices and just barely for state offices.[12] The Roper studies permitted people to name more than one medium and therefore are not easy to compare with others. A study made for the newsprint industry in 1967 (*not* a campaign year) found that people could identify more public affairs items they had seen in newspapers than they had seen on television.[13] Another study, made in 1966 in a California community where the characteristics of the population closely approximate national characteristics, revealed that from three to ten times as many people reported using the newspaper rather than television for national public affairs information between campaigns (although twice as many high school dropouts used television rather than newspapers).[14] We can conclude, therefore, that television is of major importance as a source of information on national and possibly state offices during an election campaign but of less importance in local election campaigns and *between* campaigns.

Suppose we analyze studies of other kinds of public knowledge. Newspapers are clearly used more than television for science information, and both magazines and newspapers are used more than television for information on health. And when we dig into the data in greater detail, we find that respondents whose major source of information is print are more likely than those whose major source is broadcast to answer correctly information questions on science (e.g., about polio vaccine or fluoridation) and about public affairs (which party had the congressional majority, identifying such organizations as ADA and the Birch Society, and so forth). Interesting also are two studies, 18 months apart, of the kind of information possessed before and after the launching of the first Sputnik. People reported at the same time their primary source of news about satellites. Before Sputnik was launched, the best-informed respondents said their chief sources of information on satellites was magazines. Those whose sources were newspapers were second-best informed, and television and radio came in third and fourth. This was still the rank-order after the launching, but the most interesting change was in the kind of additional information learned. After the extensive media treatment of Sputnik, every group knew more about the "science" of satellites—how they are propelled, what weightlessness is, how they maintain orbit, and so forth. That is, they knew a *little* more. Beforehand, the newspaper readers could answer 22 percent of such an information test; afterward, 34 percent. The magazine readers: before, 38; after, 47. Radio listeners: before, 10; after, 19. Television viewers: before, 16; after, 25. But every group gained sensationally in knowledge of the political implications of the launching of a satellite and the future possibilities of satellites.[15]

The launching of Sputnik, of course, was not given the amount of attention that some later American launchings received, although it made a thunderous impact on government policy makers. But suppose we take an event that had unequalled coverage: an information question asked of a national sample shortly after the assassination of President Kennedy and again about 18 months later. Respondents were asked to name three American presidents, in addition to President Kennedy, who had lost their lives at the hands of an assassin. There was no difference in the two surveys in the percentage of people able to name Lincoln as one of the assassinated three. That had probably been learned in school. But whereas 37 percent were able to name all three when the Kennedy news was still fresh, only 16 percent could name all three when the great burst of media coverage had subsided and public knowledge had reverted to a "normal" level.

On the basis of results like these, we conclude that the kind of knowledge learned from television is more likely to be related to dramatic events such as a Presidential election campaign and is more likely to consist of information on matters of the moment and relatively superficial understandings than the kind of information acquirable from the printed media. This is why people learned more about science *politics* from television and more about *science* from print.

Let us sum up. All of us emerge from school with a cognitive map, an organized life space, and certain learning skills and habits. More education means more reading skill and a better-filled-in map, which in turn means wider interests and a greater appetite for information. Through the media we continue to seek information to fill in this map. From the parade of events on television, the most vivid and dramatic of the media, we tend to fill in facts and findings, pictures and impressions and opinions, but to add concepts and understanding we are more likely to turn to the slower print media, which can somewhat more easily provide perspective and interpretation, and where we are in charge of pace and selection. The more skilled we are at reading, the better filled-in our cognitive maps are on a particular subject, the more likely we are to turn to print. That, we can assume, is one reason why the printed media are more likely to be the chief source of long-term science and health knowledge, and the broadcast media the chief source of political facts useful in an election campaign and forgettable thereafter.

# xi.
# How Communication
# Has an Effect

October 30, 1938 was a memorable day in the history of broadcasting. That was the day when Orson Welles and the CBS radio theater group put on the air a play about an imaginary invasion from Mars. Before the evening was over, thousands of listeners were in a state of panic, and some were running for the hills.

This reaction had not been anticipated. The play was intended as a gentle Halloween joke. It was adapted from H. G. Wells's novel *War of the Worlds*, which itself had caused no panic. At the beginning, middle, and end of the hour-long broadcast, the origin of the program was made clear: It was fiction, it was a dramatization of a novel by Wells, it was on *Halloween*! But the CBS switchboard lit up like Times Square. Thousands of calls went to police stations and agencies of the federal government. Thousands of people tried to warn friends. Never before in the history of broadcasting had so many people been frightened by a radio play. And it is literally true that a number of people packed the family and a few personal goods into their automobiles and drove away as fast as they could from the Eastern seaboard, where the invasion from Mars was supposedly taking place.

The next day, in varied combinations of sheepishness, indignation, and puzzlement, CBS was apologizing and explaining, newspapers were viewing with alarm, and congressmen were gravely mentioning the need of further regulation of broadcasting. Fortunately, some competent researchers were also interested and active. Hadley Cantril, a Princeton social psychologist, and Hazel Gaudet and Herta Hertzog from the Columbia Bureau of Applied Research put a study into the field to try to find out what had happened. Most of what we know about why "The Invasion from Mars" frightened so many listeners is based on their field interviews.[1]

Something that may be hard for us to remember today becomes very clear from these interviews: the atmosphere of crisis, threat, impending catastrophe that prevailed in 1938. The great war in Europe was near at hand. The threatening voice of Hitler, the martial songs of the SS troops, the ominous reports of William Shirer from Berlin were all being heard on American radio. The European powers were arming and maneuvering. In an effort to get some "inside" information on whether war was coming, H. V. Kaltenborn on one of his broadcasts had even gone to the length of analyzing a prayer of the Archbishop of Canterbury. In other words, dark clouds had gathered over the world, disaster threatened, and nowhere was the tone more ominous than on the radio.

In addition, most of us have doubtless forgotten how much people trusted and depended on radio newscasts in 1938. Even at that time radio had all but eliminated the newspaper "extra." It carried the sounds of realism—a Nazi meeting at Nuremberg, Big Ben from London, the voices of the world power figures. And in the 30s there appeared a number of most impressive newscasters and commentators—Murrow from London, Shirer from Berlin, Kaltenborn and Davis from New York. This period saw the beginning of the CBS dynasty of news reporters. For three decades these news teams had an influence on American news coverage and news habits unequalled among the networks. Because radio was first with news from troubled spots, because it had a tone of immediacy and realism, because it had effective reporters bringing the news from the places where news was happening, people were prepared to an extraordinary degree to trust anything that was broadcast as news.

"The Invasion from Mars" was written in the form of bulletins and newscasts. It was extraordinarily well done. First came a bulletin that interrupted some dance music: Astronomers had noted mysterious explosions on Mars. Ho-hum. Back to the popular music. Another bulletin. More music. The network now brought on an "expert" to try to explain the strange sightings. There were reports that objects had been observed coming from Mars toward the earth. More popular music, but by now the alleged news service was becoming worried. It brought in more "expert" opinion. Then there was a bulletin about something—perhaps a large meteorite—landing near Princeton, New Jersey. Flashing back and forth from observers on the scene to police spokesmen to scientists to the "secretary of war," the drama let people listen in on the developing crisis: the spaceship (as it was found to be) opening, proving to be unfriendly, vaporizing with a mysterious ray a force of troops that attacked it, finally spewing out gigantic mechanical figures that walked over rivers and hills, destroying anything in their path, heading for New York. Bulletins began to report similar spaceships landing in other parts of the country. And so on toward a climax.

Listening to a tape of this program today, one can hardly understand how it could have had the effect it did. It was explained carefully as a dramatization of Wells's novel. The names of the government officials and "experts" were obviously fictitious. The other networks kept on playing their usual evening programs; if a listener had merely bothered to turn to another station, he would surely have questioned whether the news bulletins on CBS were real or fictional. If he had merely bothered to look at the radio schedule for the evening, he would have found that the CBS Workshop was broadcasting a radio play. And if he had stayed with the program, he would have found that the latter part abandoned the news bulletin format and compressed many weeks into 30 minutes.

But what happened cast real doubt on the cornerstone of the American theory of mass communication: the ability of rational man, given a free and fair choice, to distinguish truth from error. For a considerable number of the audience did not question the "truth" of the presentation. Or they made an unsuccessful try to do so—they placed a telephone call and found the line busy. Or they couldn't find the radio schedule. They looked outside and saw the streets empty, and decided that everybody had gone into hiding. Or they looked outside and saw the streets full of cars and decided that everyone was running away from the danger. They didn't try very hard, if at all, to test the reality of what they were hearing. Those who did look critically at the reality of the program had no trouble. But of those who did not, some panicked and a few ran away.

About this time you may be saying: That was in 1938. It couldn't happen again. People are too sophisticated about the mass media to fall for an unsubstantiated hoax today.

Do you really think so?

On April 1, 1971, the *Saturday Review* published a letter to the editor signed "K. Jason Sitewell."[2] If readers had been on their toes, they might have remembered that the same author had appeared in the magazine on other occasions, usually around April Fool's Day. This time he wrote to urge editors and readers to oppose H.R. 6142, a bill "introduced by Representative A. F. Day and co-sponsored by 43 other Congressmen." The purpose of this bill, as stated, was to restrict the size of private parks and to democratize public parks that were sparsely used. Mr. Sitewell, however, charged that the hidden purpose of the bill was to abolish golf. The "parks" were golf courses. Mr. Sitewell said he knew from personal acquaintance that Congressman Day had a fierce, almost psychotic hatred of golf, which derived from the circumstance that his grandfather had died in a sand trap from "massive exasperation" and his father had died from the shock of hitting 19 balls into a pond on a par-three green. Therefore Congressman Day was fanatically devoted to doing away with the sport that had caused such sorrow in his family and also, he said, produces 75,000 coronary occlusions per year, 83,000 cases of hypertension, 9,300 golf cart fatalities, and 60,000 broken homes. Mr. Sitewell called upon all friends of golf to rally to the defense of the game and defeat H.R. 6142.

Norman Cousins, the witty, golf-playing former editor of the *Saturday Review*, admitted in the May 8 issue that the letter was a spoof, published appropriately on April 1.[3] There was no Congressman Day (whose first initials, one suspects, stood for April Fool). There was a bill H.R. 6142, but it had to do with taxes on national banks. There were no 43 cosponsors in the House. The figures quoted—75,000 coronary occlusions, and so forth—were without foundation. Like the Mars broadcast, the letter was extremely well written, but like the radio play, it had enough clues to cause any critical reader to put up periscope and look around.

But the most extraordinary things happened. It is reported that emergency meetings were held by the governing boards of a number of golf clubs. A leading golf magazine reprinted the Sitewell letter under the heading "A Frightening Bill." The wife of a federal judge telephoned the *Saturday Review* for reprints of the letter to send to her husband and some of his friends, who were away on a golf holiday. The editor of the *Saturday Review* reports that at least a dozen congressmen or their assistants telephoned to say that H.R. 6142 was becoming a priority target in the mail from their constituents. So it went, until the *Wall Street Journal*, chuckling up and down its front page, revealed the hoax and the *Saturday Review* itself confessed.

It is perhaps worth noting that the audience of the *Saturday Review* is generally considered a highly sophisticated and uncommonly well-educated one. And still at least an articulate minority of this audience, in the year 1971, was disturbed by what it read and failed to test it against reality.

## What Do We Mean by Effect?

What happened on Halloween in 1938 and after April 1, 1971 were obviously communication "effects." Many people were emotionally aroused, and some of them abruptly changed their behavior in a way that could never have been predicted before the broadcast.

This is the most common meaning of *effect*: Someone does something different from what he had been doing previously, apparently as a result of receiving a communication. A man hears the shout of "Fire!" and runs toward the fire escape or goes to the door or window to see for himself whether the fire is a threat. He sees a stop sign and stops. He reads "Peanuts" and chuckles. He watches a young man run down the field with a football in his arm and cheers. He answers the doorbell, and when a little girl asks him to buy cookies to help support the Girl Scouts he reaches into his pocket.

But it is perfectly clear that none of these communications brings about an effect directly. There is no direct line from a message to an action. Something happens between them. Of course, some responses have been so well learned—the reactions to "Stop" or "Fire," for example—that what happens is routine. But certainly not what happened on October 30, 1938 or in the early days of April 1971. Those required considerable information processing and deciding. And, in a less threatening way, so did the decision to buy the Girl Scout cookies.

The main effect of communication happens somewhere between the time a person turns his sensory receptors on communication signs and the time when he takes an action, if he does. Thus, it is hidden from view in the black box. The main effect communication has on us is on the pictures in our heads, our cognitive maps of environment, our images of ourselves, the beliefs and values we have accepted and are prepared to defend, the evaluations we have made of our relationships to individuals and groups—in other words, the translations of experience we have stored away in our central nervous systems.

By making some contribution to these "pictures in our heads," a communication can contribute to the probability of our making some overt response. But in order for that to happen, it is necessary to trigger off some behavioral process that will result in our doing something overtly—such as saying something, running for the hills, or buying cookies. The four steps in Figure 7, at least, must lie between a set of communication signs and an action.

There are formidable problems in the way of studying this process. We cannot directly observe 2 and 3. To some extent we can observe 1. At least we can note whether Mr. B is looking at a book or a sign or a girl, or apparently listening to the radio. If he takes some overt action after being exposed to the mes-

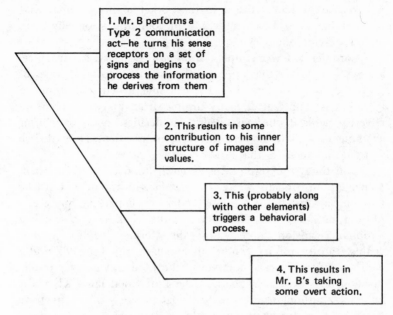

1. Mr. B performs a Type 2 communication act—he turns his sense receptors on a set of signs and begins to process the information he derives from them

2. This results in some contribution to his inner structure of images and values.

3. This (probably along with other elements) triggers a behavioral process.

4. This results in Mr. B's taking some overt action.

**Figure 7**  Steps between a message and an action effect.

sage, we can observe that action. But not 2 or 3. Those we can only infer.

One way to infer that something is going on is to observe physiological changes. We can determine whether Mr. B's pulse rate or blood pressure rises after he is exposed to the message, whether his palms sweat or he breathes faster. These are not very specific. They say that something is happening but not precisely what. If we want to try to be more precise, we can ask him questions. If he answers our questions, we can assume that the questions, at least, had an effect. We have behavioral evidence for that. We can try to project back from his answers and his behavior to the "pictures in his head." But precisely what happened inside the black box between the act of attention and the act of result we can only infer, or guess.

I remember a small boy who giggled all through the funny story his mother was reading to him at the bedtime hour. She thought the story was a great success, but when he giggled through the Lord's Prayer too she became suspicious. He admitted that he had a lizard in the pocket of his pajamas that was tickling him. The true causes of communication effect are often hidden in our pockets!

Consider a few examples. *Cumulative effects,* for instance, are overt responses that appear only after a cumulative series of exposures to communication. For example, a man may come in to buy a suit only after many urgings from his wife and from advertisements in the mass media. He decides how to vote after a whole campaign of persuasive communication. How do we sort out the causes for that kind of effect?

Sometimes the response is *opposite* to what was expected. When Upton Sinclair wrote *The Jungle,* he intended it to be a protest against the conditions under which packing-house employees had to work. The result of the book was to evoke a national revulsion, not against the working conditions but against the unsanitary conditions and lack of safeguards under which meat was packed for sale to the public. An angry public demanded a revision of some of the Pure Food laws. That was an effect, although not the anticipated one. All of us have heard of cases in which parental warnings against the dangers of drinking or smoking or promiscuous sex have apparently led to experimentation with some of these forbidden adventures. Clearly these unexpected results are as much an effect as the intended ones would have been if they had occurred. But precisely what led them to occur? Clearly, no simple S → R relationship.

*What if no response is observable at the moment?* Can we assume that there has been no effect? Certainly not. The situation may not yet be ripe for action. Perhaps a change has taken place within the receiver that will show up when the time is right or when enough change has accumulated to cause action. This is one of the chief reasons for studies of attitudes. We draw out verbal responses of some kind that may indicate a change in the inner state before any action takes place.

Suppose that our questions or tests or scales show no *attitude change* whatsoever after exposure to a message. Can we then assume that there has been no effect? No, it isn't even that easy. Suppose, for example, that the message merely confirmed what the receiver believed beforehand. Is confirmation, strengthening of belief, not an effect—perhaps a very important one?

What if all we know is that Mr. B has performed a Type 2 communication act? That is, he has turned his attention to a particular set of signs and supposedly processed the information. Is this an effect? We must call it one, although on a rather elementary level. To command the attention of an audience for a certain period of time is to have an effect on it. We must therefore distinguish levels and degrees of attention. A casual glance at a signboard is a lower level of attention than five minutes spent reading the morning editorial.

Thus, what seems simple is not at all simple. We can seldom deal with such an apparently clear and obvious case as the effect of watching the October 30, 1938 broadcast or the results of the *Saturday Review* April Fool hoax. We are usually dealing with complicated behavior in complicated situations, with multiple stimuli acting on the audience that is supposed to be affected and with many of the effects and the mechanisms of effect hidden from us. An example is the question asked so often: What effect does television have on children? As we said in an earlier chapter, this is simple to ask and desperately hard to answer.

On the basis of what has been said in the preceding pages, however, we can state a few propositions about communication effect in general. For one thing, there are many levels of effect—from attention to inner confirmation to inner change to overt action—and degrees of effect at each level. For another, much of the effect and the mechanism that creates it is hidden from us in the black box. We can only infer it from overt action (such as test responses that we ourselves elicit) or from other physical manifestations. Third, it is very likely that simple relationships between communication stimulus and effect are very few. Complex behavior usually has complex causes.

It would be reassuring to be able to deal with communication effect in classic stimulus-response terms: $S \rightarrow R$. This, of course, can be done with animals, and sometimes with humans, in a laboratory, where we can calculate the habit strength of learned responses to communication stimuli as learning theorists have done for years. In naturalistic situations, however, this primitive approach is not very helpful. At the least, we must substitute for the simple S → R model a more complicated one: S → O → R. In this case O stands for the organism in which the effect is supposed to occur. In order to understand why S is related to R, we must try to find out as much as possible about what happens within O, even though we recognize that such information must be inferred.

This is now the state of the art in studying effect. The complexity is fully recognized, and there is an effort to identify as many as possible of the variables and forces that enter into a given effect and to try to comprehend the process that combines them and leads to a result that can be predicted, at least on a statistical basis. If, for example, we can be confident that when children of a given kind are exposed to a given kind of television in a given kind of situation, a violent act has a certain greater probability of occurring than with a different kind of children or a different kind of television or a different kind of situation, we are on the way toward a usable theory of communication effect. But at present we are still blind men trying to describe the elephant from the experience of feeling his treelike leg, his ropelike tail, his snakelike trunk, or his wall-like side, and never all of them together.

## A Model of Communication Effect

What we are able to say at present about communication effect is therefore below the reliability of exact science and above the reliability of science fiction. One of the most useful models of the process is Dorwin Cartwright's. Cartwright is a social psychologist at the University of Michigan, a member of the cognitive school of Kurt Lewin.

The principles to be quoted were developed from Cartwright's analysis of research on the sale of War Bonds. This included intensive open-ended interviews with a sample of the population toward whom the bond campaign was directed. Some of the interviewees had purchased, some had not. Cartwright developed this set of principles to try to explain why the results were different in different cases:

1. The "message" (information, facts, etc.) must reach the sense organs of the persons who are to be influenced.

   1a. Total stimulus situations are accepted or rejected on the basis of an impression of their general characteristics.

   1b. The categories employed by a person in characterizing stimulus situations tend to protect him from unwanted changes in his cognitive structure.

2. Having reached the sense organs, the "message" must be accepted as a part of a person's cognitive structure.

   2a. Once a given "message" is received it will tend to be accepted or rejected on the basis of more general categories to which it appears to belong.

   2b. The categories employed by a person in characterizing "messages" tend to protect him from unwanted changes in his cognitive structure.

   2c. When a "message" is inconsistent with a person's prevailing cognitive structure it will either (a) be rejected, (b) be distorted so as to fit, or (c) produce changes in the cognitive structure.

3. To induce a given action by mass persuasion, this action must be seen by the person as a path to some goal that he has.

   3a. A given action will be accepted as a path toward a goal only if the connections "fit" the person's larger cognitive structure.

   3b. The more goals that are seen as attainable by a single path, the more likely it is that a person will take that path.

   3c. If an action is seen as not leading to a desired goal or as leading to an undesired end, it will not be chosen.

   3d. If an action is seen as leading to a desired goal, it will tend not to be chosen to the extent that easier, cheaper, or otherwise more desirable actions are also seen as leading to the same goal.

4. To induce a given action, an appropriate cognitive and motivational system must gain control of the person's behavior at a particular point in time.

   4a. The more specifically defined the path of action to a goal (in an accepted motivational structure), the more likely it is that the structure will gain control of behavior.

4b. The more specifically a path of action is located in time, the more likely it is that the structure will gain control of behavior.

4c. A given motivational structure may be set in control of behavior by placing the person in a situation requiring a decision to take, or not to take, a step of action that is a part of the structure.[4]

I find this a very usable model, given the present stage of theory and research. It is, of course, a *rational* model, emphasizing rational decision making and deemphasizing the irrational elements of choice. It pays less specific attention than I should like to the situation and social pressures in which an action necessarily takes places. But it is an unpretentious model, it seeks to explain rather than merely describe, and intuitively it makes sense.

## The Attention Effect

In practical terms Cartwright's first point means that a message must capture attention before it can make anything else happen. We necessarily make a very large number of swift decisions as to where to direct our attention. When we drive an automobile down the street we decide (let us hope) to give a major part of our attention to the road in front of us. We look relatively seldom at the houses, the lawns, the trees, the people, the dogs—even the automobiles—we drive past. We see a car going the opposite way, far over on its own side, and conclude that this is worth no special attention. We observe in the rear-view mirror an automobile coming up to pass on our left. We notice that it is in its own lane and promises to cause no trouble, so we turn our attention to other things. We pay no attention to most of the scenes beside the road, but on a certain corner we are careful to glance at a magnolia tree that has been showing signs of blooming; we look because we want to see whether the blossoms have now appeared. Out of a corner of an eye we see a movement of something light-colored on the lawn near us, and we look at it quickly because it might be a child running into the road or a puppy beginning to chase the car. We flip on the radio and quickly change stations because we have tuned in a commercial. We listen a second to the voice that comes out of our second-choice station and classify it: "Another commercial!" "That left-wing preacher at the university—more propaganda!" "The network news," or "Sounds like John Gardner; I'd better listen."

In other words, very quickly we can classify what seems to be available and decide, from previous experience, whether it is something we want to attend to at the moment. We look at the flash of color beside the road because it may mean danger. We turn away from the commercial because we don't feel like listening to a sales pitch so early in the morning or perhaps because we are tired of hearing two minutes of commercials in a five-minute news program. We turn away from the preacher because we don't want to expose our cognitive defenses to more persuasion at the moment. We may stay with John Gardner because we admire and agree with him. Our actions may not seem to confirm that we are members of a culture that believes in a "free marketplace of ideas." Ideally we ought to give the left-wing advocate and even the commercial pitch man a chance to be heard. But one of the deepest characteristics of man is to protect what he is and believes. And there is a time for all things. The busier we are, the more we are under pressure to do other things, the harder we find it to tear ourselves away from what we are doing, rouse our defenses, and invite attack.

## The Main Effect

We can call upon two main strands of psychological theory in trying to understand what happens in the black box to bring about the main effect. These are stimulus-response learning theory and cognitive theory. We are not compelled to make a "lady or tiger" choice between them; as a matter of fact, they share many concepts, and communication scholars have been quite eclectic in selecting useful elements from both.

$S \rightarrow R$ learning theory has been dominant in this country since the time of E. L. Thorndike, early in the century.[5] It has given birth to the drive-cue-response-reinforcement theory of Clark Hull, Neil Miller, Charles Dollard, and others; the contiguity-response theory of E. R. Guthrie and his followers; the operant-conditioning theory of B. Fred Skinner, which simulated the development of programmed instruction; and a number of other versions, including the neo-Hullian approach of Carl Hovland and his colleagues at Yale, who were responsible for building perhaps the most distinguished single program of communication research in our time.

The distinctions between these schools, however, may be more important to learning theorists than to communication theorists. The differences between them are mainly in the way they approach the problem of effect. If one sticks closely to the tradition of Hull, one looks for a cue that will unleash an appropriate drive in order to bring about a response that can be rewarded and, with suitable practice, learned. If one is in the tradition of Guthrie, one looks for a stimulus that can be presented in close contiguity to a desired response in the expectation that a subject can be conditioned to make the same response when the same stimulus is presented again. If one is in the tradition of Skinner, one looks for a response that begins to approximate the desired behavior, then rewards closer and closer approximations to what is desired, using a theoretically determined schedule of reinforcement so that—just as Skinner trained pigeons to play a kind of ping-pong—the subject will be conditioned to make the desired response regularly.

It has proved generally easier with $S \rightarrow R$ theory to study simple behavior like that of the rat in a maze than the complex behavior required for most communication effects. Yet present-day psychologists like Sheffield have used stimulus-response concepts to study the learning of complex behavior; Hovland was concerned with highly complex human behavior; present-day communication scholars like Lumsdaine and Maccoby have been strongly influenced by Guthrie; and followers of Skinner have demonstrated that operant conditioning works not only in animal training but in training humans by the use of "programs."[6] Concepts like response and reinforcement have been used by practically all communication scholars, whatever their theoretical roots.

Cognitive theory in this country has grown in the long shadow of Kurt Lewin and has been developed with different emphases by scholars like Fritz Heider, Theodore Newcomb, Leon Festinger, Stanley Schachter, Jerome Bruner, Brewster

Smith, and others. Lewin developed the concepts of field theory and "life space."[7] He also pioneered in studies of group communication and group effects. Scholars in this tradition are likely to be concerned, therefore, with a person's cognitive defenses, with the images he lives by and the ego structure he is trying to defend, with learning by "insight" as well as by reinforcement of responses, with the social norms one accepts and the group memberships one values or aspires to, and with the effect of group participation and social roleplaying on decisions and beliefs.

One of the most potent contributions of cognitive theory to the study of human communication has been the line of thinking and research that has come to be called "consistency theory." The concept of a "strain toward cognitive balance" or "toward inner consistency" was first developed by Heider.[8] He advanced the proposition that a person tries to keep his sentiment regarding another person consistent with his perception of their mutual liking or dislike for a third person or an object or an idea. He saw this as one of the powerful mechanisms by which cognitive organization and reorganization is accomplished. From this came Newcomb's A–B–X theory, which is now familiar to most students of communication, at least in the form of the diagrams Newcomb drew to illustrate what he called a "strain toward symmetry" in cognitive relationships. If two people, A and B, have a positive feeling toward each other and also toward an object, idea, or person, X—he said, the relationship is symmetrical.

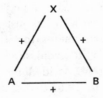

If A and B are not favorably inclined toward each other, and one is favorable toward the object X whereas the other is unfavorable—for example,

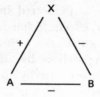

the relationship is also symmetrical. But if A and B are favorable toward each other but disagree about X, or if they are unfavorable toward each other but agree on X—

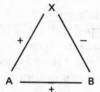 

the relationships are symmetrical, and there will be a strain to bring them somehow into balance by changing attitudes toward each other or toward X.[9]

This, in one form or other, has been basic to all consistency theory. Cartwright and Harary generalized the model to include any number of interrelationships.[10] Leon Festinger developed a theory of "cognitive dissonance" to explain such phenomena as why a person seeks further supporting information even after he has made a decision between alternatives.[11] For example, why will a person who has just placed an order for an expensive car read advertisements for it, or look for favorable opinions concerning it, and avoid reading about the less expensive automobile that he decided not to buy? Because, says Festinger, he is trying to reduce the dissonance he feels between the decision he made and the one he might have made. Dissonance, he said, acts like a drive to motivate such behavior as will reduce it.

This use of the concept of drive indicates the close relationship between cognitive-born consistency theory and S → R theory. Indeed, Hovland's last book dealt with a version of consistency theory,[12] and Charles Osgood, trained as an experimental psychologist at Yale in the tradition of Hull, developed a type of consistency theory that he called (in a book written jointly with Suci and Tannenbaum) a theory of "congruity."[13] This was based on findings that a person tries to balance his attitude toward the communicator of a message with his attitude toward the message itself. For example, if we admire a certain figure and hear him say that he espouses a political position with which we have been in disagreement, we feel a certain discomfort with this lack of consistency and usually try to make the two attitudes "congruent." We can reject the communication because we feel it is not an accurate quotation, or we can reconsider our position: Perhaps the policy is not wholly bad after all or the man is not so admirable as we had thought. Using his own semantic differential scales, Osgood was able to demonstrate that the change toward congruity depended on the strength and extremity of the respective attitudes toward the message and the communicator, and the distance between them. The most common result was in the direction of compromise: Both attitudes would tend to move together, with the one less strongly held moving the greater distance.

Consistency theory has since been developed further by McGuire and others, and has proved to be a useful way of predicting communication behavior and effect.[14] As the use of consistency by both cognitive and stimulus-response scholars indicates, there has been considerable theoretical convergence in dealing with communication effects. We can generalize in this way about where the thinking stands:

**1. If there is to be a change through communication, something must be learned: Some new element must be introduced into the cognitive structure.** The new element may be a different image of the situation. It may be a new motivation to act or new information on how to satisfy an existing motivation. It may be social pressure. It may be information that introduces enough discord into the existing structure to encourage some revision within it. The basic contribution of communication to change is to add something new to the cognitive resources and thus affect in some way the potential patterns of action.

Neither $S \rightarrow R$ nor cognitive theory has any monopoly on patterns for getting the new information introduced. Either one would try to maximize the effectiveness of all the variables that enter the message and the situation. The communicator should be as acceptable as possible, the signs of the message organized and presented in the most effective way one knows how, and the appeals chosen in the light of all we know about the potential receiver.

**2. How the new information is processed will depend on how it fits into the present cognitive structure.** Here again, there is no essential difference between the two schools as they apply to communication effect, although one side might talk about cognitive structure and the other might speak of attitudes and beliefs, or learned responses and motivations. In some ways it is easier to talk in cognitive terms about what happens.

As Cartwright points out, our ability to categorize new information helps us process it. For example, if we can quickly classify it as "just propaganda," it is easy to reject. If it can be categorized as "interesting" or "important," it is easy to accept it, at least pending further examination. If it comes into conflict with deeply held values and beliefs, our defenses spring into action.

A general principle of processing new information is that the newer it is and the less it requires us to change our cognitive structures—other things being equal—the more likely it is to be accepted. If it seems to belong in a relatively new category for us—as, for example, in 1957, when many of us heard for the first time about developments in orbiting terrestrial satellites— we are unlikely to have much information stored or very firm beliefs and attitudes in that area and can accept it without any great resistance. If we already hold firm positions in the area into which the new information fits and it does not seriously challenge them, in that case too we are likely to accept it and file it away for future use. For example, it may confirm what we already believe, clarify what we already know, or enlarge upon knowledge already accepted. Or it may suggest a *slight* change that requires no basic reorganization or reconsideration of strongly defended areas. This is what Lazarsfeld and Merton called "canalizing" an attitude—channeling existing motivations into slightly different behavior.[15] An example would be reinforcing our liking for pipe tobacco and suggesting a brand of tobacco that might be even more rewarding. In any of these cases—confirmation, clarification, extension, or canalization—there is a good chance that the information will be accepted.

But if the new element really challenges what we know and believe, strange things are likely to happen. The amount of distortion that can occur in processing information that seems perfectly clear and straightforward to an outside observer is startling. When Belson studied the effects of a British television program that was intended to reduce the anxiety of British women about traveling to a foreign country, he found that it had precisely the opposite effect: It *increased* their anxieties because they picked out the details that informed them of previously unthought-of difficulties.[16] When a public-spirited organization sought to use sophisticated campaign techniques to reduce anti-Semitism in the eastern United States, the effort backfired spectacularly. Their campaign was built around cartoons picturing a character named Mr. Biggott who was so highly prejudiced that when he was in the hospital he insisted even on having transfusions of blue blood rather than "any ordinary" blood. Many people, including the sponsors of the campaign, thought the cartoons were very funny. It was hoped that they would make readers laugh at Mr. Biggott and in so doing make it easier to laugh at some of their own prejudices and perhaps reconsider them. But what happened? A very large number of the most prejudiced people simply distorted the message to fit. They felt that the cartoons were really quite favorable to Mr. Biggott. They told interviewers that Biggott was very wise not to allow doctors to exchange his blue blood for just ordinary blood. So instead of becoming less prejudiced, many of them were actually confirmed and strengthened in their prejudices.[17] The current Archie Bunker series on commercial television and Bill Cosby's public television monologues on bigotry are in the tradition of the "Mr. Biggott" series, but no studies of their effect have yet been published.

Thus, if a new element of information is judged to be interesting and credible, and if it fits into a cognitive area where it does not have to face strong existing beliefs and attitudes or confirms, clarifies, extends, or slightly canalizes a part of one's cognitive holdings, there is a good chance of its being accepted. If it challenges the cognitive structure centrally, all the ego defenses are aroused and there is a good chance of rejection or distortion to fit. But there are ways in certain cases to combat even strong defenses.

**3. If there is to be a significant change in strongly held positions, a person must accept a significantly different view of the situation in which he is operating.** Some people *did* stop smoking after a lifetime of enjoying and approving of it. Some relatively conservative people *have* been radicalized, and vice versa. Some agnostics *have* been converted.

For this kind of thing to happen, we may be sure that something roused a drive or motivation sufficient to overpower the defenses. The fear roused in some members of the audience by "The Invasion from Mars" is a case in point.[18] Paul, had an experience on the Damascus road that completely revised his picture of the situation around him and made his previous ideas and goals irrelevant. One of my friends stopped smoking, after seeming to reject both the evidence building up around him and pressure from his family, when he heard one of his favorite movie stars report on television that he himself had lung cancer, was soon to die, and wanted to say a few words to his friends about smoking. That was enough to trigger the accumulated pressure for change.

In a sense, all of these are examples of consistency theory, although they represent forces so powerful as to be quite different from the inconsistencies studied in the laboratory. But each one introduces an element inconsistent with previous positions. Very few communicators are able to communicate a vision of God on the road to Damascus. But many can introduce some new information, credible enough to be accepted, not strong enough to be rejected out of hand, that is inconsistent with existing positions and will be uncomfortable to live with unless present beliefs and attitudes are brought into balance with it.

## The Action Effect

The main effect, Cartwright's item 2, may or may not result in overt action. Now, what about the process that triggers off an action?

Cartwright's item 3 implies that a goal becomes apparent—that some incentive to take action becomes active. This may already exist or may be aroused. For example, around 7 o'clock in the evening some of us are likely to become thirsty and hungry. The goal of satisfying these needs is already apparent. An appropriate message—about a martini or a pot roast—might arouse those drives earlier and, once received, might start some action.

It is essential, though, that the action fit an accepted goal. I like martinis but do not smoke cigarettes. Therefore, if a path toward martinis is called to my attention, that message is more likely to induce action than a suggestion that I go to the cigarette counter.

What kind of path is most likely to be accepted? Cartwright suggests that it should be a direct path, an easy path. All solicitors know this. They make it as easy as possible to contribute. You can sign one card. You can write one check or postpone paying for a certain time. You can even have the sum taken out of your paycheck in such tiny amounts that it will not really hurt.

Is it the easiest, the cheapest, the most attractive path to the goal? For example, if you feel the need to contribute to community activities, would it be better to give to the United Fund or the Red Cross, or some other combination of organizations? Would it be better to volunteer time than to contribute money?

Will the proposed action satisfy one goal or more than one—thus paying a little bonus? For instance, would buying national savings bonds be a good investment as well as a patriotic act? Would it help you do the thing most of us find so difficult—save money? Could one argue for paying the cost of going to Europe not only because the trip would be fun but also because it would be educational and provide a good rest after a hard year at the office?

Is the path to action clear and specific? This is central to Cartwright's item 4. If a person is expected to act, he is much more likely to do so when he is put into an acting situation. There must be a good reason to act *now*. (The sale ends this week. On Washington's Birthday only, all television receivers are marked down *n* percent. To be credited to our office, bonds must be bought by November 1. If you don't promise to marry me, I'll kill myself.)

Does the person who is expected to act know exactly how to act? Can he obtain his goal by doing such a simple thing as filling out a coupon or making a telephone call? The action should, if possible, be perceived as specific, direct, easy. The time must be right—and *now*. And the situation should if possible be supportive.

This may be a great deal to ask. But remember that we are describing an ideal type. Reality may be messier.

## Two Examples

In the light of this model, let us reconsider what happened in the case of the Halloween broadcast. The extraordinary thing about that event was how all elements of the situation combined to get the message accepted by at least a sizable portion of the audience. The popularity of network radio itself and the prime time of the broadcast helped get the program accepted into the sensory structures of millions of listeners. Then the stage for acceptance into the cognitive structure was set by the ominous world situation and by the uncommon trust people had developed in radio news. Some listeners, at least, were prepared to accept any newscast-like program as reality rather than fantasy.[19]

Once accepted into the cognitive structure of the people who had accepted it as reality, the "message" was relatively unopposed because most people had no firm beliefs or values about invasions from Mars; most had not even considered that possibility. There was no problem, once the program was accepted as fact, of beating down long-time defenses or strongly held values. The obvious question was, Are the invaders friendly? The program speedily made clear that they were far from friendly. Then the existing cognitive patterns pointed to trust in the police, and if necessary the army, to handle the situation. When the program demolished these alternatives—the police could do nothing and the army was destroyed by mysterious weapons—the gullible listeners were left without defense, without precedent for action, in a completely new situation.

The result was to arouse an overpowering fear drive. This was so strong that sensible, educated people, who would have checked up on an ordinary rumor or a stranger's story, failed to do so or when they tried to do so fumbled and failed or misinterpreted what they saw.

What to do? If an authoritative source had made a suggestion at that moment, it might have been readily accepted, just as any panic crowd or emotional mob will tend to follow a strong voice or example. And this was indeed a typical panic situation: people faced with a fearsome threat to which there seemed to be no real answer. Consequently a number of people behaved as people usually do in a panic. They took the most direct path of action they could find at the moment. They ran.

Let us now look at another event in which communication had a spectacular effect of a far different kind. This was the extraordinary success of the popular singer Kate Smith in selling war bonds by radio. One of her broadcasts was studied in detail by the sociologist Robert Merton and reported in a book entitled *Mass Persuasion.*[20]

Miss Smith was able to bring about the purchase of many millions of dollars worth of bonds by means of a radio "marathon" in which she appeared at intervals during a number of hours, singing and making appeals for people to purchase bonds.

In sharp contrast to "The Invasion from Mars," the Smith program was planned with meticulous care to accomplish exactly what it did. The choice of Miss Smith herself was well thought out. Some campaigners might have chosen a sex symbol or a beauty queen. Miss Smith was not glamorous. She was, to put it impolitely, fat. She was middle-aged. But, as the planners believed and Merton confirmed in later interviews, she projected a most unusual image of sincerity. The reason for wanting this kind of image is easy to understand: It distinguished her message

from that of the commercial pitchmen and the fast-talking salesmen, and consequently kept the communication relationship from
being one that required the buyer to "beware."

Moreover, she was a very popular performer. Millions of
Americans tuned in her program each week and hummed her
theme song, "When the moon comes over the mountain." She
was therefore assured of a large audience for any radio appearance.

The style of the program was planned to take advantage
of these things. It was a mixture of entertainment and "amateur"
salesmanship. It was designed to keep Miss Smith on the air so
long that it was a challenge to her strength and endurance, and
many people actually stayed with the program out of sympathy
for Kate Smith and because they wondered how long she
could last.

This type of program fitted ideally into the main theme
decided on for the messages: Sacrifice. Miss Smith was "sacrificing"; she received no money for the program; she was putting
herself to a great physical strain for a patriotic motive; people
who bought bonds could feel that they were sacrificing along
with her.

Many of her messages made use of this *sacrifice* appeal.
Many others used the theme of common effort: Forget private
differences and work together for America! But listeners could
hardly forget that they were being asked to work together with
Kate Smith. Sacrifice. Work together. Help bring the boys
home. Surprisingly little attention was paid to the economics of
bond buying; rather than trying to prove it was a good investment, the designers of the program preferred to keep the arguments emotional.

So the program itself was designed with great care and skill
to achieve acceptance. In the wartime situation it was unlikely
to strike great cognitive opposition; patriotic values ranked
high. And many listeners already had planned to buy bonds
anyway; 38 out of 75 who were interviewed after they had telephoned pledges to station WABC, New York proved to have
been emotionally involved and to have planned, even before the
broadcast, to buy bonds. The program's effect on them was

merely to catalyze an action already decided upon. Of the group of 75, 28 already were involved but had not decided to buy. In these cases, it appeared that Miss Smith succeeded in arousing them emotionally, creating enough dissonance between their feelings and their lack of decision to lead them to act. There was another small group who were rather indifferent to the ideas expressed but had decided to buy. The effect of the program on them was simply to provide a suitable and easy way of carrying out the intention. These people were more likely than others to consider economic reasons important. They were also likely to be admirers of Miss Smith and susceptible to her pleas. We can assume that the mechanism working here was a kind of identification with the star rather than an arousal of conscience or a change of mind.

Finally, there was a still smaller group—3 out of 75, or 4 percent—who before the program had not been deeply involved nor had intended to buy. These people apparently went through a real change of mind and heart. The program introduced enough inconsistency between their former position and the new ideas they were absorbing, the emotions they were made to feel, to bring about a reorganization and an action. This was the nearest thing to a real change, or "conversion," that the program accomplished. The other 72 people were merely directed into paths of action that were not really incongruent with their previous ideas and feelings.

Great care was taken not only with the themes and with the projection of Miss Smith's personality but also to make the path of action easy and direct. Purchasers had merely to telephone the radio station, give name and address, and pledge a certain amount. They stood a chance of earning an additional bonus: having Miss Smith read their names and thank them on the air. Or, if they preferred, they could write a letter. It was not even necessary at the time to send money.

Furthermore, action was put into the context of time. How many pledges could Miss Smith win during her marathon? By pledging that night, it was possible to contribute to her effort—to break the record, to do honor to Kate who was doing honor to them.

Looked at with hindsight (which is often 20-20), the Smith campaign seems to have been carried out with great skill and care. But it is noteworthy that, spectacular as the effect was, most of the changes themselves were not spectacular. They were changes of a few degrees rather than 180 degrees.

# xii.
# Components of Effect

## Attitude Change and Action

It may seem extraordinary that we have come this far without saying much about attitudes. We have talked about them many times, however, although sometimes by other names.

No one has ever seen an attitude or touched it or smelled it. We aren't even sure that attitudes exist. Yet, as someone has said, if no one had invented the concept of attitude we would probably have to invent the same thing by another name. For attitudes are an imaginary thing, a hypothetical construct that has been used in hundreds of studies to help explain what happens in the black box between the communication and the response.

Gordon Allport said that the concept of attitudes is "the primary building stone in the edifice of social psychology," and went on to define it as "a mental and neural state of readiness, organized through experience, exerting a directive or dynamic influence upon the individual's response to all objects and situations with which it is related."[1]

Rokeach's definition is simpler: "An attitude is a relatively enduring organization of beliefs about an object or situation predisposing one to respond in some preferential manner."

Attitude *change*, then, would be "a change in predispositions, the change being either a change in the organization or structure of beliefs or a change in the content of one or more of the beliefs entering into the attitude organization."[2]

It is evident that the only way we have of studying attitude is to study their reflection in behavior, verbal or otherwise. Like all other hypothetical constructs, the existence and nature of attitudes have to be inferred from the answers to attitude scales or tests, from verbalizations around some stimulus like an ink blot, or from nonverbal behavior.

DeFleur and Westie have pointed out that there are two main ways of looking at the evidence from which we infer the existence and nature of attitudes, and that these amount really to two concepts of attitudes. They call them the *probability* and the *latent process* concepts.[3]

"The primary inference in probability conceptions," they say, "is that attitude responses are more or less consistent." That is to say, when a person is confronted with a set of stimuli of a given kind, his responses are likely to be predictable. If he rejects an idea several times, he is more likely to continue to reject it than to change. The attitude, then, "is an inferred property of the responses, namely their consistency. Stated in another way, attitude is equated with the probability of recurrence of behavior forms of a given type or direction."[4]

An observer studying someone's attitudes in this way would ascertain on what topics the subject's responses are consistent. These consistencies would be his attitudes. Nothing would necessarily be said about causality or the mechanism involved; attitudes would serve merely to map out the consistencies in the response behavior and, by inference, the cognitive structures that lie behind them.

However, most students of attitudes do not stop there. They begin with response consistency but go beyond it and, according to DeFleur and Westie, "postulate the operation of some hidden or hypothetical variable functioning within the behaving individual, which shapes, acts upon, or 'mediates' the observable behavior. That is, the observable organization of behavior is said to be 'due to' or 'can be explained by' the action of some mediating latent variable." Viewed this way, an attitude is considered not the responses themselves, not their probability, "but an intervening variable operating between stimulus and response and inferred from the overt behavior."[5]

This is the favorite form in which attitudes have entered into communication research. They are conceived to be an intervening variable, probably the most powerful variable readily available to us to study, and therefore instrumental in determining what response is made to a given communication. Most scholars assume that the direction of the attitude (favorable or unfavorable) will, other things equal, determine the direction of action. Therefore attitude change has been used again and again as a dependent variable in communication studies. Because attitude tests are relatively easy to administer and action is relatively hard to isolate and measure, scholars have again and again accepted a measure of attitude change as a communication effect pointing to action. For example, literally hundreds of family planning surveys in many countries have measured attitudes toward contraception, family size, and the like; if these are more favorable than before the campaign, the campaign is regarded as a success.

The trouble is that it has proved extraordinarly difficult to match attitudes with action. In the family planning surveys just mentioned, it is very common for 70 to 90 percent of the respondents to express favorable attitudes toward family planning and contraception but for only 10 to 15 percent of them to go to the clinic for treatment or materials.[6] Festinger, speaking to the American Psychological Association, said that he could find only three controlled studies in which attitude change had been shown to predict action.[7] Vroom found that "job attitudes have only a slight and often insignificant relationship" with job performance and absences from work.[8] Reviewing the studies of attitudes and behavior toward minority group members, Wicker found "little correspondence between the two types of variables, and in several cases there are reversals of expected relationships."[9] Summing up the entire literature on attitude change and overt action, Wicker concluded: "The present review provides little evidence of the postulated existence of stable, underlying attitudes within the individual which influence both his verbal expressions and his actions."[10]

These findings are troublesome, not only because they diminish the usefulness of a great many studies that have employed attitude change as a dependent variable, but also because they cast doubt on a concept that intuitively seems to be a good one for explaining what goes on between communication stimulus and response.

Why do we not get consistently reliable predictions of action from verbal measurements of attitude? A number of scholars have wrestled with this question. Some of them have questioned the validity of the verbal measurements. One of these is the sociologist Richard La Piere. In the early 1930s, when there was a considerable amount of anti-Chinese feeling in the United States, he made several long automobile trips accompanied by a Chinese couple. They stayed in many hotels in many different states and ate in many restaurants. Only once were they denied service, and La Piere felt that their treatment was above average in perhaps 40 percent of the cases. When he returned home he wrote to the approximately 250 hotels and restaurants they had visited, inquiring whether these places would accept Chinese guests. More than 90 percent of the respondents said they would not serve Chinese—even though they had done that very thing a few weeks or months earlier when La Piere and his Chinese friends had visited them.[11]

La Piere wrapped a stone in the snowball he threw at attitude change research:

> The questionnaire is cheap, easy, and mechanical [he said]. The study of human behavior is time consuming, intellectually fatiguing, and depends for its success upon the ability of the investigator. The former method gives quantitative results, the latter mainly qualitative. Quantitative measurements are quantitatively accurate; qualitative measurements are always subject to errors of human judgment. Yet it would seem far more worth while to make a shrewd guess regarding that which is essential than to accurately measure that which is likely to prove quite irrelevant.[12]

Quinn McNemar, the redoubtable psychological statistician, also took aim at the questionable validity of attitude measurements. He pointed out that "the degree of relationship between overt nonverbal and verbal behavior is not known and apparently is of little interest to most investigators."[13] Practically all research, he noted, is on the verbal level, whereas research on the validity of these verbal measures is "direly needed." It still is.

However, there is another reasonable explanation for some of the failures of verbal measurements of attitudes to predict action. There are many more constraints on social action than on private answers to questions. It was much easier for the hotel and restaurant proprietors to say verbally that their policy was not to house or feed Chinese than to turn down La Piere and his Chinese companions when they had actually come, thus risking a "scene" and unfavorable publicity. It is easy to give a favorable answer to a question about what one thinks of contraception (indeed, in many countries a favorable answer is culturally required). On the other hand, to go to a clinic for a vasectomy, to have an IUD inserted, or even to accept and use the pill regularly is an entirely different matter. It requires special effort. It may threaten future ability to have more children. It may require persuading one's spouse. It may be contrary to what one's friends or neighbors or mother-in-law or other acquaintances think is acceptable behavior. And there are always rumors and reports about the bad side-effects of these devices.

In a well-known article Carl Hovland worried about why it was relatively easy to achieve a communication effect in the laboratory and very difficult to do so in the field.[14] One reason, of course, is that the laboratory experimenter pretests and tries and reconstructs his measure until he develops one that will show an effect; he is basically concerned not with proving that there can be an effect but rather with finding how one variable or another *relates* to effect. A more obvious reason, as Hovland noted, is that there are in the field social pressures and constraints, competing messages and actions, that are not present in the private laboratory.

Fishbein points out that the verbal expression reflects a generalized attitude but that an action must necessarily be specific. For example, he and his colleagues have measured racial attitudes and attempted to predict whether a white person who expressed given attitudes would ride with, work with, or cooperate with blacks. When the prediction has failed, he says, it has usually been owing to the fact that a white subject's beliefs about blacks in general may be unlike his beliefs about a *particular* black with whom he comes into contact. Actions are always addressed to a specific situation and usually to a specific person.[15]

Rokeach suggests that it would be desirable to study not only a person's attitudes toward an object but also his attitudes toward a situation in which the object is likely to be encountered.[16] In other words, much more than attitude toward a person or a thing or a concept would be required to predict how one would act toward it.

Perhaps it has become evident by this time why we have not made a major use of the concept of attitudes in these pages and instead have tried to focus as much as possible on other measures of behavior. This is not to say that the study of attitudes is not useful at this stage of communication research or that it cannot be useful in the future. What we have reported, however, carries a warning: We must be very cautious about assuming that any given communication effect measured in verbal attitudes is necessarily a predictor of action or that any "attitude changes" are necessarily socially significant.

## Other Elements in Communication Effect

The variables that contribute to communication effect have never been studied in a more sophisticated way than by Carl Hovland, Irving Janis, and others in the Yale Program on Communication and Attitude Change.

In large part this program was an outgrowth of World War II, when a number of able psychologists and sociologists were recruited into the Army Information and Education Branch and put to work studying problems of communication effect. The leadership of Samuel Stouffer, a sociologist at Chicago and Harvard universities, and Carl Hovland, then a young and promising experimental psychologist, gave a tone and an approach to the work that has seldom been equalled in government social science.

One of the group's first assignments was to find out whether the Army orientation films on the Battle of Britain were having any effect. From this task they moved to many other studies of learning and attitude change in this country and overseas, and when the war was over they reanalyzed much of their data and, under Stouffer's general editorship, published four volumes entitled *The American Soldier*. These have been influential in the study of communication, the study of morale and organizations, and research method. They introduced Guttman scaling, latent-process analysis, and some considerations of research design that have been highly useful. The third volume of the four was *Experiments on Mass Communication*, by Hovland, Lumsdaine, and Sheffield; it might be considered the first major product of the Yale Program.[17]

Studies of the variables in persuasive communication had been conducted long before the Yale studies and have been conducted at many other places. The contribution of the Yale Program was a continuity and sophistication of approach that set a model for communication research. During the more than twenty years in which the program was actively funded, it was possible to design a series of experiments around a single variable and to modify it in connection with other variables until there was some hope of understanding how it contributed to effect. When a finding proved puzzling—for instance, when the group found a "sleeper effect," in which the effect of a communication actually seemed to *increase* after an interval of time during which the effect should have been decreasing—there was enough continuity in the program to follow up the result and learn something about why it happened. For the most part, the study used very carefully designed experiments in laboratories, schools, or military units. They examined one variable after another in different combinations and situations, with attitude change as the usual dependent variable. The result of these experiments was to set the stage for what might be called, with due respect to Aristotle, a new scientific rhetoric, in which there was an attempt to set forth principles of communication effect in scientific terms backed by scientific evidence.

Most of what we know about the part played by different variables in communication effects comes from studies like these, which are basically studies of learning. It is, of course, impossible to review this very large literature in any detail here, but let us try to give a general idea of what variables in persuasion have been studied and what the present state of knowledge is concerning them.

**What is the best source of a message?** Earlier in this book we spoke of the communication relationship as one in which Mr. A, as he saw himself, related to Mr. B as he saw Mr. B, and Mr. B, as he saw himself, related to Mr. A as Mr. B saw him. The research has borne out the importance of this rather peculiar relationship. One of the surest ways of making a difference in the amount of attitude change has been to vary the receiver's picture of the communicator.

This has been done in countless ways. Long before the Yale Program began, Irving Lorge tested the effect of identical messages attributed in one case to Nicolai Lenin, in another to Thomas Jefferson. With American subjects the message had much more effect when attributed to Jefferson; supposedly, the opposite result would have come about with Russian subjects.[18] Hovland and Weiss presented identical articles on the atomic bomb attributed in one set of cases to a distinguished American atomic scientist, in the other to the Soviet newspaper *Pravda*. They found four times as many attitudinal changes (among American readers) agreeing with the article when it was attributed to the American source.[19] Kelman and Hovland studied the result of having the same speech on delinquency given by an individual who was introduced in one case as a judge, in another as a lay member of the studio audience, and in a third as a layman who was alleged to have certain shady chapters in his record. These communicators were rated by the audience as positive, neutral, and negative, respectively, and the amount of attitude change was proportional to the differences in rating.[20] This kind of thing has been done literally dozens of times, and the general result has always been that a source who is seen as prestigious in the field he is talking about will have more attitudinal effect than a low-prestige source.

However, as research has developed in this area, it has been possible to identify components of prestige: notably expertise and disinterestedness. If a communicator is seen as an expert in what he is talking about or as not in a position to profit from the change he is advocating, he is more likely to have an effect than a communicator who is not perceived as expert or objective. The greatest effect comes when a communicator is perceived as having both of those characteristics—as being both credible and trustworthy. Especially with involved and rather suspicious people, it is sometimes more effective to arrange to have a message *overheard* so as to do away with the suspicion that the communicator is trying to manipulate the listener.

As far as they have been tested, the suggestions advanced earlier in this book about "contractual relationships" brought about by the roles people in the communication relationship see themselves as playing—for example, the relationship of teacher to student or salesman to prospective buyer—are supported. For example, the negative effect of introducing a communicator as someone who stands to gain by "selling" his idea to the receiver and the positive effect of introducing a communicator as an authority on the subject indicate that in one case the receiver comes to the relationship with his defenses up, in the other prepared to listen and learn.

Suppose a person is confronted with conflicting messages from authorities and from peers; for example, a physician tells the school assembly that cigarette smoking is bad for one's health, whereas one's friends later laugh at that viewpoint and offer a cigarette. What happens? In general the laboratory experiments show an advantage to the expert source; field studies show an advantage to the peer group. This is another case in which there are serious doubts that the laboratory situation can be used to predict naturalistic effects. The controlled situation is often perceived as somewhat contrived, and the full pressure of peer group influence as it operates in real life can seldom be reproduced.

What is the effect when the source of a message is perceived by the receiver as a person similar to himself—the quality Rogers calls *homophily*? Other things being equal, the receiver is likely to be influenced more by a person he sees as similar. This leads to the persuasive strategy that Kenneth Burke calls "the strategy of identification," in which a persuader tries to convince his audience that he is "their kind of person."[21] But it makes a difference whether the subject is one in which expertise is required; if the "similar" communicator knows no more about it than the receiver, he is not likely to be persuasive. There is also an element of "liking" that interacts with similarity. As McGuire says, it is a two-way street; a feeling of real similarity produces liking, and liking tends to increase the feeling of similarity. The more the source is liked, the more effect his message will probably have. However, Zimbardo has found that this too is subject to qualification.[22] For example, if a person will commit himself to listen to a communicator he dislikes, that is likely to encourage some change on his part because he will have to get rid of his dissonance by arguing internally that the message is *worth listening to*.

One of the more interesting findings in this area is that people tend to forget the sources of ideas they have stored away. This was the implication of the "sleeper effect" experiments mentioned previously. The first experiment compared the effect of a source perceived as trustworthy with one perceived as untrustworthy. As expected, the subjects became more favorable to the idea proposed by the "trustworthy" source. But when the subjects were retested some weeks later, it was found that their attitudes toward the position of the trustworthy source had become less favorable, whereas they were more favorable toward the position espoused by the untrustworthy source, so that the original change was almost blotted out. When the experiment was done over again with suitable additions, it was concluded that they had simply forgotten where the different ideas had come from. When they were reminded of what the "trustworthy" source and the "untrustworthy" source had said, their attitudes returned to what they had been after the original exposure to the two sources. The implication of this, and of most of the other findings reported in the last few pages, is the great importance of how the source of the message—the other person in the relationship—is perceived. In effect he becomes part of the message, and when he is removed from the scene (through forgetfulness or anonymity) the message is not quite the same.[23]

**What is effective persuasive style?** One of the somewhat surprising things about the study of message variables is how seldom laboratory experiments have been able to show any large effects due to what is usually considered "good rhetoric." This may be an artifact of the way the experiments have been done or the way the effects have been measured. We all know from experience, for example, that we are more likely to want to hear, and enjoy hearing, some speakers more than others. Yet this may affect attention, or liking or entertainment value, rather than persuasion.

Whatever the reason, the general skill of a speaker has not been experimentally proved to be a very powerful determinant of persuasion. Lewin, for example, found little difference in the effectiveness of trained and untrained speakers in bringing about group decision.[24] Thistlethwaite, De Haan, and Kamenetzky found that well-organized messages affected comprehension rather than opinion change.[25] Humor, in general, has been found to affect liking for the speaker or the communication experience, but there is not much evidence of its contribution to attitude change. Repetition of a point (preferably with some variation) contributes to learning and change, but the limit of its persuasive effect seems to be reached rather quickly.

"Dynamic" style has not proved to have as much effect as one might expect. Dietrich found no significant differences in attitude change brought about by dynamic versus conversational style.[26] Hovland, Lumsdaine, and Sheffield found no significant difference in attitude effect between a radio commentator and a dramatic version of the same material.[27] McGuire reports only a slight effect produced by a dynamic "hard sell."[28] One of the key points seems to be how a high-key or low-key style is perceived. For example, a low-key presentation may be interpreted as low expertise, negating any advantage gained from its being interpreted as objective. A high-key style may be interpreted either as "propaganda" or as vigor and expertise. Depending on which interpretation is held, it might accomplish *more* change by attracting closer attention or *less* change by encouraging rejection.

**Should a message draw its conclusions explicitly or let the receiver decide what they are?** Here we have another contrast between laboratory and field results. The laboratory experiments typically find that more change occurs and more desired points are learned when the conclusions are stated explicitly. On the other hand, many psychotherapists, especially followers of Freud, are committed from their experience to letting the patient discover the conclusions for himself. The situation may be the determining factor.

**Should the main points be placed first or last?** Does the first speaker or writer have an advantage over the second? The results do not entirely agree. For example, in 1925 Lund obtained results that led him to proclaim a "law of primacy in persuasion."[29] Cromwell, in 1950, found an advantage in recency.[30] Hovland and Mandell, in 1952, found no advantage in either primacy or recency.[31] As the matter has been further studied, however, the relationships have been found to be more complex than originally believed, and a number of other variables have had to be introduced in order to give any very useful advice about primacy and recency. Perhaps the most general statement is that arguments placed first have some advantage in attracting attention; arguments placed last have some advantage in being remembered. But even this is not enough. If one has arguments that are likely to be well accepted by an audience, there is some reason to present them first and establish attention and a favorable climate for later arguments that may not be so easily accepted. If contradictory and possibly confusing information is being presented, that presented first has a better chance of dominating what is finally accepted. If one is presenting information that arouses needs and other information that suggests a way to satisfy them, it is clearly better to arouse the needs first.

**How can one build defenses against counterarguments?** As in other areas of this field, these small rhetorical points have proved to be relatively insignificant in determining effect compared to certain processes and mechanisms of change that lie behind them. The matter of primacy-recency, the question of one- to two-sided presentation, the question of whether to ignore or try to refute an opponent's arguments have all led researchers into the study of how defenses against change are built, and from this have come some general and important ideas.

The first experiments on one- or two-sided presentations were interpreted mostly in terms of audience characteristics. The finding seemed to be that if an audience was already on the desired side of the argument there might be an advantage in merely strengthening the arguments in favor of that side; if opposed, it would be better to present the opposition side also in order to give an impression of fairness and also to be able to present counterarguments. There was some reason to believe that a highly intelligent audience would respond better than a less intelligent one to a presentation that included both sides (although, of course, there had to be a weakened presentation of the other side). The most important conclusion, however, was that if an audience is going to hear the other side anyway, it is better to let them hear it from you first. This finding has been developed in an interesting set of experiments based on the idea that if a person can be given arguments to rehearse in advance he is more likely to be able to resist persuasion. This has been called "immunization against propaganda." McGuire has both contributed to this line of research and reviewed it in the *Handbook of Social Psychology*.[32]

The general conclusion is that one can help build resistance against later persuasion by "inoculating" an individual with counterarguments in advance. Then the question arises, How can such counterarguments be overcome? A fascinating experiment by Festinger and Maccoby suggests a possible answer. They showed groups of experimental subjects two versions of a film with the same persuasive message on the sound track. The message opposed college fraternities. The audiences were themselves fraternity members and, therefore, expected to have counterarguments ready to defend their membership. One of the films had a picture track that showed the persuasive speaker delivering his message; the other film, delightful but irrelevant, was "The Day of the Painter." One film, that is, was a coherent, realistic persuasive situation; the other, a persuasive sound track grafted onto a film to which it had no relation. What would you predict about the relative effectiveness of these two versions?

The fraternity men who saw the coherent film showed less attitude change, less readiness to accept the arguments against fraternities than did those who heard the persuasive message with the unrelated film. The researchers interpreted this result as indicating that the unrelated film had distracted the subjects from rehearsing their counterarguments for use against the persuasion.[33] Later research and discussion has cast some doubt on this interpretation. For example, the greater effect of the message with the unrelated film may have come about because the audience enjoyed "The Day of the Painter" and responded out of general good feeling. In other words, they were nearer the *entertainment* than the *persuasion* relationship. They may have perceived the purpose of the experiment and let that partly determine their response. But it is clear that the tendency to maintain and defend what one has already accepted into his cognitive structure and values is very strong, and the effectiveness of devices like one- or two-sided presentations and other rhetorical tactics as well can better be interpreted in terms of an underlying process of that kind than in terms of any specific advantages of the rhetoric itself.

**What appeals should one use?** The choice of appeals for effectiveness in persuasion is something that seems to depend very much on the subject matter and on the audience rather than on specific tactical principles. There has been some research (for instance, that of Menefee and Grannenberg in 1940[34]) and a great deal of experiential lore to indicate that emotional appeals are more likely to change attitudes than are logical ones. However, in practice it is uncommon to separate the two kinds of appeals entirely. The Kate Smith program, for example, depended largely on emotion but not entirely. A trial lawyer argues as logically as possible from the law but is not averse to calling upon emotion where he can. And he is more likely to direct emotional appeals to a jury in a county court than to the U.S. Supreme Court.

However, one area of emotional appeals has generated some very interesting research that promises to lay bare some of the underlying processes of change. In the early 1950s Janis and Feshbach conducted a study on the effectiveness of fear appeal in persuading people to brush their teeth. They presented arguments at several levels of fearsomeness. The most fearsome had gruesome pictures of the results of gum disease. They found that these strongest appeals tended to be rejected and that the minimum appeals actually accomplished the most change.[35]

Replications of their experiment did not obtain precisely the same results, and later studies of fear appeal have complicated rather than simplified the relationship. An experiment by Chu showed that it makes a difference how easily a person can do something about the thing he is being encouraged to fear. If the solution is relatively easy and simple, and consequently the message can be simple and clear, then the stronger the appeal the more effect it is likely to have. If, on the other hand, the solution is difficult and complicated or the result in doubt, the strongest messages tend to be rejected.[36] McGuire, in reviewing this literature, suggests that there is probably an interaction between the degree of fear arousal and the subject's level of anxiety, leading to a relationship that is not linear and consistent in all cases.[37]

Questions like these have obvious practical importance. Whenever we make a decision on how to try to affect attitudes and behavior on health problems like cigarette smoking, policy problems like pollution, or population problems like family planning, we must decide what appeals to use and how high to key them. Yet on many such questions communication theory is not yet able to provide simple and practical guides. The best guidance is to examine the situation and the audience as deeply as possible and try to decide how best to stimulate the process that must operate. And then pretest!

**What are the effects of surroundings?** Every lover knows that situation makes a difference. A moon, a balmy night, a happy evening, the odor of spring flowers, a car—these help influence both attitudes and behavior. There is a significant amount of research evidence on the effect of pleasant architecture and decor on human responses. These contributory effects of surroundings can be accepted without great question, but the most interesting research on situational variables in communication effect has to do with human relationships.

**What are the effects of group membership?** Among the shadowy participants in every communication relationship are certain groups to which the participants belong or aspire to belong, whose norms they share and will defend. There are different kinds of groups—family, work, social, class, professional, political, and so forth. The important thing is that most individuals need the support of such group memberships and value it. Therefore, in predicting communication effect it helps greatly to know what groups a person values and what their norms are.

An experiment by Kelley and Volkart demonstrated that

such norms are not influential unless the particular membership is brought to mind at the moment when the information leading to change is being processed.[38] For example, if an individual is led to see the relationship of a persuasive argument to his membership in, let us say, the Catholic Church or the Republican party or the Rotary Club, he will probably test the persuasion against the beliefs he shares with those groups. If he does not see the relationship, he will probably not call upon whatever defenses or support might derive from such group norms. Therefore it has always been considered good tactics not to attack frontally any group loyalties or valued group memberships.

When a major change is achieved in a man's values and behavior, it usually has to be accompanied by a change in his valued groups. For example, it was reported that one principle of Chinese and North Korean "brainwashing" at the time of the Korean War was to remove the POW as far as possible from the group support to which he was accustomed. Officers were separated from enlisted men and often from each other. Mail from home was not delivered. Publications and news reflecting the norms of old groups were cut off. The POW was put into new discussion groups, and every attempt was made to build up new friendships and dependencies. Similarly, after "conversion" takes place during a religious campaign, one of the first steps in any well-planned revival is to put the convert into a group of believers who will support him in his moments of dissonance and reinforce him in his new values.

Background groups thus blend into active, foreground groups. A series of experiments by Asch, Sherif, and others have been conducted to measure the effect of social pressures on an individual. Asch put an individual into a group that had the task of judging which of three lines was the longest. The experimental subject did not know that all his fellow group members were stooges in the pay of the experimenter. They went around the circle, the stooges speaking first, each giving the opinion that line B was the longest. Obviously it was not. But by the time the poor experimental subject had his turn, he was beginning to wonder about his own judgment. And the pressure to conform was so strong that more than 30 percent of the experimental subjects went along with the stooges and said that line

B was indeed the longest—though the answer was patently wrong. However, if even one of the stooges gave the right answer, the experimental subject was reinforced in his own judgment and much less likely to yield to the example around him.[39] This effect has been demonstrated a number of times. Sherif, for example, did it with a different stimulus, the auto-kinetic affect—the circumstance that a point of light in a dark room seems to move—and the participants were required to judge the direction and distance of the apparent movement. Unfortunately, we do not know whether the socially induced responses were real changes in belief or merely conformity to the group for sake of conformity.

**Does role playing help persuade?** There are interesting studies on role playing in public. For example, a subject is induced or paid to improvise a talk or write a paper in support of a viewpoint with which he does not agree. Merely improvising arguments for the other position will tend to influence his attitudes in the direction of the position he has been led to take. There are two ways of explaining this. One is that his act has roused some dissonance in him that he has to get rid of by bringing his private feelings more into accord with his performance—consequently deciding that there is something to this other viewpoint after all, and therefore some justification for doing what he did. The other explanation is that the act of improvising the talk led him to find out more about the other side than he had known before and that in so doing he learned and stored some of the arguments he used. But it was the act of *improvising* that made the difference. Improvising the talk or the paper had more effect than merely reading the same kind of material aloud or silently. If the subject was praised for his performance or given a high grade by the instructor, that made him feel happier but did not change his attitudes any more. The key part of the change mechanism was his creative activity, which necessarily had to be done in empathy with opposing viewpoints.[40] If you notice any resemblance between these experiments and the long custom of giving prizes for schoolchildren's essays in support of some good cause, the resemblance is not coincidental.

**Can group decision be used to affect individual decision?** Lewin was one of the first to study the effect of group decision on individual attitudes and behavior. He found that a group of housewives who came together in wartime, when the best meat was being shipped to the troops, to discuss the possibility of cooking unpopular cuts of meat were much more likely actually to use such meat than if they merely read about it or heard a talk about the need of doing so. In particular, they were more likely to change their practice if they made a public commitment in the group to do so.[41] This has been tested in different experimental situations and has been used practically in successful change programs like that of the Radio Rural Forum, in which farmers meet in groups to listen to a radio broadcast and then discuss whether or not to put into effect the changes suggested by the broadcast. The Forum idea has been used in India and other developing countries, and has often resulted in an increased rate of adoption of new practices.

What is the underlying process in group decision? Partly, it must be the experience of talking over the proposed change and learning about it. More important, it must represent the promise of social support and approval if one decides to change. And when one commits himself in public, he is risking some uncomfortable dissonance, along with loss of public credibility, if he does not bring his behavior into line with his promises and then bring his viewpoints into line with his behavor.

It hardly needs saying that many other elements of the situation may, under suitable circumstances, enter into the effect. To take one example out of many, consider the effect on an evangelistic group of singing together, the effect of linking arms and swaying bodies, the effect on a protest group of marching together, the effect of "touching" as it is done in some encounter groups. These are suggestive devices and, other things being equal, make it easier for a member of the group to accept a suggestion in accord with the shared norms of the group. The range of suggestive devices like these is very wide, from background music to hypnotism.

## The Quiet Effects

I am a bit uneasy about ending this section with such a long treatment of attitudinal effects, which makes it seem that the significant results of communication are mostly persuasion and that the effects we are most interested in are quick and easily measurable ones.

I doubt that this is true. Unless I am mistaken, the effects of communication that have most to do with determining what we are and do are the quiet effects of the never-ceasing flow of information to us, through us, from us. Our ways of seeking information and giving it determine a great part of our life patterns and the way we spend our time. They determine our picture of our environment and our image of ourselves. They determine many of the skills we possess and the borders of our knowledge and understanding. These include our skills in communication, which is one of our most important possessions. They underlie all the change effects we have been talking about in this chapter, but because they accumulate and are in a constant process of being added to, clarified, revised, and confirmed, they do not invite the kind of short-term change studies that attitude researchers like to do.

Communication researchers, however, have to face up to the need of studying quiet continuing effects that, in perspective, overshadow the more spectacular and more easily measurable ones. And there is no better place to make their importance clear than in their relation to the effects of mass communication, which we take up in the next chapter.

# xiii.
# Some Special Effects of Mass Communication

**Do Mass Media Really Have an Effect?**

Ask that question in a college classroom, and you will probably have on your hands an argument that goes something like this:

*Pro:* Look at the amount of time people give to media. Greenberg found that a white child of 9 or 10 in a relatively well-off family, spends about 5 hours and 48 minutes a day on TV, records, and radio. Subtracting sleep time, school time, and mealtime, that leaves him about 3 hours a day free for other things. And a disadvantaged child spends anywhere from half again to twice as much: on the average, 9 hours and 30 minutes for a black child from a disadvantaged home. Furthermore, Greenberg and Gerson and others found that children from poor families were more likely than others to use TV as a "school of life"—to find out things they couldn't learn in school. Can you possibly believe that all this isn't having an effect?

*Con:* All right, if you want to count time as in effect. But the sociologists say that the media really don't have much to do with changing anybody in an important way. La Piere decided

—remember?—that "social control is exerted through interpersonal influence, not the mass media."

*Pro:* Then why do the political experts fight to get their message into the mass media? Why do the Republicans and Democrats spend over a hundred million dollars on the media during a Presidential campaign? Why does the Vice President become so angry over the way the media cover the national administration?

*Con:* Oh, they may have some effect on the information that gets out. But election studies show that the people who really change their opinions during the campaign are usually influenced by other people, not by the media. The rural sociologists find that the media are helpful in telling farmers about new crops, but when it comes to the point of decision, farmers depend on personal advice. And all the development campaigns find out that they can't accomplish much with media alone; they have to use field staffs.

*Pro:* Why do parents and psychiatrists and psychologists get so uptight over what violence and crime on television may be doing to children? Why do people try to commit the crimes they see on television—for instance, using the altitude-pressure bomb? As soon as that program went on the air, somebody extorted half a million from an Australian airline with the same trick, and others tried it in the United States and elsewhere.

*Con:* But has anybody ever proved that television or any other medium was the *real* cause of anything like that? It may have helped plant an idea, but only two or three people out of three billion did anything about it. That doesn't sound like a very potent effect! There was something else wrong with those two or three people.

*Pro:* Do you deny that almost everything you know about faraway places, people, and events you learned from the media?

*Con:* People don't believe everything in the media. They use them mostly for entertainment, anyway.

That is the way the debate is likely to go. It has gone the same way in print, with psychiatrists like Frederick Wertham[1] almost hysterical over the probable effects of entertainment media on children, with parents and congressmen expressing concern, with psychologists reporting rather ominous studies of the effects of media violence on aggressive behavior. On the other side, sociologists insist that personal influence is vastly more important than media influence, and television spokesmen insist that the research does not prove anything bad; the news media are not at all loath to hear that they may be having an effect on knowledge and opinions or that people are increasingly depending on them for political information; finally, most behavioral scholars advise caution in drawing conclusions from the evidence at hand.

In the following pages we will try to sort out these arguments and identify, insofar as we can, what the mass media can be expected to do and what cannot be expected of them. Perhaps the best place to start is with the brilliant group of sociologists around Paul Lazarsfeld at Columbia; this group has won a unique right to assess the effects of mass communication, for, unlike many sociologists, they have studied *both* personal and media influence in depth. Over a period of twenty years this group contributed, among other things, the first voting studies, a series of opinion leader studies, some of the best audience research, the study of the Kate Smith telethon, and the principal book on personal influence. They have stayed with the problems of effect long enough to put insights and observations to the test.

The Columbia group, too, has been quoted as disparaging the power of mass communication to make any substantial change in social behavior. However, a closer look at the writings of Lazarsfeld and his colleagues and former students shows that this is not precisely the position they have taken. Let us begin with an admirably thoughtful essay by Lazarsfeld and Merton entitled "Mass Communication, Popular Taste, and Organized Social Action."[2] Now, nearly twenty-five years after its publication, this essay still stands as one of the classics in its field and as a summary of what the Columbia communication sociologists had concluded, even at that early time, about the effects of the mass media.

It begins with the statement of a lecturer that the "power of radio can be compared only with the power of the atomic bomb." The size and ubiquity of the media encourage "an almost magical belief" in their enormous power.[3] This is chiefly because the media are seen as an instrument of propaganda, and Americans have a peculiar dread of propaganda. The essay recalls what William Empson, a British philosopher and critic, said "[The Americans] believe in machinery more passionately than we do; and modern propaganda is a scientific machine; so it seems to them obvious that a mere reasoning man can't stand up against it. All that produces a curiously girlish attitude toward anyone who might be doing propaganda. 'Don't let that man come near. Don't let him tempt me, because if he does, I'm sure to fall.' "[4]

The Columbia sociologists have little sympathy for that viewpoint and in this respect are in agreement with most scholars who had written about mass communication since the time of their essay. But they go on to analyze certain other concerns about the effects of the media. A more realistic basis for concern with the social role of the media, they say, arises from the changing tactics of powerful interest groups in society:

> Increasingly, the chief power groups, among which organized business occupies the most spectacular place, have come to adopt techniques for manipulating mass publics through propaganda in place of more direct means of control. Industrial organizations . . . engage in elaborate programs of "public relations." They place large and impressive advertisements in the newspapers of the nation; they sponsor numerous radio [now it would be television] programs; on the advice of public relations counsellors they organize prize contests, establish welfare foundations, and support worthy causes. Economic power seems to have reduced direct exploitation and turned to a subtler type of psychological exploitation, achieved largely by disseminating propaganda through the mass media of communication.[5]

With this concern they are more sympathetic, not because they fear that the media may be changing values and viewpoints but rather because mass communication may be encouraging a social and economic *status quo*. We will say more about this later.

A third concern expressed in the essay is with the effects of the media on the esthetic tastes of their audiences. Bright hopes for a major contribution to the level of public taste have not been realized. For generations men fought for more leisure, "and now they spend it with the Columbia Broadcasting System rather than with Columbia University." They recognize that there is "substantial ground" for concern about immediate social effects but that the possible use of mass media for raising public taste is little understood and needs long-term study. Lazarsfeld has repeatedly urged long-term operational research on raising tastes through the mass media, but it has never been funded.

The authors analyze some things they feel the mass media *can* do:

1. **Mass media can confer status.** Favorable attention in the mass media raises and legitimizes the status of persons, organizations, policies. One has "arrived" when he is singled out by the media. He is worth paying attention to. And citing the "men of distinction" advertisements for Calvert whiskey, they point out a circular process of status conferral that seems to operate: "If you really matter, you will be at the focus of mass attention, and if you *are* at the focus of mass attention, then surely you must really matter."[6]

2. **Mass media can enforce social norms—to an extent.** Malinowski observed about the Trobriand Islanders that no organized social action was taken about deviation from social norms unless there was *public* announcement of the deviation. Publicity can close the gap between "private attitudes" and "public morality." The media can reaffirm social norms by exposing deviations from norms to public view. As Boss Tweed is said to have remarked about Thomas Nast's sharp political cartoons, "I don't care a straw for your newspaper articles: My constituents don't know how to read, but they can't help seeing them damned pictures!"

3. **Mass media can act as social narcotics.** The Columbia sociologists feel that the enormous flood of information tends to narcotize rather than energize the average reader or listener. Media absorb time that might better be used for social action. *Knowing* something about problems tends to be confused with *doing* something about them. Thus, although the media have

clearly raised the level of information, they may have contributed to superficiality of knowledge and lack of participation.
In this respect, Lazarsfeld and Merton say, mass media may
be "among the most respectable and efficient of social narcotics. They may be so fully effective as to keep the addict from
recognizing his own malady."[7]

Furthermore, commercial ownership and support of the
mass media, they feel, tends to encourage the status quo rather
than change, both because status quo is in the interests of
business and finance, and because the support of the media
depends on attracting large audiences through entertainment
programming. "To the extent that the media of communication
have had an influence upon their audiences it has stemmed not
only from what is said, but more significantly from what is *not*
said. For these media not only continue to affirm the status quo
but, in the same measure, they fail to raise essential questions
about the structure of society."[8]

Let us note that this is far from saying that mass communication has no effect!

Is it possible to use the mass media actively for desirable
social objectives rather than as a "narcotizing dysfunction"?
Lazarsfeld and Merton feel that one or more of the following
conditions must be fulfilled before the media can have such an
effect: There must be (1) monopolization rather than real competition of ideas, (2) canalization rather than an effort to change
values in a basic way, and/or (3) face-to-face contact supplementing the media exposure.

They believe that political campaigns largely neutralize
media effect because the arguments and programs of one cancel
out the programs of the other. If, on the other hand, the media
were to be taken over by a single viewpoint—as happened, for
example, during World War II—there might be "discernible
effects." Similarly once a basic pattern of attitudes and behavior
has been established, it can be turned slightly in one direction or another. Advertising has learned to do this effectively in
brand competition (for instance, encouraging a smoker to try a
new brand). But social-change campaigns usually require far-
reaching and basic changes rather than canalization. If mass

communication is unable to achieve monopoly or to be satisfied with mere canalization, it can still achieve some effect by supplementing media with personal and/or group communication.

Thus, for example, Lazarfeld and Merton believe that the propaganda success of Father Coughlin was due not so much to his broadcasts as to his local organization, which brought people together to hear the radio talks and then discuss them. The propaganda successes of Nazism were also attributable not so much to capturing the mass media as to "the use of organized violence, organized distribution of rewards for conformity, and organized centers of local indoctrination." And although Lazarsfeld and Merton wrote their paper before economic and social development in the new countries had really come to public attention, if they had written a little later they could have cited discussion groups built around broadcasts or print, field staffs supported by public information campaigns and the use of organizations like national parties to bring about adoption of new practices—all demonstrating the potency of a *combination* of approaches.

We have reviewed the Lazarsfeld and Merton essay at such length not only because it is a cogent and important paper but also because it represents the considered conclusions of a group of scholars who have spent a long time studying mass communication and who are predisposed by scholarly background to be doubtful about its ability to bring about a social effect. However, as they have made clear, under certain conditions it *can* have a significant effect. And the fact that even without special conditions it can confer status, enforce social norms, and help *inhibit* change in social norms and practices —this adds up to considerable effect.

A dozen years after Lazarsfeld and Merton published their essay, one of their students, Joseph Klapper (who has become director of social research for the Columbia Broadcasting System), summed up his view of existing research knowledge in a much-quoted book entitled *The Effects of Mass Communication*. He was able to state his conclusions with admirable brevity, and they are worth reporting here as a later development of the strand of theory that gave rise to the paper we have just discussed. Klapper proposes these generalizations:

1. Mass communication *ordinarily* does not serve as a necessary and sufficient cause of audience effects, but rather functions among and through a nexus of mediating factors and influences.

2. These mediating factors are such that they typically render mass communication a contributory agent, but not the sole cause, in a process of reinforcing the existing conditions. (Regardless of the condition in question—be it the vote intention of audience members, their tendency toward or away from delinquent behavior, or their general orientation toward life and its problems—and regardless of whether the effect in question be social or individual, the media are more likely to reinforce than to change.)

3. On such occasions as mass communication does function in the service of change, one of two conditions is likely to exist. Either:
   a. The mediating factors will be found to be inoperative and the effect of the media will be found to be direct; *or*
   b. The mediating factors which normally favor reinforcement, will be found to be themselves impelling toward change.

4. There are certain residual situations in which mass communication seems to produce direct effects, or directly and of itself to serve certain psycho-physical functions.

5. The efficacy of mass communication, either as a contributory agent or as an agent of direct effect, is affected by various aspects of the media and communications themselves or of the communication situation (including, for example, aspects of textual organization, the nature of the source and medium, the existing climate of public opinion, and the like) .[9]

Klapper says that he submits these generalizations "very gingerly." He adds a word of caution lest they be interpreted as implying the impotency of mass communication. "It must be remembered," he says, "that though mass communication seems usually to be a *contributory* cause of effects, it is often a major or necessary cause and in some instances a sufficient cause. The fact that its effect is often mediated, or that it often works among other influences, must not blind us to the fact that mass communication possesses qualities which distinguish it from other influences, and that by virtue of these qualities, it is likely to have characteristic effects."[10]

It is hard to quarrel with this viewpoint, except when it is interpreted to mean that mass communication necessarily has little impact on human behavior. Experiments with mass communication in the laboratory, where other influences are controlled as completely as possible, readily produce attitudinal change and sometimes behavioral change. Outside the laboratory it is rarely possible to separate mass communication from the other influences that bear on every individual. These are the elements that Klapper refers to as "mediating factors." He names some of them: the receiver's predispositions; the selective exposure, selective perception, and selective retention that supposedly support those predispositions; the groups to which audience members belong and the group norms to which they hold; personal influence and personal communication that supplements or counteracts persuasion by mass communication; and (in words reminiscent of Lazarsfeld and Merton) the nature of commercial mass media in a free enterprise system which makes it more likely that they will operate to reinforce and maintain existing social and political beliefs rather than to change them.

The complexity of social communication effects is now generally agreed upon. Complex behavior almost always has complex roots. Outside the laboratory a person is always more fully aware of social constraints and alternative behaviors than he is within the laboratory. His cognitive defenses are more easily roused in a naturalistic situation than in the laboratory, where there is often an aura of unreality about the questions he is made to answer and the decisions he is asked to make.

As Klapper recognizes, the media are quite efficient in implanting information and in contributing to new values and beliefs in areas where no strongly held positions already exist. But the images, knowledge, and values that accumulate in every individual through exposure to mass media are likely to appear only after a series of cumulative exposures or as a result of a combination of stimuli. Therefore, causation is hard to measure, and it is very difficult to isolate the elements that bring about the behavior finally observed.

What Klapper says is that mass communication undoubtedly has an effect on men and society, but it is much more often a contributory than a sole effect; it is seldom conversion, but more often a reinforcement of ideas already held or a contribution to areas in which the cognitive defenses are not strong. And occasionally—as in "The Invasion from Mars"—it does have a quick and spectacular effect on some people. But even here the acceptance of the new information and the action triggered can be understood only in terms of the cognitive structure of the individual and his interpretation of the situation.

## The Developing Theory of Effect

The well-reasoned conclusions of Lazarsfeld, Merton, and Klapper are not only correctives to the "no effect" viewpoint but also healthful counteragents to some of the almost frantic fears concerning mass media propaganda that have been expressed ever since Americans became aware of mass propaganda during World War I. As a matter of fact the change in viewpoint toward mass media effect since 1920 has been one of the really spectacular developments in communication theory.

For nearly thirty years after World War I, the favorite concept of the mass media audience was what advertisers and propagandists often chose to call the "target audience." A handbook was written during this time for the United States information services under the title *Are We Hitting the Target?* In the earlier years of the postwar period, this is precisely how the audience was conceived of: a passive, relatively defenseless target which, if the mass could hit it, could be knocked over.

Along with this image of the audience went a concept of communication as the transferring of something—ideas, feelings, facts, thoughts, or some other cognitive baggage—from one mind to another. Because the analogy to this was the electric current that could flow over a wire and light up a bulb or the marksman shooting a bullet from a gun into a target, this theory of communication effect has sometimes been called the "bullet theory." A propagandist could shoot the magic bullet of communication into a viewer or a listener, who would stand still and wait to be hit!

However, this conception proved to be less than satisfactory. The audience, when observed closely, usually refused to fall over and play dead. It even refused to play target. Sometimes the bullet bounced off, and at other times the audience actually seemed to be trying to catch the bullet in its hands and eat it like chocolate.

Trying to explain these phenomena in the early years of intensive audience research, sociologists and advertisers began to use an approach some people have called the "category theory." The advertisers needed some simple way of categorizing the audience so that they could more easily predict responses to mass media. It was quickly discovered that highly educated people responded differently from poorly educated ones, young people from old, men from women, Chinese from British, rich from poor. As attitude measurement developed, it was found that attitude tests would also help predict responses to messages related to those attitudes. This categorical approach was descriptive rather than explanatory, but it demonstrated that more than the mass media stimulus entered into the effect of "propaganda."

Lazarsfeld and his colleagues, and Lewin and his colleagues, observed that people in the audience belonged to groups and would discuss new ideas with other members of these groups. In the absence of group activity, they would recall "reference groups" and test some of the messages of mass media against the norms of that group. This led to the study of group influence and more generally of personal influence as a supplement and sometimes counteragent to mass media influence. "Opinion leaders" were discovered, and the two-step flow hypothesis was proposed to explain the combined influence of these leaders and the media. The general conclusion of this line of research which was summed up in *Personal Influence* by Katz and Lazarsfeld, published in 1955) was that, far from being a sole cause or an irresistible influence, mass communication was less likely than personal influence to have a direct effect on social behavior.[11] The rural sociologists supported this finding with studies of the adoption of new agricultural practices. They concluded that mass communication was important in spreading awareness of new possibilities and practices but that at the stage where decisions were being made about whether to adopt or not to adopt, personal communication was far more likely to be influential.

In the late 1940s and 1950s, Hovland and others studied a number of other variables related to communication effect and began to tease out the interrelationships of these variables.[12] (We mentioned some of these in the preceding chapter.) Some people have called this the "individual differences theory."

In other words, by the late 1950s the bullet theory was, so to speak, shot full of holes. Mass communication was not like a shooting gallery. There was nothing necessarily irresistible about mass communication or mass propaganda. Many influences entered into the effect of the mass media. The audience was not a passive target; rather, it was extraordinarily active.

Raymond Bauer, a social psychologist at Harvard contributed a title that typified some of these new ideas when he wrote about the "obstinate audience"[13]—the audience that simply refused to be pushed around as old theories said it should be by the supposedly omnipotent mass media. In addition, he conducted several experiments that further demonstrated how nonpassive the audience really is. Perhaps the most striking of these was done in collaboration with Claire Zimmerman. This was designed to find out what an individual would seek out and remember from information available to him. A group of journalism students and a group of teachers in training were given some printed material, supposedly to help them with a talk they were to prepare for one of two fictitious audiences: the National Council of Teachers or the American Taxpayers Economy League. The talk and the reading material were on the subject of raising teachers' salaries. Supposedly the teachers' group would be in favor of this, the Taxpayers Economy League opposed. There were also two versions of the reading material, one strongly weighted in favor of raising salaries, the other against. Half of the experimental subjects were given the favorable arguments, half of them the unfavorable arguments. Of each group, half were told they were to prepare a talk for the Taxpayers Association, half for the Teachers Council. The question was, What relation would there be between the expected use to be made of the material and what was learned?

As might be expected, there was a very strong relationship. When a person read material that was not in agreement with the anticipated viewpoints of the audience he was to address, he remembered much less than from material he thought the audience would probably agree with. Journalism students, who were supposedly taught to be objective in their reporting but were also expected to be more aware of their audiences than were the other subjects, were actually able to remember only about half as many points from the material they expected the audience to disagree with than from the other versions.[14] This circumstance raises certain questions about the objectivity of news coverage. But the important implication of the experiment is the *activity* of the audience: not soaking up the arguments like a sponge but searching among them for arguments that they *want to find*.

So in forty years communication theory moved from the concept of a passive, helpless audience to that of an obstinate, self-reliant, *active* one; from the concept of mass communication as an irresistible force to the concept of mass communication as one force among many, interacting with the others. The obvious next step in this development is the kind of theory presented in Chapter III, in which the two participants in a communication relationship are conceived of as equally active, making their own uses of the communication signs they momentarily share.

As we have rejected the idea of the magic bullet of propaganda, however, so must we avoid overreacting to it. Mass communication isn't irresistible, but it does have effects. Few of them are as direct and immediate as what happened after the broadcast of "The Invasion from Mars." More of them are "quiet effects," long-term, cumulative, hard to isolate from related causes of behavior. Nevertheless, they are a major factor in determining what people know, believe, and do. In the following pages we shall look more closely at some of these effects.

## What Is the Effect on Individual Living Patterns?

I was talking recently about the effects of mass media with an old broadcaster, a man who before his retirement was a pioneer in bringing radio and television to the American West. He said, "If you worked for me 7 days a week, 40 to 45 hours, wouldn't you say that I was having some influence on your way of life?"

It is sometimes hard to see the most obvious things. There is a game for example, in which players compete in finding names on a map. New players give their opponents obscure names to search out, but the old hands often choose names printed in large type and spread over the page with a great deal of space between the letters. And in the same way we sometimes miss the large effects and notice more subtle ones.

Television, as we know, is now turned on over 6 hours a day in the average American home and absorbs 3 hours a day or more of an average individual's time. Of course, there is no average home or average individual, and therefore some use television less, some a great deal more. Let us not think that American behavior in this respect is wholly different from that in other countries. In Japan, for example, one of the few countries for which we have reliable measurements, average daily television viewing time is even longer than in the United States. In any situation like this a mass medium is bound to have an effect on the way a family arranges its living patterns. If the network news comes on at 7 o'clock, there is good reason to have dinner late or to put a television set in the dining room. The late afternoon children's programs, the daytime women's programs, the favorite prime-time entertainment, the weekend football games, the special events like a broadcast from the moon or election night reports—these are likely to be fixed points around which individuals organize their leisure and families arrange their schedules.

Add 40 to 60 minutes spent each day on the newspaper, one or more hours on radio (often as a background to other activities), some time on magazines and books, and an occasional movie, and the total adds up to 6 hours or more a day—the 40 to 45 hours a week my broadcaster friend was talking about. Mass media are the chief components of leisure time, not only in America but elsewhere. They absorb more time than the average individual gives to any activity other than work or sleep, and if he works only a 40-hour week or sleeps no more than 6 hours a night, he may make his single largest allocation of time to mass communication. Let me warn again that these are average figures, which may or may not apply to any individual. But unless he retires from modern life he is certain to allocate a substantial portion of his time to mass media and organize his living patterns partly around them.

Disregarding for the moment any possible effect on our stock of information and ideas, what does this do to our way of life? Some of us can still remember, with a twinge of nostalgia, the experience of a family singing together or playing its own instrumental music instead of depending on radio and stereo phonographs for music at home; hiking or picnicking on Sunday rather than driving or watching television; living in houses with front porches designed for conversations with one's neighbors rather than houses designed to close out the street in favor of more private activities. But there is nothing to be gained by considering what life might be like if the electronic media had never come into our homes and our lives. We will never go back to those premedia days. South Africa, the last economically advanced country on earth to resist television, has finally decided to introduce it. Even among the developing nations and the remote countries and territories, all know radio and movies, and many have television. American Samoa, which fifteen years ago might have been thought of as one of the last strongholds of the primitive life, now has six channels of VHF television and "Bonanza" and "Sesame Street" are seen there as well as here.

Therefore it is of no use to speculate as to whether, if the electronic media had never been invented, people might spend more time with each other rather than with the media; more time on high culture rather than popular culture; more time in libraries, museums, discussion groups, at symphony orchestra concerts, or simply talking with their families and their neighbors than with the media.[15] Of more interest is the question. What activities do the mass media displace? Such changes have taken place in our own time, and we have been able to observe them.

The growth of films, large-circulation magazines, and radio in the first forty years of this century came at a time when leisure was expanding steadily. The 6- or 7-day work week gave way to the 5-day week; the 10- or 12-hour work day to the

8 hour day and the 40- or 36-hour week. The growth of media use during that period, therefore, undoubtedly shifted some emphasis from group and social activities to activities within the home but operated principally to fill up the additional leisure time that was becoming available.

Television, however, was something else. It came in after the 8-hour day and 40-hour week were already established and consequently had to displace existing leisure activities of some kind or other. What conclusions can we draw from television history as to what a new medium does to leisure time?

When Dr. Hilde Himmelweit of the London School of Economics and two of her colleagues studied the impact of television on English children, they suggested three principles to explain its effects on other activities.[16] These principles have been confirmed by other studies in other countries. With a little paraphrasing, they seem just as applicable to adults as to children:

1. **If some activities have to be reduced or eliminated to make room for a new medium, the ones curtailed are likely to be marginal ones.** What is marginal, of course, depends on an individual and a culture. Dr. Himmelweit found that television at least in the early years, had little effect on outdoor play, social activities, or hobbies but reduced the time spent doing "nothing special"— just "passing the time." In the United States however, both Maccoby in 1951 and Mahoney two years later found that television was reducing children's playtime. But in this case also the kind of play that was curtailed was not the kind most enjoyed or valued. For example, television was not likely to keep a boy from playing Little League baseball or building his own ham radio. It was not likely to keep youngsters away from the movies when they reached the age at which it became important to be with their friends and to see and be seen by members of the opposite sex.

Similarly, for adults television has not displaced golf, although the game is probably scheduled for hours other than those of the favorite weekend television programs. It has not kept the people of Hawaii from surfing or from going to the beach. But adults now have a good excuse to spend more time at home, to see movies on the picture tube rather than in the theater; and it it becoming more common now than it used to be for young people to spend a great deal of time at home in front of the television set instead of going out—until they come to the stage of courtship when they cannot find sufficient privacy at home.

This principle, then, seems to be that, given an attractive and useful new medium, people will use it to replace the leisure activities they value least and will maintain (sometimes reschedule) those they value most.

If within the next two decades we have a communication development like the "new medium" suggested in Chapter IX we may expect more far-reaching changes in life patterns. For example, how many conferences, meetings, seminars, and annual meetings of learned societies can then be held more conveniently without leaving one's home or office? How much travel will be replaced by this kind of contact? How much shopping will be done by a voice-and-picture channel? How many learning and study activities will be transferred from the school and the classroom to the home? Will we finally have the mechanism for truly "lifelong" learning? What will be displaced if we have to pay as much for an "information center" as we now spend to purchase an automobile? What will be the effect on public events, sports, concerts, and theater? It is evident that the social changes, if and when *this* projected "medium" arrives, may be considerable.

2. **Time given to media that are functionally similar to the new medium but not so interesting will be reduced in favor of the new opportunities.** We sometimes forget that before television the radio receiver was the family entertainment center. The situation comedies, adventure dramas, family serials, and public events that we now get from television we used to get from radio. The average family then spent almost as much time on radio as it now spends on television, and its living patterns were organized around the Fred Allen and Jack Benny programs, "Amos 'n' Andy," amateur hours, "One Man's Family," the CBS Workshop, the soap operas, the sports broadcasts, the New York Philharmonic and the Metropolitan Opera, the popular singers from Rudy Vallee to Frank Sinatra, the election

night *radio* broadcasts, and the newscasts, just as they are organized today around similar programs on television.

Will any of us who lived in the great days of radio ever forget Edward R. Murrow beginning his news report: "This . . . is London!" And, on a lower level, I remember a newscaster who came on the air at 1 P.M. in a certain midwestern state; we sometimes called him the "voice of doom" but seldom failed to listen to him. After his program radios clicked off and lights turned out all over the state. When this man left his station, he ran for governor of the state, though he had no previous political experience, and came within a few votes of being elected. Then he ran for Congress, was elected, and stayed a long time.

The portions of this radio experience that television replaced tell us something. The comedians are chiefly on television now. The fantasy theater, the adventure shows, the variety hours featuring big-name stars are on television because show business is more interesting when you can see as well as hear it. The big money and the big audiences for sports broadcasts are in television now, although many people still listen to sports on radio if they can't take the time to sit in front of the television set or if the program is not televised. News events and news personalities are likely to be on television, but news summaries are just as likely to be on radio. If people have a chance they will watch an election night summary or a moon shot on television, but if not they will settle for radio. I remember sitting in Paris during one Apollo crisis with television tuned to the French broadcast and radio to the BBC—lest I miss something.

In other words, we are saying that for the kinds of programs in which the visual element is an essential part of the interest, television tended to displace radio. When the picture is less important—as in news summaries—many people still held to radio. If the visual element is of relatively slight importance— as in music—radio maintained its popularity; today the music audiences, for either popular or classical music, are largely with radio.

Why, then, did television displace so much movie going? Television does drama or fantasy no better than films, but it doesn't require the viewer to go out or pay an admission fee. Television also offers a variety of programs that no single movie house could duplicate. In an evening at home one can see adventure drama, a comedy, perhaps a variety show, current news from the network and a choice of several movies. Therefore, television offers *more*, though not better, entertainment.

Why did not television displace newspaper-reading time? Clearly because it does not do the detailed job of news coverage that newspapers do. As newscasters like Huntley and Cronkite have often noted, the total content of a 30-minute TV news program is less than that of one page of a newspaper. Radio and television replaced the extra but not the basic service.

Why did television tend to displace magazines of general interest rather than specialized magazines? Because it, too, offered a general entertainment and information service for the family, and offered it with all the advantages of movement and color and liveness and sound. It did not replace magazines that dealt with flying, cooking, golf, teen-age problems, movie stars, or political and social commentary; its service is more generalized. The genius of commercial television, at least as it has developed, is in show business and events. These it has taken over. Therefore, a golfer will watch the telecast of the Masters Tournament or the U.S. Open, but he will go to a golf magazine or a golf textbook for more systematic information or instruction.

**3. In order to continue to attract attention, media that are adversely affected by a new medium will be transformed to satisfy needs the new medium does not meet.** We have been talking about the effect on the audience. There is a concurrent effect on media. When television took over the show business side of radio, radio moved into two areas for which television had no special fitness: listening while one's eyes are occupied elsewhere, and listening to music. Consequently, 70 million automobiles in the United States now have radio to help combat the boredom of long drives. Some stations carry nothing but news items all day. Almost every large city has one or more classical music stations, and some thousands of radio stations in the United States exist mostly for popular music. Another development in which radio has led is the "talk show," in which listeners are invited to call up and air their opinions, often in conversation with a studio host and sometimes with a guest expert. Radio is not making as much money as television, partly because of the vast number of stations trying to divide the advertising dollar; but it is still carrying out important functions and attracting audiences.

Motion pictures too have been reacting in predictable ways to the loss of audience to television. They have been able to profit from filmed entertainment that television would have great difficulty showing—"adult" movies and semiprivate pornographic movies. They have turned their skills and facilities to making programs for television. And finally, they have used television as an extension of the theater by selling their backlog of old movies to be shown on the picture tubes, interrupted by parades of commercials.

Both from the side of the individual and from the side of the media, then, living patterns and services tend to be organized and reorganized around the apparently best ways to meet needs and interests. It is hard to think of a *new* need introduced by the mass media, but they have made some needs more salient and raised expectations that were hardly thought of half a century ago. For example, in 1920 few people would have expected to participate, at least as observers, in every public event of world importance as they now do. Hardly anyone would have expected the President of the United States to show himself at regular intervals to all the people of the nation; indeed, people now begin to be suspicious if he does not do so. Hardly anyone would have expected a United States senator or representative or cabinet officer to submit himself to interrogation by newsmen in full view of the people of the country. Hardly anyone would have expected to have delivered to his home, free of apparent cost, the kind of entertainment that was formerly available only in the theaters of great cities or the stadiums of universities—or to feel mistreated if, for some reason, an important game was not broadcast or the network cancelled a show he liked.

These interests are not new, but the expectations of people that their interests will be satisfied is of an entirely different order than previously, and consequently living patterns and schedules, bedtimes and social life, media habits and nonmedia activities have been reorganized. This is an effect of mass media that is obvious to us every time we switch on the news in the automobile or see our preschoolers rush to the television set when it is time for *their* programs.

## What Is the Effect on Knowledge?

If there is one thing we know about the effects of the mass media, it is that they absorb a very large amount of time and consequently rearrange the leisure time of a very large number of people. If we can say confidently that we know a second thing about mass media effects, it is that people learn an enormous amount from them. We are not passing a value judgment on what is learned. Rather, we are saying that if a person exposes himself to six hours of concentrated information flow each day from the mass media, much of that information is likely to be processed and a considerable part of it stored away.

Give yourself a brief test. Where have you learned most of what you know about these topics or people?

| | |
|---|---|
| The Vietnam war | Bob Dylan |
| The appearance, ideas, and policies of the President of the United States | Muhammad Ali |
| | Joan Baez and her political activities |
| The circumstances of the assassination of John F. Kennedy | The Cannes film festival |
| | Willy Mays |
| The nuclear bomb | Leonard Bernstein |
| China | The Bolshoi ballet |
| Antarctica | The "top twenty" |
| The green revolution | Bob Hope |
| Fidel Castro | Norman Mailer |
| The present leadership in the Soviet Union | César Chavez |
| | Ralph Bunche |
| What Latin American countries think of the United States | |

As you have observed, some of these items are concerned with public affairs, others with entertainment topics. I have refrained for the most part, from asking for small details such as what Castro looks like, what the Concorde looks like, what John F. Kennedy sounded like, or the latest events and characters in any of the broadcast serials or movies—things you could hardly have learned elsewhere than from the mass media. Instead, I have asked about a number of people, events, and ideas that are or have been important to public affairs in the United States and elsewhere, and about a number of artists, entertainers, and productions that are widely known and in many cases highly praised in the world of entertainment.

Unless I am mistaken, you have answered that the chief source of your knowledge of most, if not all, of these topics has been the mass media.

Of course, if you have served a tour in Vietnam, that may overbalance what you have learned about the war from the media. If you work for the Atomic Energy Commission, you will probably have better sources of information about the Bomb than are provided by the mass media. If you are a personal friend of Bob Dylan or Leonard Bernstein or Willy Mays, or usually attend the Cannes festival, you will not have to depend on the media for information about them. But if you are like most Americans, I suspect that you have met these people, problems, events, and organizations chiefly through mass communication.

I am not asking how *much* you know about them, how well informed you feel on the topic, or whether one is more worth knowing about than another. The question is merely how this public affairs and entertainment information came to you.

If the situation is, as I suspect, that most of this information has come through the mass media, we can agree that it is a most significant effect. Whether you are deeply or shallowly, narrowly or broadly informed is a part of the effect.

This circumstance does not necessarily mean that the mass media have any special advantages over other channels as a teaching device. Man is an extraordinarily efficient learning machine. He can learn from nearly any source and any experience. When he exposes himself six hours a day to such an enormous flow of information and entertainment as the mass media carry, there is bound to be a great deal taken in and retained.

Literally hundreds of experiments have demonstrated that students learn a great deal from any of the media—from the textbooks on which our public school systems have been built, from instructional films, radio, television, language laboratories, any application of mass media tools to teaching and learning. For example, no single one of the dozen or so fully controlled experiments on teaching with television has found any significant difference in the amount learned from instructional television and the amount learned from a live and present teacher doing the same thing as the teleteacher. There are results of face-to-face instruction that are not being measured by that design, but as far as learning the subject matter of a course is concerned, that is the evidence.

In the laboratory too, there have been scores of experiments showing that subjects learn attitudes and facts efficiently by reading them, hearing them on radio, or viewing them on television or films. One of the most interesting findings, as we noted in Chapter IX, has been the amount of *incidental* learning—incidental meaning facts, ideas, and attitudes that were not intended to be part of the learning from the message. This means that such information can be acquired—*is* acquired—from programs intended to entertain rather than inform.

These things are sometimes a bit harder to demonstrate in life than in the laboratory, but even here the evidence is extensive. Fads like the hula-hoop have run like wildfire through the country once they have appeared in the mass media. Berelson and others, studying the 1940 election, and Trenaman and Mac-Quail, studying a British election twenty years later, presented evidence that the issues presented in the mass media in an election campaign are the ones that are learned.[17] Stewart in 1964, and many advertisers before and after him, found that newspaper, magazine, and television advertising correlated very closely with what people knew of new consumer products and brands.[18] In a Central American country researchers have found that exposure to television has resulted in a notable rise in career aspirations among young people. Fujitake studied the reaction of the Japanese people to the Tokyo Olympics and found that the involvement of the people in the games at a given time was parallel to the density and content of media coverage.[19]

Somewhat surprising is the evidence on how much credence is placed in the incidental learning from entertainment media. For example, in the early 1960s when at least half of the screen time throughout the world and a substantial amount of television time was taken up with American films and tapes, the USIA sponsored a survey in eleven countries which found out that, on the average, 28 percent of the people in those countries considered American movies a major source of their information about this country.[20] In 1962, 40 percent of the people surveyed in four NATO countries said that they felt American films gave a true picture of American life. A survey in Santiago, Chile, in 1964 found that 56 percent of the moviegoers in that city believed that the films from the United States and Mexico, the countries that provide a high percentage of the movies in Chile, faithfully represented everyday life in those two countries. Holaday and Stoddard found that American children, too, believed that films about foreign countries were factually true and used the films as sources for their answers to questions of fact about those countries.[21] Visitors to Bangkok have sometimes reported that they can walk down a street in the evening and hear gunfire on both sides—from the sound tracks of American westerns being shown on Thai television! It is not entirely surprising, then, that we should hear of foreign visitors landing in New York or San Francisco and looking for frontier scenery and cowboys riding into the sunset.

With all this incidental learning and an amazing amount of exposure to a broad flow of information through the mass media, why are people not better informed? Why are there so many blank areas in the public affairs knowledge, the health and science knowledge of the public? The evidence is considerable:[22]

At the height of Senator Joseph McCarthy's widely covered proceedings against alleged communists in government, almost one-third of a national sample could not name any senator or congressman who had played an important role in the investigation of communism.

At the height of a Presidential campaign in the 1950s, nearly half the electorate could not name *either* Vice-Presidential candidate.

For two years, every time the name Bundesrat was mentioned in a news broadcast over Radio Stuttgart, the station explained to its listeners what this part of the German Federal Republic is. Nevertheless, a survey found almost no one able to explain what the Bundesrat is or does.

During a campaign intended to make the people of Cincinnati better informed and more interested in the United Nations, a slogan—Peace begins with the United Nations—the United Nations begins with you—was broadcast about 150 times a week. At the end of the campaign more than half of the people surveyed were unable to recall the slogan, and only one-third had much idea what the main purpose of the UN is.

In a national survey in 1947, 80 percent could say in general what a Presidential veto is, but only 70 percent of those knew that Congress could override the veto, and only 44 percent of those who knew about the override were aware of the majority required to accomplish it.

In 1950 almost 20 times as many people had heard of Truman's Point Four program as could remember any of its purposes.

In 1955 only 7 percent of a national sample could name the planet nearest the sun, and two years later only 38 percent were sure that the moon is smaller than the earth.

Figures like these may be shocking, except to scholars and politicians who know that there will always be a considerable amount of ignorance on any topic of public interest. But they illustrate that, inadequate as mass media coverage of public affairs and science may be, it is better than the result. The mass media carried much more about each of the topics represented in the sad little list we have just given than was reflected in public knowledge. Why were the blank areas so large?

The scholars who studied the Cincinnati campaign came to the discouraged conclusion that there always has been, and probably always will be, a certain number of "know-nothings" among the public.[23] Individual interests are narrow and often self-centered. People don't care to explore any more deeply than they have to into problems and knowledge not directly related to them. Their media time is given preponderantly to entertainment. They commonly scan the news for "new" developments, for some significant change in the parade of events that passes day after day, and tend to see most of the day's events, no matter how full of war and crime and social problems and political changes, as "more of the same" because they have become used to it and are not deeply interested in most of the details. They tend to be selective—to pick out experiences from the enormous menu they have before them that will meet their needs at the moment. These are likely to consist largely of relaxation or diversion, or solutions to their own particular problems. For example, a woman carrying her first child will be more likely to select material on childbirth or child rearing than most other people in the audience will be. The Cincinnati evaluation discovered that most of the people who made use of campaign programs or reading material were merely following a long-time interest in the UN and international relations; people who did not share this interest usually did not expose themselves and risk having their viewpoints changed. Finally, it must be remembered that field studies of general knowledge are usually conducted some weeks or months after the exposure that might have implanted the knowledge being tested. People forget. The details with which they might have answered the questions tend to slip back into a general sense of awareness of what is going on, unencumbered with many facts.

This is the people side of the interaction. The result, however, depends also on what the media choose to report and how they report it. We have discussed the power of the gatekeeper function and some of the instances in which television, among other media, has proved to be far less than a "clear lens" on reality. In an interesting study of a television editor's reasons for choosing the news he did, Buckalew found five main qualities the editor seemed to be looking for—conflict, significance, timeliness, proximity, and visual availability. Except for the visual requirement, the same factors would probably rank high in any radio or newspaper news editor's choices. He looks for something that has the tension of competition or a fight, something that seems "big" and important, something that is recent and timely, and something that comes as close as possible to his own audience's interests and experiences. His coverage tends therefore to be of events rather than ideas, today's excitement rather than tomorrow's significance, "facts" rather than interpretation, and a heavy diet of feature material to leaven the seriousness of events. Moreover, the media as a whole are devoted largely to entertainment, and the time or space left for public affairs and matters of social and intellectual interest is sufficient only to carry a small part of the available information that might be carried. Because the information must often be telescoped and must be presented in such a way as to be understood by a large audience, it tends to take the form of a stereotyped reality in which the situation can be understood more easily (although less accurately) as a conflict between "them" and "us" or the good guys and the bad guys.

What the mass media do not report may be as significant as what they do report. The *Los Angeles Times* has been praised for its coverage of events and problems in Watts, yet the editors of that paper are frank to admit that if they had covered it as well before the violent events as later the problems might have been understood better and there might have been less likelihood of a Watts riot.

Another matter of concern is what use is made of the media to report public affairs. We have read a great deal recently about the image makers who "create" a candidate for presentation on television. Daniel Boorstin has written of the pseudo-events that show up in such numbers within the media—demonstrations, meetings, protests, promotional press conferences, and so forth.[24] These are simply examples of using the media for one's own interests, and to the extent that media officials allow their picture of reality to be overbalanced by this sort of thing they might as well be working for the manipulators. Street demonstrations, which supposedly represent wide public indignation, have sometimes been abandoned because the television stations did not send crews to photograph them. And I watched with some interest as a group of campus protesters delayed a planned "invasion" of a trustees meeting until the television truck arrived. I am not implying that manipulation of the media is on one side of the political fence rather than the other. The alleged riot at San Jose in the fall of 1970, when television stations and newspapers spread over the country the word that the President and his caravan had been attacked after a public address, looks in retrospect like a rather synthetic event. Reporters who investigated afterward could find almost no fire beneath the smoke. The guardians of the law did not find it necessary to take any action. But it got on the network news and into the headlines, and therefore—as far as many people were concerned—it was true.

Lest this be misunderstood, though, let me repeat that there is a great deal more information in the media than the public ever absorbs. The knowledge effect of the mass media outside the classroom or the equivalent is probably a general one: awareness of what is going on and who is doing it, and a chance to follow one's own special interests into more detail. An analogy of some pertinence here is that a very high proportion of the intelligence information on China during the years when it was so tightly closed came from no more glamorous or mysterious activities than reading the newspapers from inside the country and the official publications of the government. One can find a great deal of information in the mass media if one wants to.

A reasonable hypothesis is that the most powerful effect of the mass media on public knowledge—comparable even to the effect of the realism with which it can present distant events and places—is the ability of the media to focus public attention on certain problems, persons, or issues at a given time. This may be an effect controlled in part by people who are able to use the media skillfully, but it is clearly important. It feeds the conversation that goes on interpersonally. It stimulates other viewing, listening, or reading. It encourages reporters to dig deeper and commentators to interpret a problem in greater depth. For example, the developments during the past two years in the field of ecology could hardly have taken place unless the mass media had raised ecology to a level of public attention and kept reporting on it day after day. The drug problem in

Vietnam or the events at Mylai would hardly have been in the public eye so long if the media had not kept attention focused on them. This is a great power the media have in their hands, and an especially potent one considering the glut of news, the vast river of information that flows past us all the time at a rate that allows none of us to comprehend it all any more than a man can drink up all the Amazon as it flows to the sea.

We can be confident, then, that the mass media do have a significant effect on the organization of our leisure time and a significant effect on what we know, and when and in what detail we know it. The effect on knowledge is sufficiently important to cause some troubled thoughts about what appears in the media and how what appears is determined. We have good reason to believe, also, that under certain conditions (such as "The Invasion from Mars") the media can have a direct effect on social behavior and that under other conditions they may function to inhibit social change. But the best place to examine social effects of these latter kinds is in some of the social laboratories where we might expect to see media effects, if at all, under real-life conditions. We are going to look next at one of these "social laboratories"—politics.

# xiv.
# The Political Impact of Mass Communication

It would be unfortunate if the last few chapters were to leave the impression that the study of the effects of communication is something "academic," conducted in a laboratory, expounded by a theoretician.

It is that, but it is more than that. There are a number of real-life situations in which communication is tested constantly against such measures of effect as the choice of leaders, the expansion of commerce, the state of the national economy, the condition of health care, the level of agricultural practice in developing villages, and social behavior. I mean election campaigns, advertising, economic and social development, and the effect of television violence on children. There is nothing "merely academic" about these activities. They are deadly serious, and researchers join with political and economic leaders in trying to understand how communication works and to make it work toward a given goal.

In all of these real-life laboratories, the effects of communication must undergo a pitiless and continuing examination. It is true that the state of the art in using communication for politics or economic development, or ameliorating the effects of its violence is still far below the level of science. Yet trial and error, the lore of experience, and occasional research are beginning to coalesce into something more than trial and error, and there is much to learn from any of these fields about how communication works and what it does.

In Chapter IX we spoke briefly of the emerging knowledge of television's effect on children. It is unfortunate that we cannot examine each of the other social laboratories, and at greater length. Economic development now represents the largest movement of planned change in the world; it depends on the mass media, supported by face-to-face communication, to offer educational opportunities where they are not now available, to push back the horizons of undeveloped villages, and to carry the flow of knowledge without which people cannot participate in the remaking of their countries. Indeed, the spread of transistor radios throughout the developing regions, overleaping illiteracy and remoteness, is itself one of the dramatic chapters of communication history. Advertising is perhaps less dramatic, because we are more accustomed to it, but it provides a situation by which different appeals and different presentations can be gauged very specifically in terms of sales and changes in taste. It would be interesting to look hard at these areas and others, but here let us concentrate on one life laboratory only—the arena of politics.

Politicians have to be communication "experts" because they must offer themselves, make issues known, and persuade voters and decision makers to their way of thinking. This has been the case since long before the mass media came into being, but the increasing dependence on media in political campaigns has forced politicians to become media experts too. As media politics has become more complex, they have had to bring in other experts to guide them—political public relations specialists, media specialists, public opinion pollsters. Under the guidance of these individuals, more and more of the campaigns have been fought out in the mass media, and particularly (in recent years) television.

The bill for political broadcast advertising in 1968 was $58 million. This is the Federal Communications Commission's conservative estimate. Less conservatively, Herbert E. Alexander, director of the Citizens' Research Foundation of Princeton, New Jersey, estimated that at least $300 million went into the 1968 campaign, including the primaries: about one-third of it for electing a President, the remainder for state and local campaigns.[1]

This money was spread over the entire spectrum of public communication. Television and radio got the lion's share among the media, but large amounts went to newspapers, printing, billboards, direct mail, meetings, travel, telephone calls, organization expenses, local staffs, and all the symbolic paraphernalia of a campaign. For example, the Nixon-Agnew organization ordered 9,000,000 bumper strips, 560,000 balloons, 400,000 posters and placards, 28,000 straw hats, and 12,000 paper dresses, to be designed, warehoused, and supplied by one New York advertising agency alone.[2]

Campaign expenses have increased sharply. Alexander estimates that the 1968 election cost approximately 50 percent more than that of 1964. Why? For one thing, an increased portion of the money went into television. Strangely enough, the actual amount of television time bought for campaign purposes was less in 1968 than previously, but more of the money went for expensive spot announcements, rather than program time, and advertising rates have been going up. Another reason for the increased expenditure is the rise of the advisers and organizations described in *The Selling of a President 1968* and *The Political Persuaders*, whose job it is to create a favorable public image of a candidate, study the currents of public knowledge and opinion, and guide the messages that go out from a campaign headquarters.[3] Few major candidates now feel able to go into a campaign without such professional and expensive advice. A third reason for rising costs is the ineffectiveness of legislative controls on campaign contributions and expenditures.

All in all then, an enormous amount of money is spent every two years in the United States to deliver information and persuasion to the voting public. What kinds of assumptions lie behind this outpouring of mass media, and what can we learn from them about mass media effects?

## Communication Strategies in Political Campaigns

Suppose you were sitting in the chair of one of the media experts retained to advise a Presidential candidate. You would be aware that perhaps one-third of the voters are safely in your camp: You can't afford to ignore them, but unless you make great mistakes you are not likely to lose them. Perhaps another 10 percent lean toward your candidate. You must be more careful about these people than about the loyal third, because they are potentially vulnerable to the opposition's arguments. Only 10 or 15 percent of the total are really undecided, really neutral, equally open to the arguments of both sides. By early October, in a close election, the number of truly vulnerable voters may be as low as 5 percent, and they represent the main battleground on which victory must be won.

Consequently your strategy will be to try to hold all your loyal voters and win as many as possible of those who are not firmly committed. If you are advising the Republican candidate, you will be aware that you start with a handicap because more people are registered as Democrats than as Republicans. If you are advising the Democratic candidate, you will be aware that you have a problem in holding your army together because it is a tenuous coalition of unlike groups—southern conservatives, northern liberals, big-city political machines, minority groups, and labor unions. So in either case you cannot afford to neglect either the votes that must be held or the votes that can possibly be won. Your problem is how to select the appeals, how to present the candidate in the most favorable light, how to apportion the effort.

You will try to see that local organizations are active, that personal influence is exerted through local meetings, door-to-door canvassing, and endorsements by prestigious persons and organizations. As you look at the mass media, you will be aware of an impressive set of figures compiled from national studies by the University of Michigan Survey Research Center. In every election between 1952 and 1964 they asked a large sample of American adults from which media source they felt they had obtained the most political information during the election campaign. The results are presented graphically in Figure 8.

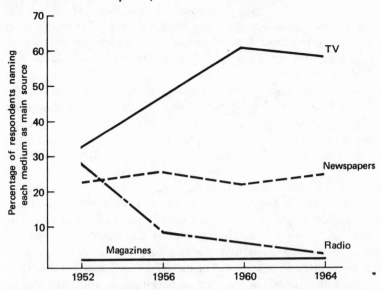

**Figure 8** Major sources of information about election campaigns, 1952–1964. (W. Schramm and S. Wade, *Knowledge and the public mind.* Stanford, Calif.: Stanford University Press, 1967, p. 200)

In other words, the use of newspapers for campaign information has remained about steady, the use of radio and magazines has declined, and the use of television has increased sharply. The Roper organization asked a national sample in 1964 and 1968 how they had become best acquainted with local, state, and national candidates (Table 10).

**Table 10** Major Sources of Information about Different Levels of Candidates (by Percent)

|  | Local Candidates | | | State Candidates | | | National Candidates | | |
|---|---|---|---|---|---|---|---|---|---|
|  | 1964 | 1968 | 1971 | 1964 | 1968 | 1971 | 1964 | 1968 | 1971 |
| Newspapers | 42 | 40 | 37 | 41 | 37 | 30 | 36 | 24 | 24 |
| Television | 27 | 26 | 32 | 43 | 42 | 50 | 64 | 65 | 62 |
| Radio | 10 | 6 | 6 | 10 | 6 | 6 | 9 | 4 | 4 |
| People | 18 | 23 | 20 | 8 | 9 | 9 | 4 | 4 | 5 |
| Magazines | 1 | 1 | 1 | 1 | 1 | 1 | 6 | 5 | 4 |

Source: Adapted from B. W. Roper. *An extended view of public attitudes toward television and other mass media, 1959–1971.* New York: Television Information Office, 1971, pp. 8–9.

The farther the campaign and the candidates are from the voter's own location, the more he depends for information on television, the less on other people, and the less on newspapers.

You will also be aware of what Dan Nimmo said in *The Political Persuaders*—that the campaign audience includes two main groups: one makes considerable use of and trusts the printed media and tends to be loyal to one party or the other; the other, larger group, relies primarily on radio and television, tends to have less education than the print-using group and is less than deeply interested in politics.[4] This latter group, as Rivers, Peterson, and Jensen point out, are more experienced "with TV, film, and recording personalities than in deciding public issues."[5] You will be interested in the latter audience, as all political "packagers" have been. If you can get their attention, you have a good chance to sway their votes; and you can make a shrewd guess that the way to get their attention is to present them with the kind of material that already draws their attention to television—attractive personalities and hard-hitting, well-packaged material.

You might well decide, therefore, that every effort should be made to present your candidate on television as attractively as possible. President Lyndon Johnson tried to avoid large press conferences and television appearances, where he was not at his best, and preferred small and informal meetings. "Johnson is formidably ingratiating—in private or semi-private gatherings," wrote Ted Lewis of the *New York Daily News*. "He easily dominates any group where he can look a man in the eye, grab lapels, poke chests, and talk about what happens to be on his mind."[6] Richard Nixon made extremely careful and controlled use of television during the 1968 campaign and has continued to do so since. He felt that his television appearances against Kennedy in 1960 had helped him lose the election. Therefore in 1968, under guidance of the best advisers he could get, his television performances, as James Reston of the *New York Times* described them, were

> masterpieces of contrived candor. He seems to be telling every-
> thing with an air of reckless sincerity, but nearly always in a
> controlled situation, with the questioners carefully chosen, the

questions solicited from whole states or regions, but carefully screened.

He is now complaining publicly about how he and Mr. Agnew are misrepresented in the columns of the New York *Times,* but he has been refusing to be questioned on the record by editors of the *Times* and most other major newspapers ever since the very beginning of the campaign.

Mr. Humphrey and Mr. Wallace submitted to questions by CBS, but Mr. Nixon sent tapes of replies made in his carefully prepared broadcasts. And his refusal to debate Mr. Humphrey on television is merely one more incident in a long campaign of packaged broadcasts.[7]

The Republican Presidential campaign of 1972 will undoubtedly be scrutinized and analyzed for a long time by students of politics and communication. It was controlled and orchestrated so skillfully, using the full power of the Presidency to make news, control the flow of information from the national government, and influence media coverage, that the President scarcely had to leave the White House. He could assign surrogates to argue with the opposing candidate, while he remained "above" the arguments, negotiating with China and the Soviet Union, working toward peace in Vietnam, and announcing policy actions toward goals that had clearly demonstrated their popularity. It is too early at this writing to see the 1972 campaign in perspective, but it was clearly a classic in its field.

No one can argue with the wish of a candidate or an official to present himself to the public in the most favorable manner and, when using a universal and potent medium like television, to take special care what image is projected to the public. This requires of the candidate a professional performance usually guided by professionals. This kind of image engineering—and the increasing use of short, hard-hitting, carefully packaged political advertisements—is what has been happening to political communication in recent years.

As you consider what the mass media can do for your campaign, you are likely to decide that their ability to *focus public attention* is what makes them most interesting and useful to you. If you can succeed in having one set of issues rather than another talked about, if you can bring a less-known candidate into the public eye and present him in the most ingratiating way, if you can bring complicated issues down to simple ones, for example focusing attention on a charge of corruption or mismanagement on the part of one candidate or group, then you can take charge and impose your own game plan.

The mass media can focus attention on candidates as well as on issues; both Stevenson and Kennedy moved from relatively obscure positions in the wings out to center stage in the political theater. In the 1948 campaign, the Republican candidate Thomas Dewey was so confident that he concentrated on "stylistic" rather than "issue" campaigning—that is, he chose to present himself as the kind of man who ought to be President, and his party as the best qualified to lead the nation—whereas Truman, the Democratic candidate, stuck doggedly to issues. As the media reported these arguments day after day, people began to be concerned about them, and this is at least part of the explanation for the Democrats' unexpected victory. In the 1952 campaign, media coverage was instrumental in making the Korean War and national security the chief issues of the campaign. Between January and October of 1952, according to Roper surveys, twice as many people had come to consider the Korean War an important political issue as previously, and an unknown but substantially greater number had come to think that the national security was threatened and that someone like General Eisenhower was needed to take care of the national interest. That was the year in which "image makers" first came to political prominence. They were instrumental in presenting the immensely likable Eisenhower as a figure of national affection and trust. They advised him to announce that, if elected, he would go to Korea with the intention of bringing that war to a close. That statement was generally regarded as the high point of the campaign.

## Some Generalizations

If you were to talk with professionals and research scholars, you would find that they tend to agree on at least three propositions about the effect of communication on electoral politics. First, a campaign is such a complex thing that no single cause can ever explain the result. Local issues are intertwined with national ones, issues with personalities, previous experiences and viewpoints with the new experiences of the campaign, unplanned events with planned tactics, rational with irrational reasons for voting choice, and above all the unpredictable parade of news events during the campaign. Therefore, no act of communication or even communication strategy can ordinarily be credited with swinging an election. Eisenhower's Korea announcement is generally regarded as a masterly political stratagem, but he would doubtless have won without it. The highly skillful television performance of the former broadcaster and movie star Ronald Reagan, constrasting as it did with that of his opponents, is widely credited with his election as Governor of California in 1966 and 1970; yet many other forces influenced the voting.

Second, you would find general agreement that a realistic political strategy today must be based on mass media *and* personal communication rather than on either one alone. The professionals feel that the most important support a state or national candidate can have is from local organizations, people who will ring doorbells, have neighborhood coffee hours and community meetings, transport voters to the polls on election day, and thus get out the maximum potential vote for their candidate. On the other hand, as we have said, campaign directors spend enormous amounts of money on broadcasts and considerable sums on printed materials, posters, direct mail, and other mediated persuasion. Many gubernatorial or senatorial candidates now budget hundreds of thousands, sometimes more than a million dollars for mass media, and even local candidates expect to spend thousands, chiefly on television and radio. There have been many movements to limit such expenditures and to bring the American electoral system in this respect nearer to the British one, in which opposing candidates and parties receive equal time, free of cost, on BBC. But the American tradition of hands off private enterprise and public communication is against it. And the political professionals, despite their reliance on local organization and personal persuasion, are generally opposed to any regulation that would keep them from spending as much as they can afford on mass media. The passage of the relatively innocuous Federal Election Campaign Act of 1972, therefore, which requires reporting of political contributions and sets certain limits on individual giving, was a remarkable accomplishment by its sponsors in Congress.

Third, professionals and scholars agree that actually not many voting intentions are changed during an election campaign. The campaign serves to remind many people of political loyalties and ideological interests, to reinforce party allegiance, to persuade people who might not otherwise do so to vote— along the line of previous party loyalty. Not many are actually converted, despite all the money put into a national electoral campaign. But a shift of even a few hundred thousand votes would be enough to change the results of many Presidential elections.

Most of the survey research indicates that two-thirds to three-fourths of the voters have made up their minds how to vote before the formal campaign begins. Those who have not made up their minds include those less interested and those who have conflicting pressures on them or have become aware of conflicting loyalties and interests. (One inner conflict that has been written about frequently is that of Protestant Democrats and Catholic Republicans, many of whom saw the election in 1960 as a test of whether a Catholic could be elected President.) In 1956, 76 percent of American voters are estimated to have known by the time of the national party conventions whom they would support in the election. This doubtless reflected the wide popularity of President Eisenhower. In 1960, however, only 60 percent had decided by convention time, probably because there was no such widely known and dominant figure as Eisenhower. In 1948, according to Berelson, only 63 percent of the Democrats as compared to 87 percent of the Republicans had decided for whom they were going to vote by August, before the formal campaigns began.[8] Truman's campaign obviously had to run on an uphill grade. He had to revive the loyalties of his own party and rally them behind the issues he so doggedly presented. In 1972 the leaders of both parties agreed that most voters had already made up their minds by August.

In a thoughtful review of studies of political decision, Sears concludes that Americans typically reach late adolescence without strong commitments to any political party. Because they grow up in the same social milieu as their parents, they tend to have the same party preferences. This is not a very strong or stable loyalty. Their own loyalties tend to be formed in the late teens or early 20s, when they move away from parental influence and support.[9] If at this time they are put into a very different climate of opinion, as were the students at liberal Bennington College who were studied by Newcomb in his classic book *Personality and Social Change*,[10] they are likely to be "liberalized." Today, when they are thrown into contact with radical peer groups on the college campus, they are likely to react strongly one way or the other to these political challenges. If a liberal-leaning young person joins the administrative staff of a large industry or a stockbroker's office, he may become more conservative. If he encounters a charismatic candidate like John Kennedy in 1960 (or, 28 years earlier, Franklin Roosevelt), he is likely to be swayed toward the candidate's ideas. In other words, the key period in determining political loyalties and tendencies is probably the end of adolescence and the beginning of adulthood, when an individual needs to find his own identity and his career, and rejects parental influence or guidance.

This is the time of life in which planned peer-group organizations like those of the Hitler Youth, the Chinese Red Guard, and the Soviet Young Communists have apparently exercised a strong influence on the political leanings of their members. It is worth considering, therefore, what may be the influence of young activists and their organizations in the United States and elsewhere. Bandura points out that under conditions of "rapid social and technological change" like the present, "many parental interests, attitudes, and role behaviors that were serviceable at an earlier period may have little functional value for members of the younger generation." In other words, one cannot expect that a conservative background will be so likely to predict a conservative younger generation,[11] as it has been in the past, or even that political behaviors are likely to take the form they have in the past. The new frequency and respectability of public demonstrations and civil disobedience seem to support that prediction. But however we interpret the present set of political influences and behaviors, we can be quite sure that the political preferences and trends of the next decades are being formed in our young people by what is happening to them today.

As we grow older we settle into a comfortable pattern of beliefs and behaviors that serve us well with our careers, our families, and our social groups, and we are willing to defend these beliefs against change. In the 1972 national election, therefore, much political communication was directed to the new 18- to 21-year-old voters. But 1972 was a rather unusual campaign in that there were early signs of widespread disaffection among the Democrats. Therefore, the chief Republican goal was to appeal to the disaffected and provide a new political home for them, and the chief Democratic goal was to try to rekindle party loyalties.

What do we know about exposure to political content in the mass media during an election year? Exciting events, like the national conventions, the Kennedy-Nixon debates, Nixon's defense of his personal "fund" (and consequently of his political integrity) attract the great audiences. Except for these, attention is rather low from convention time until a week or ten days before the election, when people are facing the need to make voting decisions and seek more information from the media as well as from their friends. In 1960 about one out of every three persons viewed the election-eve broadcasts of his party. The figure was apparently somewhat lower in 1968. This helps explain why political professionals have turned away from long political broadcasts to short "commercials" and newsworthy "events."

Nevertheless, this is a rather extraordinary development. One might expect that candidates would try to avoid the patterns of commercial advertising. But quite the contrary. For example, in the last gubernatorial campaign in New York, the airwaves were saturated with brief spot announcements in behalf of Nelson Rockefeller. Some broadcasters considered them "old-fashioned." Mostly they were "talking faces." They showed Rockefeller briefly answering a question, talking to a constituent, saying a few "sincere" sentences to New York voters. And they seemed to be effective.

"Sincere" comes close to being a keynote for this type of

political advertising. In 1969 and 1970 Michael Rowan and Joe Napolitan studied the expectations of voters who would have only electronic contact with candidates before election time.[12] Their studies in several states found a fairly high level of agreement in what the voters said they were looking for in a candidate. They said they wanted to feel that the candidate is:[13]

| | |
|---|---|
| Honest, a man of conviction | 47% |
| An understanding, compassionate man | 14 |
| A capable, qualified person | 9 |
| A good person, familistic | 7 |
| A leader | 5 |
| Bright, intelligent | 4 |
| A man who perceives the "vital issues" | 3 |

It may well be, therefore, that the old rule in agency advertising that salesmen and account executives should wear a "sincere tie" is not a bad one. However, Rowan and Napolitan urge that the results just quoted should not be interpreted to mean that people are not concerned about issues. They are. The point is, say Rowan and Napolitan, "that when it comes time to choose the person to be elected, voters are looking for the man best capable of *dealing* with the issues." And here they greatly respect the kind of honesty and sincerity that, by coincidence, can be projected perhaps even more effectively from a brief spot announcement than a long program.

This is what they think happened in the 1970 election that made William Egan Governor of Alaska.

> In 1970 a highly talented team was assembled to elect a bright businessman Governor of Alaska, Larry Carr. After being routed in the election by about 2 to 1, Carr's staff went into the field with research to discover why. They found that people thought Carr had surfaced the right issues; people thought Carr had the best media; people thought Carr delivered the most information; and people thought Carr was a very bright, capable person. When asked why they voted for Bill Egan, the majority said because they felt Bill Egan was a sincere, nice guy.[14]

This contributes something to our understanding of "packaging" a candidate, about which so much has been written in the last few years. The packaging is nothing arbitrary; it is intended chiefly to make a candidate reflect the voters. Someone has said, "I must follow the people because I am their leader." Thus, the problem is to make the candidate seem to fit the people's image of the leader they want, to make him say what they want him to say. The brief spot announcement can be more easily controlled than a press conference program or a longer speech. In carefully made and recorded 30-second statements, the candidate can be made to project honesty, sincerity, and competence on whatever issue seems to concern the voters most. The question we can ponder is, In this kind of situation what is leadership?

Two British researchers who studied campaigns in England report that the voters they interviewed felt that qualities like "straightforwardness," "sincerity," and "confidence" are easily revealed by television, whereas characteristics like "strength" or "hardworking habits" are not. Lang and Lang report, on the basis of American election studies, that people's judgments of a televised candidate tend to be made on three scales: "performance," meaning how well he speaks and acts on television; "political role," meaning his skill in presenting a political argument or fielding a question; and "personal image," the personality and character traits that television brings out.[15]

We know very little in a scientific way about image formation on the mass media. In general, it can be assumed that the less people know about the candidate before the campaign, the more likely television and the other media are to shape his image. In the case of Reagan's first campaign for the California governship, for example, the candidate was well known as a movie star but not as a political figure, and the campaign task was to build an image for him as a competent political leader. We know also that television often leaves different images than does radio. There has been considerable discussion, for example, as to whether FDR's image would have been as favorable if his medium had been a visual rather than an auditory one.

Every candidate faces the problem of selective exposure: Voters listen to their own party's candidates, go to their own party rallies avoid the opposition. Does this apply to media politicking also?

Studies in Britain have found relatively little evidence of selective exposure to the media in national campaigns. This may be due to the tradition of British politics, to the scrupulously even time provided candidates on British television, or to the relative brevity of the British campaign—5 weeks instead of 9 or 10 as in the United States. In this country, however, the evidence on selectivity is consistent if not spectacular. More Republicans than Democrats listened to Wilkie in 1940, more Democrats than Republicans to Roosevelt. The great majority of newspapers were for Wilkie; Republicans, consequently, were more likely than Democrats to expose themselves to political material in the press and more likely to consider the press "impartial." Roosevelt was an eloquent and attractive speaker; hence Democrats used the radio for political information more than Republicans did. In 1952 more Republicans than Democrats heard Eisenhower, more Democrats than Republicans heard Stevenson, but the difference was not great.[16] In 1958 Senator William F. Knowland conducted a 20-hour telethon as part of his unsuccessful campaign to be elected Governor of California. The survey and audience figures are instructive. Only 10 percent of a survey sample in the area of the telethon tuned in to it at all. There were about twice as many Republicans in the audience as in the sample, about the same number of Democrats as in the sample, and about one-third as many Independents (self-designated) as in the sample. Republicans watched, on the average, about twice as long as Democrats did. They were twice as likely as Democrats to report that they had tuned in intentionally rather than by accident. In both parties, some people said that their voting intentions were strengthened by the telethon. But only a tiny percentage said that they had changed their vote as a result of the program.[17]

There is mostly anecdotal record and little research evidence as to how the image of a candidate that is projected during a campaign, with or without the ministrations of a professional "image maker," affects voting. As a matter of fact, the general conclusion of all voting studies is that communication during the campaign probably changes few votes, and is more likely to strengthen party preferences, reinforce decisions already made, and contribute less than dramatically to knowledge of arguments or issues.

However, in determining the political effect of the media we must consider some other possible effects. What about the influence of broadcasts and print on the loyalties of party members, their financial contributions, and their willingness to engage in precinct work? What about the long-term effect on the political socialization of children who will not vote for several years? A study by Chaffee and others indicates, for example, that what children in their mid-teens know of political arguments and political positions relates closely to their attention to public affairs content in the mass media.

Still more important, what about the effect of media between campaigns? If two-thirds to three-fourths of all voters have made up their minds by convention time, have their decisions not been swayed at all by the reporting of political news and the formulation of political questions in the mass media between elections? When Franklin Roosevelt was informed that 75 percent of all the newspapers that had taken editorial positions had declared for his opponent, he laughed heartily. The editorial columns belong to the publishers, but the news columns belong to the people, he said. As long as he could continue to fill the news column for three-and-a-half years with the dramatic news of the New Deal, he was willing to let the publishers advise their readers on the editorial page for the six months before the election!

## Two Case Studies of Political Communication

In the fall of 1960 John F. Kennedy and Richard M. Nixon agreed to a series of four radio and television debates. Many of Nixon's advisers considered this an unwise decision because it gave additional public exposure to Kennedy, who was the lesser known of the two candidates. However, Nixon accepted the arrangement. Free time was provided on all the networks. In the tradition of the Lincoln-Douglas debates, but before vastly larger audiences, the two candidates presented themselves and their ideas to the broadcast audience.

The experiment was of the greatest interest to the public and to professional observers alike because it seemed to be a way of getting around selective exposure. If debates became a common practice, no longer would it be possible for Republicans to hear Republican arguments only while Democrats stuck to Democratic arguments. If a voter tuned in to the debates he was compelled, by the nature of the program, to hear both candidates and the positions taken by both parties. Of course, there was no guarantee that people would attend with equal care to both presentations or refrain from filtering the opposition arguments through their previous preferences, but if Americans truly believed in a free marketplace of ideas this seemed a long step toward that ideal.

The audiences were enormous: 27 million homes for the first debate, 24 and 25 and 24 million, respectively, for the other three. About 1 out of 4 people who watched any of the debates watched all four; 2 out of 4 watched three debates. There was much discussion of the debates, and they served to focus the whole campaign.

Carter found that viewers who were interested in and attentive to the first debate, on the average, remembered each candidate's arguments equally well; those less interested and less attentive remembered more of what their own candidate had said. People who felt that both candidates had presented effective arguments remembered most; those who thought that only their own candidate had been effective remembered the next largest number of arguments; those who felt that neither candidate had been effective remembered least. Only the third group showed biased recall in favor of the candidate or their own party.[18] Therefore, as an invitation to a free marketplace of ideas the debates seemed to work quite well.

There was an interesting finding about the discussion generated by the debates. About 56 percent of the people in a panel interviewed by Deutschmann reported that they had talked about the debates afterward.[19] Forty-seven percent of these talked only with people who agreed with them politically; 42 percent talked both with people who agreed and people who disagreed; and only 11 percent talked solely with people of different political persuasions. But among the people who said they had talked with no one, 30 percent said their voting intentions had been affected, as compared to 19 percent of those who had discussed the debate.[20] The implication seems to be that the personal communication generated on a political topic by the mass media is more likely to inhibit than to encourage change.

What was the effect on the election? Many observers have credited Kennedy's narrow victory to the debates. Lang and Lang concluded, however, that in an election as close as the one in 1960, no single factor could be identified as the sole reason for Kennedy's victory.[21]

The Roper polls found that about half the people in their sample reported that the debates had affected their voting intentions. However, a number of panels conducted during and after the debates concluded that this effect was not to bring Republicans, in any large number, to the Democratic side, or vice versa, but rather to strengthen members of each party in their convictions. For example, Deutschmann found that the net gain in favorable attitudes toward Kennedy among the Democrats was considerably greater than the net gain for Nixon among the Republicans, but the Democrats had been less certain originally.

Ben-Zeev and White found when they compared viewers of the debates with nonviewers, that there was a slight net change to Kennedy among viewers but no change to Nixon. Lang and Lang found few conversions to either candidate after the first debate. Some of the most interesting findings had to do with the contributions of the debates to the public images of the two candidates. After the first debate, according to the chief study of this topic, the number of people who ascribed the adjective "experienced" to Kennedy increased greatly. Throughout the debates the image of Kennedy (as measured by the researchers) moved slowly but steadily toward the cluster of adjectives that people tended to use when they were asked to describe "the ideal President." In contrast, Nixon's image, measured in that way, moved erratically, and at the end of fourth debate it was a bit further from the "ideal" pattern than at the beginning of the series.

What is the most reasonable conclusion we can draw

about the political effect of the debates? As in most examples of political change brought about by the mass media, there were few "conversions" few changes of party or candidate. But the Democrats went into the campaign with a candidate who was much less well known than the opposition candidate. Moreover, some of them had reservations about him—because he was a Catholic, because he was young, because he had sought the office (in American folklore the office and the voters must seek the man), or because he seemed to be inexperienced in the administrative and policy-making qualities required of the chief executive. This is why the great increase in the number of people who called Kennedy "experienced" after seeing him in action against Nixon was especially noteworthy. His performance in those debates helped relieve many people of their doubts about him. He *could* hold his own with the Vice President, he did *not* seem to be too young for the job, he gave the impression of seriousness of purpose, wisdom, and broad information. Therefore, the debates contributed to a trend toward Kennedy that was in evidence even beforehand; they rallied doubtful Democrats to his support and reassured many voters who knew little about him that he had the qualities of a President.

Through most of this chapter we have discussed *electoral* politics. This is because most studies of political communication have dealt with election campaigns. However, as we have suggested, the most significant effect of mass media on political life and beliefs probably takes place between campaigns. At this time it might be well to describe another event in the career of John F. Kennedy that suggests some of the ways the mass media can function politically outside electoral campaigns.[22]

This is the record of something that is still fresh and poignant in the memories of many of us. What happened on November ber 22, 1963 was not the first assassination of an American President, but it was different in certain ways from the earlier ones. This assassination struck down a young and vital leader who had become known in an unusually personal and intimate way through the mass media, notably television. The sorrow of his death was very deep. The majority of 1300 respondents interviewed after the assassination said that they could not recall any other time in their lives when they had felt this way. Among those who could think of times when they had had similar feelings, the majority mentioned the death of someone near and dear to them. And, just as Kennedy had become well known through television, so was television at hand to report his death with a vividness and intensity unequalled in previous coverage of such events.

The news had reached more than half the people of the United States by the time the President died, 30 minutes after he was shot. Ninety percent of Americans heard it within an hour, and almost everyone by the end of the afternoon. Then for the next 3½ days there was in all America practically no other news story. All the media concentrated on telling the story, but television was chief among them. So immediate, so detailed was the coverage that millions of Americans saw Oswald, the suspected assassin, himself killed, and heard the shot before it had finished echoing through the entranceway to the Dallas courthouse. So great was the public attention to television that at times during the 4 days in which the media concentrated on the story *more than half* of all Americans were looking at the same events on their television sets.

The Kennedy assassination provides a remarkably good illustration of how communication works to serve and preserve a social system. There was the first emergency message from Dallas. At once came a swift flow of information to and from the point at which society had been hurt. Urgent administrative communication swiftly involved the local and national security agencies, and the appropriate agencies and individuals of the national government. The machinery of news coverage organized itself as best it could to explain what had happened and to answer the troubled questions that were asked in every corner of the country. The *New York Times* promptly turned its great resources to the task of investigating what lay behind the mystery of the actions in Dallas. Network television cancelled its entire schedule from Friday noon to Monday evening and devoted itself to enabling the American people to participate in the events that were so far from most of them geographically but so near to them psychologically and spiritually. On the part of the people who heard, there was first incredulity, then anger, then sorrow, then the need to glue oneself to television and take part in the ceremonies of farewell. The media turned, bit by bit, to the problem of reintegrating society, resolving the doubts, closing ranks around a new President, turning attention to new problems and continuing responsibilities. One can compare what happened with what happens in a biological system when part of it is hurt and the blood flows quickly to do what it can, and then to heal the wound.

The really remarkable media relationships during the events of late November 1963 were between viewers and television. Between November 22 and November 25, the average American home had its television receiver tuned to broadcasts related to the death and burial of the President for an average of 8 hours a day. According to Nielsen figures, 166 million Americans in 51 million homes (more than three-quarters of the entire population of the country) were tuned in at some time to the Kennedy broadcasts. A little less than half heard the news first on radio or television, a little more than half from some other person who had heard it on television or radio, or from a third person who had heard it from someone who had heard it on the air. But once the news had been heard and ongoing responsibilities could be dropped for the time being, there was a rush to radio and television to confirm what had been heard. When the news was confirmed, there was for most people a period of shock. Some people wanted to talk it over, some to be by themselves. The streets of New York for once lost their tumult and much of their hurry. Newsdealers reported their customers said "Don't wanna believe it." People wandered around instead of hurrying to their offices or their next appointment. And then people settled down in front of the television set.

Why? First they were seeking answers. Who was the assassin? Would he be caught? What was behind his action? Four out of five people named a suspect immediately. For most of them it was a political figure and a political action: The assassin was probably a communist, a Castroite, a leftist of some kind, or if not that a right wing person who opposed the President's politicies on segregation and civil rights. These suspicions and anxieties passed remarkably soon, although the questions of whether the man apprehended was really the murderer and whether he was alone in the crime are still being asked. But there was very little anxiety after the first few hours about whether a foreign or a conspiratorial American political group might be guilty. This was taken care of by the enormous flow of news from Dallas, the frank statements of officials, and the general impression that nothing was being held back. People felt that they were being told the whole story. A principle of public communication seems to be that full and frank disclosure is more effective than secrecy in alleviating anxiety, suspicion, and political disquiet. Thus when President Eisenhower had his heart attack in Colorado, his able press secretary, James Haggerty, had the President's physician go on television, explain the illness, give a candid prognosis, and answer newsmen's questions. On the other hand, covering up some events in Vietnam in recent years has resulted only in a "credibility gap."

The story of the President's killing and the succeeding events was told in massive detail. And then the media performed two other services for the American people: They provided reassurance as to the immediate future, and they furnished a way in which Americans could experience the catharsis of grief that would prepare them to return to normal life. The first of these was done by exposing the new President and showing that he was taking over competently, that the machinery of government was continuing to function with a new leader. They presented national leaders, chapters out of national history, the career of the dead President, the rituals and norms of American life enacted by some of the most admired people in the nation. In other words, they reassured the shocked people who had just heard that their President had been slain.

The media provided catharsis by permitting Americans to participate in such numbers as never before in the ceremonies surrounding the funeral of their lost leader. People were shown the symbols of grief and patriotism—the flag-draped casket, the beautiful young widow and her children appearing at the White House door to join in the sad walk to the church, the terribly slow drum-beat of the funeral march. Reports from many of the homes where television was turned on during the funeral said that people were wiping their eyes and many were weeping openly.

The extraordinary feature of this experience was that 150 million Americans were doing it together. At one time during the funeral, audience measurements indicated that 90 percent of all the television sets sampled in New York were tuned in to the scene as the cortege passed over the bridge to Arlington. And many people apparently had a sense of participating in a national act for the first time in their lives, feeling a sense of nationhood and unity with other Americans such as they had never felt before. Many of those who passed through that experience will remember it as one of the remarkable things in their lives.

In other words, the function of the media, and especially of television, at that time was to heal and reintegrate society. We have been speaking of the effect of mass communication in the competitive and argumentative setting of electoral politics; it is well to remember this other aspect of its political effect. Owing to mass communication and especially to television, the American people closed ranks around their new President and for a time abandoned business as usual and politics as usual in a spirit of national dedication. It is unfortunate that this has been lost in disagreements over the events and policies in Southeast Asia.

## Summary and Questions

What can we learn about the effects of mass communication in general from its particular effects on politics? Clearly, there is no special magic about mass communication. By itself it does not convert many people. Principally, it offers a menu from which voters can select what they wish to support positions to which they were originally inclined. Even in the midst of the great flood of communication during election campaigns, it is the activity of the receivers of communication that determines its effect. The "target" audience is active, independent, alert to its own interests, picking and choosing what *it* wants from all the available communication.

While denying magic to the mass media, let us nevertheless not lose sight of their power. The two cases presented in this chapter are illustrations of this power. The media in general and television in particular can introduce candidates for leadership with a clarity and vividness unmatched except for personal acquaintance—and do this for an entire population rather than the few individuals privileged to know the candidates personally. That is what the Kennedy-Nixon debates demonstrated. Visitors to the United States often express their amazement at the spectacle of national leaders and their critics being subjected on national television to close questioning concerning their plans and policies. Mass communication has always brought candidates closer to the mass electorate, but this particular power of the electronic media is so different from that of the printed media that it represents a political effect unique to this century.

The meaning of the communication events following the assassination of President Kennedy is that the mass media can teach national norms and provide a rallying place for political consensus. Anyone who lived through those days in November 1963 could hardly have emerged without heightened respect for what the media can contribute to national life. Yet we must remember that in those particular days the mass media spoke with a unanimity almost unparalleled in American culture. Monopoly, as we have earlier noted, is one condition for strong mass communication effect. The Soviet Union and the People's Republic of China make use of their communication monopoly to teach the national norms they call, respectively, the "new Soviet man" and the "new Chinese man." Given unanimity, the media have that kind of power; the use to which it is put depends on the goals of the national culture. In the United States such unanimity is quite rare. The media are likely to rally together in a national crisis or around a national hero, but seldom around an issue. A few days after the Kennedy funeral, mass communication went back to business as usual, with the press assuming its usual adversary relationship to government and the news filled with the customary give and take, arguments and counter-arguments, of American political life. Yet during those few historic days the media gave a most impressive performance.

It might seem unnecessary to say again that the media provide a great voice for the flow of communication, whatever its goal. Yet we hurry over that fact because we are so used to it. Without the continuing attention of the mass media, how could the events at Mylai have been kept before the American people? Without mass communication bringing the Southeast Asia war daily into American living rooms, would not that war have seemed merely a small and distant event rather than the focus of public opinion it came to be? Without the mass media, how could the problems of ecology and environment have come so quickly to be of national concern?

This potential for broad national effect always resides in the mass media, but it is not always realized. It may be diffused or trivialized. It may be used to distract a nation from crucial problems. In cultures where the media are under authoritarian guidance, this is less of a worry to leadership than it is in a country where government is supposed to keep hands off and the media themselves are expected to speak for the public interest and reflect policy alternatives. No matter how it looks to us from the outside, the leaders of a country where the media are subordinate to government are confident that they are using the mass communication system for the good of their people. Our own newsmen were astonished to find the Chinese media almost completely silent on the visit of President Nixon to China early in 1972. The President was received in an almost deserted airport, and the event that brought several hundred press and television representatives all the way across the Pacific and led to the installation of a satellite communication station in Peking went unnoticed in the Chinese press. Unnoticed, that is, until Chairman Mao received the President and thus gave the signal that the newspapers could publish some of the pictures they had been taking and that the visit could be covered in news stories. This was a policy decision on the part of Chinese leadership. In contrast, the American government had to go to most elaborate lengths—even inventing a fictitious stomachache for Henry Kissinger—to keep the American press from discovering the fact that the President's representative had visited China. From our point of view, as noted in Chapter IX, such controls on mass communication are unacceptable; from the Marxist-Leninist point of view, they are both acceptable and desirable. The potential power of the mass media are the same whatever the system, but the effects of the media are necessarily judged against the political philosophy in which they operate.

Our own political philosophy places difficult requirements on our mass media and raises considerable problems for all of us. For example, we ask our media to turn a clear lense on the men, events, and issues about which an intelligent electorate needs to be informed. At the same time, we ask our media to support themselves and thus keep themsleves free of the influence of government. But suppose that the media grow so large, so costly, so essential to election campaigns that some candidates could not afford the cost of using them. Would this not necessarily fog the lense? Would it not create a situation in which the media could, in effect, be "bought"—or at least in which some persons and viewpoints could not afford to buy adequate exposure? And if so, would not this necessarily discriminate against lower economic classes, minority groups, and new parties?

Suppose that expertise becomes so important in political use of the mass media that image makers, political public relations firms, and media experts can be employed to manipulate the lense to show only "packaged" candidates. The practical result of this might be to have voters deciding between purely imaginary candidates. For the "packaged" candidates would say only what the public opinion polls reported that the voters wanted to hear. They would be made up to look like the candidate the voters are thought to admire. They would be trained to speak (or perhaps given a dubbed-in voice that sounds) like the political speakers voters are thought to like to hear. This may sound like fantasy, but the trend is in that direction and the possibility is frightening.

For this amounts to using the great voice of the media not to inform people but to manipulate them.

Suppose that the mass media, because they have grown large and expensive and eliminated much of their competitive ownership and with it their contrary political viewpoints, might insert a built-in filter into their reports on politics. This is the charge that has been made ever since the 1930s: that most dailies are owned by conservatives and that consequently their readers see only conservative editorial opinions. Minority groups charge that their members are underrepresented on the staffs and their viewpoints underrepresented in the products of the media. The emergence of "underground" and other special interest papers is a reaction to this feeling, but all of the new outlets represent only a whisper compared to the voice of big media. On the other hand, Vice President Agnew and other administration spokesmen have charged that many large newspapers and national network news services are staffed predominantly by leftist reporters and commentators who do not fairly report Administration policies. As long as both sides feel mistreated, we can perhaps discount the crisis nature of the charges, but the problem remains and people remain worried about it: How can we be sure that all the people and policies on which we need to vote or express our opinions are fully and fairly represented to us?

This is a vexing problem for a political system that prides itself in keeping hands off the media and a population that believes in a free marketplace of ideas. We have typically depended on private ownership and competition to keep a diversity of intellectual goods in the marketplace, but what happens when competition shrinks, professional image makers come into widespread use, and people begin to doubt the objectivity of the news?

We have tried to handle the problem of free access for all candidates and viewpoints by requiring media to sell time or advertising space to all candidates or viewpoints that avoid libel or sedition. However, as we have said, this tends to discriminate in favor of wealthier individuals or groups. A country like Britain handles the problem by allocating equal time, free of charge, on the publicly owned BBC to all recognized parties. We have shied away from a procedure like this, but it is clear that either a strict limitation on total campaign expenditures, or at least on the most expensive component of modern electoral campaigns—television time—will become necessary.

We have tried to prevent political dominance of the airways by providing that people or parties attacked in broadcasts shall have the right to reply on the same channels. This is less than an ideal solution; it may actually be counterproductive, for it makes broadcasters loath to stage political debates or express political viewpoints lest they have to give time for reply to an unknown number of offended spokesmen.

Our principal answer to the problem of the unclear lense has been to expect professional skill and responsible performance of newsmen. Despite the objections of the party in power (*either* party objects to the news coverage when its man is in the White House), the adversary relationship of press to government is probably more informative for the citizenry than *no* such relationship would be. The attempts to "package" candidates are distasteful but hardly new; politicians have always tried to show their best face to the electorate, and the government in power uses to the full its formidable power to time news events and to stage them in the most favorable way. In any political system in which opposition is allowed to surface, there will be competition for the most popular channels of information. We continue to believe that skeptical, fair, diligent, investigative newsmen will be able to cut through the ficitious images and the controlled news events and expose attempts to misuse the media and delude the public.

In general terms, then, we can conclude that the media always have the power to affect political beliefs and behavior but that what actually happens depends on the way the media are used. To use them for one goal, one gives up something else. It is easier to obtain political consensus with a monopolized mass communication system than with an open system, but to us it seems worthwhile to face all the problems of an open system in order to try to reach political consensus through that somewhat idealistic construct we call the open marketplace of ideas.

To the limits of its ability and resources, any culture uses the great power of the mass media to obtain the effect it wants. Or, as many observers have said, every country has the mass communication system it deserves.

# Coda

If one theme has been dominant over others in this book, it is that communication is behavior and must be understood as behavior. It is not something that exists by itself. It is not something shot by an active communicator into a passive receiver, nor something produced in multiple copies by a machine interposed in the communication process. It is people coming together in a relationship built around a set of signs they momentarily share. It is not an active-passive relationship; both participants are extraordinarily active, making such use of the signs as their needs and goals urge on them and rejecting the signs they do not want.

It is not a simple relationship; the participants in an act of communication behave with their whole bodies and their whole personalities so that the message is always more than words. It is a tenuous relationship, because each participant brings to it the cognitive map of his own cultural experience, and one's meanings are never entirely like another's; consequently every communication relationship is truly an intercultural one. It is not a relationship that produces an automatic effect; everyone defends his own cognitive structure, his beliefs, his image of himself and his environment, and there must be changes in these before any action can be triggered. The "effect" of communication is therefore usually the effect of an amalgam of forces and stimuli, and social effect in particular is often cumulative and hidden in a skein of events and experiences: Complex behavior usually has complex roots. But communication behavior occupies a large part of our waking hours, fills in the cognitive maps by which we live, allows us to relate to our environments and our fellow men, and keeps information flowing through society wherever it is most needed. This behavior represents one of man's greatest skills, which he has developed much more completely than has any other animal.

We know more about communication than we show. We know more about the effects of mass communication than we use. Our communication troubles are not with the process or with the machine interposed in the process; they are with man's use of these things. There is no magic in communication per se. When we report, as we do so often today, that there has been a "failure in communication," we really mean that there has been a human failure. And more often than not, the true failure has been not in the communication behavior but in the *pre*communication behavior—the formation of beliefs and attitudes and policies that provide the reason for communicating and the substance to be communicated.

Some of the illustrations we have given in the last few chapters demonstrate both what communication does in society and the limitations on what it can do. We have been talking about true-to-life, deadly serious problems. Two billion people in the developing regions must make wise and skillful use of communication if they and their children are going to keep up with the world's knowledge, get enough to eat, enjoy happy and healthy family lives, and still avoid overcrowding their spaceship Earth. In the "developed" regions we have challenging and frightening problems of our own. We wonder whether we are maintaining the kind of intellectual marketplace in which man can freely pursue truth. We have a glut of information and still no very good ways of finding out quickly what we need to know when we need it. We wonder what is the effect on our children of the entertainment television to which many of them typically devote more time than to any other waking activity.

The topics we talked about in the last few chapters were

illustrations only. We could just as well have chosen others. But communication is the life blood of all of them.

Establishing a communication relationship is merely a necessary, not a sufficient, condition for a particular effect in any of the situations mentioned. It is not sufficient merely to establish communication with voters to win their votes. It is necessary also to present a candidate and a policy to their liking. A few notes about a communication problem familiar to all of us in the United States may illustrate the effects and limitations of communication in a social problem situation.

Every culture has difficulty in trying to talk with its disadvantaged groups. In recent years this has been especially disturbing in the United States, where the heart of the difficulty has been communication with the urban poor and the ethnic minorities among them. We know a great deal about the communication behavior of these groups. We know, for example, that the mass medium of the urban poor is, overwhelmingly, television. They view an enormous amount of it—adults, according to one study in Michigan, view two and one-half times as much TV as the general adult population; children, somewhere in the neighborhood of one and one-half times as much as middle-class children, who themselves spend a great deal of time on television. A black child of 9 or 10 from a disadvantaged home may spend as much as $9\frac{1}{2}$ hours a day on the mass media, of which nearly 7 hours will be on television. (Of course, he does other things during some of the viewing or listening time.) Furthermore, most of them trust television—certainly to a much greater degree than they trust the mass-circulation press, which they feel does not represent them either fairly or adequately. Their own press is more to their taste, but television is still their number one source of information outside the immediate vicinity. Children and teen-agers from low-income families are more likely than other children to believe that television is "true to life" or "realistic," and study after study reports that they use it as a school for growing up in the world—learning things they do not learn in school, how to act in a certain situation, how to solve certain problems.

This leads one to ask what kinds of programs children of the inner city watch. Most typically the television receiver is turned on and left on without much selection of programs. No matter how much these children "trust" television, they do not watch any great amount of news or public affairs programs. They typically watch the most highly rated general-interest programs. They watch more suspense, more conflict, more excitement and violence, more family serials and comedies, than the general population. They watch more of the content that some writers call "fantasy" as distinguished from news, documentary, or public affairs, and this is what many of them consider realistic and a school for life.

For really local news, of course, the urban poor depend on personal networks of communication. These networks are rather more local and more restricted than the typical ones in middle-class society and certainly more restricted than those described in Chapter V. Ghetto people tend to have a deep distrust of personal communication from "outside"—the "establishment" in general, the police, the welfare workers, the merchants who come in to sell to them. The same attitudes can be seen in a village of Southeast Asia, where, until recently at least, the most frequent visitors from outside have been policemen or tax collectors.

What can we say about what is probably happening in that communication situation? In the first place, the picture of the world that a ghetto child imprints on his mind as he grows up must come largely from (1) the restricted, embittered personal networks to which he belongs and (2) television. As much as anyone in our society can be said to be a "product" of television, that can be said of the emerging young person in the urban ghetto. Obviously television is having some effects, and it would be interesting and helpful to know just what they are. Is it, for example, acting as "circuses" to distract these unhappy groups from their dissatisfactions and perhaps from their lack of "bread"? Or is it working in the way that McLuhan predicts, to bring about a global village, a healthier balance of sense perceptions, more participation, less privatization, and so forth? And what are the inner-city viewers learning from television about how to solve problems and meet needs—with weapons and violence or by other means?

In the second place, it is evident that the pathways of

communication make it difficult for any outsider to break into the networks of the urban poor. The lion's share of their communication time is devoted to sitting in front of a television set. They distrust representation from the outside and especially from the establishment. They are not typically very articulate: The frequent insertion of "you know" or "know what I mean?" in their conversation is an attempt to reach for an understanding beyond the words they have at hand. On television and radio they tend to close out public affairs in favor of entertainment. In other words, it takes rather special efforts for an outsider to enter into a significant and meaningful communication relationship with them.

But suppose someone does accomplish this—and indeed, it must be accomplished if there is to be a solution to the social problem of the urban poor and the ethnic minorities. Then *intercultural* communication begins. A middle-class white professional man and his family, and a black family from the urban ghetto have grown up in cultures that are just as surely different as the cultures of the United States and China. It is dangerous to accept this difference as superficial. Learning a few phrases like "Right on!" is merely a start at mastering the problems of communication with a different culture. This is, so to speak, only the ribbon on the package. The important differences come from the experience of growing up in an inner city or a suburb, in poverty or comfort, in a school that aimed at a respectable career or one that probably seemed increasingly irrelevant to the kind of opportunities that lay ahead. The same signs, the same sentences, the same motions or gestures or actions may mean quite different things in the ghetto and in the suburb. And it is not surprising that the two sides of such a conversation may run on parallel tracks and never meet.

If we are sensitive to this situation, we can at least be wary of easy interpretations. We can learn to listen harder. We can select the most promising pathways of communication. If we really want to establish a dialogue between the disadvantaged and the more advantaged groups in our society, we know enough about communication to make it possible with a minimum of misunderstanding and mischance.

It is terribly important to do so, but it is not enough. Communication by itself will not solve the problems of the urban ghetto. As we have found out in this book, it will not solve many basic problems of any kind by itself. It is no substitute for adequate principles, policy, and action. It serves only to relate men to each other. *Men* must solve those problems.

We have to *want* to get rid of the conditions that create the urban ghetto and the inequalities and isolation that lie so heavily on the urban poor. We have to be willing to take the social action that will bring these changes about and will in turn establish mutual respect and make the communication relationship easier and more rewarding.

It is essential in a troubled time like the present, when people seek easy and magical solutions, to recognize the limitations on what social communication can do. It is no substitute for policy and social action. It is not magic. There is no magic in communication except the magic that has enabled man to learn such a skill. There is no magic in shiny tools like television or communication satellites.

There is no magic, but there is hope. If human beings really want to relate to each other and will try to understand both the opportunities and hazards of the communication relationship into which they enter, we may succeed in sharing our understandings, revising our cognitive maps so that they are not mutually contradictory, and solving some of the problems that plague us.

Ultimately, therefore, we have to depend on man's ability and willingness to use his most human skill for the general good of humankind.

# Appendix

**A Note on Models
of the Communication Process**

It is interesting to see how some of the influential writers on the communication process have described or diagrammed it. For example, Claude Shannon and Warren Weaver, in their book *The Mathematical Theory of Communication,* which introduced so many scholars of human communication to the electronic approach, called human communication "all the procedures by which one mind may affect another." This is very far from "thought transference," and therefore anyone who has derived that idea from information theory has probably done so by analogy from the diagrams of electronic systems. Shannon diagrams the process thus:[1]

He also introduces the ideas of feedback as a return message to the source and noise as anything in the channel not intended by the source to be there. The idea of encoder and decoder is a useful one, because the Type A act of information clearly in-

cludes encoding of internal states into signs that may be put
out for others to use and respond to, and the Type B act clearly
includes the decoding of information from those signs so that it
can be absorbed into the receiver's internal states. Osgood, who
has contributed so much to the psychological study of meaning, has adopted this distinction and diagrammed the process
as follows:[2]

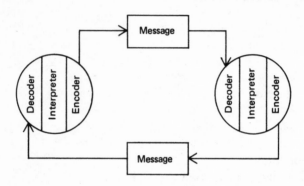

The return message, of course, may be feedback or a formal
response. To do him justice, we must record that Osgood does
not think that what happens in the black box is as simple as
this diagram, and he has elsewhere advanced a brilliant "media-
tion model" of what may be inferred to occur. His definition of
communication is somewhat like Shannon's. "In the most general sense," he says, "we have *communication* whenever one
system, a source, influences another, the destination, by manipulation of alternative signals which can be transmitted over the
channel connecting them."

Thus, both Shannon and Osgood are highly sophisticated
about the way in which human communication has an effect:
One mind influences another through signs or signals that one
person makes available for another. No thoughts are transported
or transferred. On the contrary, a source, drawing upon his
internal resources, encodes something that becomes separate
from him, and a destination decodes some or all of those signs
to be interpreted and added to the destination's internal re-

sources. We must be cautious only about drawing too literal an analogy from their terminology and their diagrams. For example, there is undoubtedly no such separation in the human black box as there is between the source and the encoder in one of Shannon's electronic systems, or between human decoder and destination as there is between the listener and the telephone instrument that decodes the electronic signals into sound waves. Also, it is well not to think too literally about channels. The telephone wire is a channel, and an assigned frequency over which a station broadcasts is a carrier that is modified so that it can be decoded into sound and/or sight. But this is obviously a far different kind of communication channel from a newspaper or from what is created when someone puts up a poster to be seen by passers-by. We will have more to say about channels, but here let us merely note that this idea, too, is an analogy to electronics and must be defined carefully when used in connection with the human process of communication.

Westley and MacLean,[3] drawing upon Lewin's idea of the gatekeeper and Newcomb's A—B—X model[4] (of A communicating to B about topic X), have also developed a useful approach to the communication process. They see it as including (1) "advocacy roles," meaning a personality or a social system engaged in selecting and transmitting messages purposively; (2) "behavioral system roles," meaning a personality or social system "requiring and using communication about the condition of its environment for the satisfaction of its needs and the solution of its problems"; and (3) "channel roles," which are gatekeepers[5] like the mass media or teachers who act as agents of receivers in selecting and transmitting "nonpurposively" the information that receivers require. Critics of the mass media or people who question the objectivity of teachers might ask whether information always is transmitted nonpurposively, but it is nonetheless clear that these three roles exist and play significant parts in the flow of information through society, whether for social radar, communication management, instruction, or entertainment.

Westley and MacLean also use the concepts of encoding and feedback. They diagram the process as follows. (We have simplified it slightly so that it can stand alone without their full explanation.)

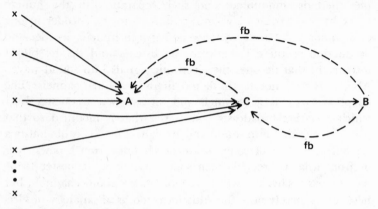

The x's are messages in the environment, and the fb's represent feedbacks. A represents source or "advocacy roles," C the gatekeeper or "channel roles," and B the receivers or "behavioral system" roles. This is obviously a very general model that can include most of the ideas and concepts we have talked about. Note that some of the same information that stimulates the original communicator also reaches the gatekeeper (and probably the ultimate receiver) and that feedback occurs all along the line—from the gatekeeper to the source, from the receiver to the gatekeeper, and from the receiver to the source.

All of these "models" are good. All are useful in pointing out some aspect of the process: Shannon, the sequence of events; Osgood, the different kinds of information processing involved; Westley and MacLean, the different roles assumed in the process. If we were to diagram the process in the way we describe it in Chapter III—as a set of communication acts focused on a set of informational signs within a particular relationship—we could do so as shown on the facing page.

A and B are two participants. S represents the signs one puts out and the other makes use of. In this case feedback is merely one's perception of the signs he himself has created or his early reading of the reaction from the other participant. The vertical line between A's and between B's indicates that some of the following communication act is determined by the images A carries and the needs he feels, as well as by his reaction to the signs he has most recently processed.

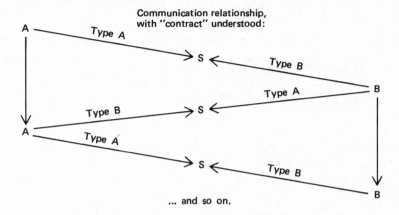

... and so on.

Perhaps the feature of this diagram most at variance with the others is the fact that the arrows all run *toward* the signs rather than *to* the signs from the sender and *from* the signs to the receiver. We distrust the idea of a "passive" receiver— a person who is acted upon, who can easily be manipulated by a propagandist or a mass medium. As we have tried to indicate, we see the process quite differently. Except in cases in which a receiver has agreed to a willing suspension of disbelief (as in one's response to fantasy entertainment) or is very naive or is "ready" for a substantial change, we perceive no such passive acceptance, no helplessness in the face of persuasive communication. Rather, acceptance is in the hands of the receiver. The messages does not enter automatically into his decision making apparatus. First it must be selected from among many other possibilities, many more than any individual can accept and process. Then it must be perceived and interpreted, not in terms of the images that the sender has tried to build into it but rather against the stored images and needs of the receiver.

In other words, receiving and processing a collection of signs, which constitutes a message, is just as active as what happens when those signs are created and sent out to be received. The message, once created, once sent, is on its own, and nothing happens until someone acts on it.

# Notes and References

## Chapter I:
## How Communication Developed

For further reading on the topic of Chapter I, the reader may be interested in M. Fabre. A history of communications. *The new illustrated library of science and inventions*, vol. 9 (New York: Hawthorn Books, 1963) and L. Hogben, *From cave painting to comic strip* (New York: Chanticleer Press, 1949).

Useful readers in the general field of mass communication include: B. Berelson and M. Janowitz, (eds.), *Reader in public opinion and communication*, 2d ed. (Glencoe, Ill.: The Free Press, 1966); L. A. Dexter and D. M. White, (eds.), *People, society, and mass communication* (New York: The Free Press, 1964); A. G. Smith (ed.), *Communication and culture* (New York: Holt, Rinehart, & Winston, 1966); W. Schramm and D. Roberts, eds.), *The process and effects of mass communication*, rev. ed. (Urbana: University of Illinois Press, 1971); W. Schramm, (ed.), *Mass communication*, 2d ed. (Urbana: University of Illinois Press, 1960).

There are a number of relevant articles in G. Lindzey and E. Aronson, (eds.), *Handbook of social psychology*, (Reading, Mass.: Addison-Wesley, 1969) and *The international encyclo-*

*pedia of the social sciences* (New York: Macmillan, 1969). The prime reference source, summing up scholarship in this field, is I. Pool, W. Schramm, et al., (eds.), *Handbook of communication* (Chicago: Rand McNally, 1973).

[1] C. Cooley. *Social organization.* New York: Charles Scribner's Sons, 1909, p. 61.
[2] E. Sapir. Communication. In *Encyclopedia of the social sciences*, 1st ed. New York: Macmillan, 1935, vol. IV. p. 78.
[3] K. Davis. *Human society.* New York: Macmillan, 1949.
[4] K. Boulding. *The image: knowledge in life and society.* Ann Arbor: University of Michigan Press, 1956, esp. pp. 15 ff.
[5] M. McLuhan. *Understanding media: the extensions of man.* New York: McGraw-Hill, 1966.
[6] For an interesting, brief treatment of this material, see Fabre, op. cit., pp. 12 ff.

# Chapter II:
# What Communication Does

A classic article in this area was written by Harold D. Lasswell and first published in L. Bryson, (ed.), *The communication of ideas* (New York: Institute for Religious and Social Studies, 1948). It is also reprinted in Schramm and Roberts, *The process and effects of mass communication*, rev. ed., (Urbana: University of Illinois Press, 1971), pp. 84 ff. Other useful general reading includes: M. DeFleur, *Theories of mass communication*, 2d ed., (New York: David McKay, 1970); C. Wright, *Mass communication: A sociological perspective* (New York: Random House, 1959); and W. Stephenson, *The play theory of communication* (Chicago: University of Chicago Press, 1967).

[1] E. Sapir. Communication. In *Encyclopedia of the social sciences*, 1st ed. New York: Macmillan, 1935, vol. IV, p. 78.
[2] B. Berelson. What "missing the newspaper" means. In P. Lazarsfeld and F. Stanton, *Communications research, 1948–1949*. New York: Harper & Row, 1949.
[3] R. K. Merton. *Social theory and social structure*, rev. ed. New York: Free Press, 1959, esp. pp. 51, 61–66.

4 E. Piaget. *The language and thought of the child.* New York: Harcourt Brace Jovanovich, 1936.

5 E. C. Tolman. *Purposive behavior in animals and men.* New York: Appleton, 1932.

6 F. Lorimer. *The growth of reason.* New York: Harcourt Brace Jovanovich, 1929.

7 Stephenson, *op. cit.*, esp. chs. 4 and 11.

8 J. Huizinga. *Homo ludens.* Boston: Beacon, 1950.

9 T. S. Szasz. *Pain and pleasure.* New York: Basic Books, 1957.

10 Stephenson, *op. cit.*, p. 45.

11 *Ibid.*, p. 46.

12 *Ibid.*, pp. 48 ff.

13 See, for example, Stephenson, *op. cit.*, pp. 45 ff.

14 Lasswell, *op. cit.*, reprinted in Schramm and Roberts, *The process and effects of mass communication*, 2d ed. Urbana: University of Illinois Press, 1971, p. 87.

15 Lasswell, *op. cit.*

16 Wright, *op. cit.*

17 DeFleur, *op. cit.*

## Chapter III:
## The Process of Communication

Most of the readers cited at the beginning of the notes on Chapter I contain useful papers on the communication process. D. K. Berlo's *The process of communication* (New York: Holt, Rinehart, Winston, 1960) deals directly with the topic. Boulding's *The image: knowledge in life and society* (Ann Arbor: University of Michigan Press, 1956) is well worth reading in connection with this chapter. Useful sources on information theory are: C. E. Shannon, and W. Weaver, *The mathematical theory of communication* (Urbana: University of Illinois Press, 1949) and C. Cherry, *On human communication* (New York: Wiley, 1957).

1 Shannon and Weaver, *op. cit.*

2 W. Weaver. In Shannon and Weaver, *op. cit.*, p. 103.

3 Shannon and Weaver, *op. cit.* N. Wiener. *Cybernetics.* New York: Wiley, 1948.

4 See Plato, *The republic,* Book VII.

[5] W. Johnson. *People in quandaries: the semantics of personal adjustment*. New York: Harper & Row, 1946, p. 472.

[6] Quoted in S. Langer. *Mind: an essay on human feeling*. Baltimore: Johns Hopkins Press, 1967, p. 284.

[7] *Ibid.*

[8] See the remarkable discussion of this topic in Langer, *op. cit.*, pp. 257–306.

## Chapter IV:
## The Signs of Communication

For general reading in this area: R. Brown, *Words and things* (New York: Free Press, 1958); G. A. Miller, *Language and communication* (New York: McGraw-Hill, 1951); C. Morris, *Signs, language, and behavior* (Englewood, N.J.: Prentice-Hall, 1946); C. K. Ogden and I. A. Richards, *The meaning of meaning* (New York: Harcourt Brace Jovanovich, 1936); C. E. Osgood, G. J. Suci, and P. H. Tannenbaum, *The measurement of meaning* (Urbana: University of Illinois Press, 1957).

[1] A. L. Campa. Language barriers in intercultural relations. *Journal of Communication*, 1951, *1*, 41–46.

[2] W. Johnson. *People in quandaries: the semantics of personal adjustment*. New York, Harper & Row, 1946, pp. 137–138.

[3] D. Krech and R. S. Crutchfield. *Theory and problems of social psychology*. New York: McGraw-Hill, 1948. For a later version see D. Krech, R. S. Crutchfield, and E. L. Balachey. *The individual in society*. New York: McGraw-Hill, 1962, pp. 20 ff.

[4] Johnson, *op. cit.*, p. 109.

[5] Osgood, Suci, and Tannenbaum, *op. cit.*

[6] A. Mehrabian. Communication without words. *Psychology Today*, 1968, *2*, 53–55.

[7] See E. Goffman. *The presentation of self in everyday life*. Garden City, New York: Doubleday, 1959, p. 2.

[8] P. Ekman, and W. Friesen. The repertoire of nonverbal behavior: categories, origin, use, and coding. *Semiotica*, 1969, *1*, 1, 49–98.

[9] J. Gunther. *Roosevelt in retrospect*. New York: Harper & Row, 1950, p. 22.

[10] Reported by P. F. Secord, Facial features and inference processes in interpersonal perception. In R. Tagiuri and L. Petrullo, (eds.), *Person perception and interpersonal behavior.* Stanford, Calif.: Stanford University Press, 1958.

[11] See R. L. Birdwhistell. *Kinesics and context.* Philadelphia: University of Pennsylvania Press, 1970.

[12] G. W. Allport and P. E. Vernon. *Studies in expressive movement.* New York: Macmillan, 1933.

[13] E. Goffman. *Behavior in public places.* New York: Doubleday, 1963, p. 35.

[14] G. Simmel. Sociology of the senses: visual interaction. In R. Parl and E. Burgess, (eds.), *Introduction to the science of sociology.* Chicago: University of Chicago Press, 1921, p. 358.

[15] See D. C. Barnlund. Introduction—nonverbal interaction. In Barnlund, D. C. (ed.), *Interpersonal communication: survey and studies.* Boston: Houghton Mifflin, 1968, pp. 511 ff.

[16] F. Deutsch. Analysis of bodily posture. *Psychoanalytic Quarterly*, 1947, *16*, 211.

[17] Mehrabian, *op. cit.*

[18] N. Maccoby and G. Comstock. *Instructional television for the in-service training of the Colombian teacher.* Stanford, Calif.: Institute for Communication Research, Stanford University, 1966.

[19] G. Fairbanks and W. Pronovost. An experimental study of the pitch characteristics of the voice during the expression of emotion. *Speech Monographs*, 1939, *6*, 87–104.

[20] See D. Fabun. *Communications: the transfer of meaning.* New York: Macmillan, 1968, esp. pp. 20 ff.

[21] R. Brown. *Social psychology.* New York: Macmillan, 1966, p. 102.

[22] W. McKeachie. Lipstick as a determiner of first impressions of personality. *Journal of Social Psychology*, 1952, *3*, 241–244.

[23] Fabun, D., *op. cit.*

[24] J. A. M. Meerloo. *Unobtrusive communication: essays in psycholinguistics.* Assen, Netherlands: Van Gorcum, 1964, p. 166.

[25] R. Sommer. Further studies of small group ecology. *Sociometry*, 1965, *28*, 337–348.

²⁶ Quoted by S. Rodman. *Conversations with artists*. New York: Capricorn Books, 1961, p. 84.

²⁷ Barnlund, *op. cit.*, p. 512.

## Chapter V:
## The Codes of Communication

In addition to the titles suggested for Chapter IV, W. Johnson, *People in quandaries: the semantics of personal adjustment* (New York: Harper & Row, 1946) and S. I. Hayakawa, *Language in thought and action* (New York: Harcourt Brace Jovanovich, 1946) are useful general reading in this area.

There are a number of general books about language. Because of his present importance in the field, N. Chomsky, *Syntactic structures* (The Hague: Mouton, 1967) is suggested.

¹ See Chomsky, *op. cit.*

² This is quoted in a popular exposition of Chomsky by J. Ved Mehta in Easy to please. *New Yorker*, May 8, 1971, pp. 44 ff.

³ The easiest place to find this is in Ved Mehta, *op. cit.*, p. 46.

⁴ J. Greenberg, (ed.). *Universals of language*. Cambridge, Mass.: M.I.T. Press, 1966. See especially Greenberg's chapter, "Some universals of grammar with particular reference to the order of meaningful elements."

⁵ *Ibid.*

⁶ J. B. Carroll. In S. Saporta, *Psycholinguistics*. New York: Holt Rinehart & Winston, 1956.

⁷ E. Sapir. The status of linguistics as a science. *Language*, 1929, 5, 207–214. See also quotations in J. B. Carroll, (ed.), *Language, thought, and reality*. New York: Wiley, 1956.

⁸ See D. Krech, R. S. Crutchfield, and E. L. Balachey. *The individual in society*. New York: McGraw-Hill, 1962, pp. 296 ff. Also Whorf, in Carroll, *ibid.*

⁹ B. L. Whorf. Science and linguistics. *Technology Review*, April 1940, 62–6, 247–248.

¹⁰ N. Chomsky. *Language and mind*. Berkeley, Calif.: University of California Press, 1968.

¹¹ S. I. Hayakawa. *Language in thought and action*. New York: Harcourt Brace Jovanovich, 1949, p. 169.

¹² Johnson, *op. cit.*, pp. 174–175.

[13] *Ibid.*, pp. 9–10.

[14] K. Boulding. *The image.* Ann Arbor, Mich.: University of Michigan Press, 1956, pp. 109–111.

[15] Johnson, *op. cit.*, p. 394.

[16] Hayakawa, *op. cit.*, p. 118.

[17] *Ibid.*, pp. 290–291.

[18] Quoted by Hayakawa, *op. cit.*, p. 96.

## Chapter VI:
## The Pathways of Communication

For general reading see E. Rogers, *Diffusion of innovations* (New York: Free Press, 1962) and M. L. DeFleur and O. N. Larsen, *The flow of information* (New York: Harper & Row, 1958). Useful material can also be found in D. C. Barnlund, *Interpersonal communication* (Boston: Houghton Mifflin, 1968), pp. 227 ff.

[1] H. J. Leavitt. Some effects of certain communication patterns on group performances. *Journal of Abnormal and Social Psychology*, 1951, *46*, 35–80.

[2] *Ibid.*

[3] J. Thibaut. An experimental study of the cohesiveness of under-privileged groups. *Human Relations*, 1950, *3*, 251–278.

[4] Dube. In D. Lerner and W. Schramm, (eds.), *Communication and change in the developing countries.* Honolulu: East-West Center Press, 1967, pp. 131–132.

[5] How communication works. In W. Schramm, (ed.), *Process and effects of mass communication.* Urbana: University of Illinois Press, 1954, pp. 19 ff.

[6] See G. K. Zipf. *The psycho-biology of language.* Boston: Houghton Mifflin, 1935.

[7] D. O. Sears and J. L. Freedman. Selective exposure to information: a critical review. In W. Schramm, and D. F. Roberts, *The process and effects of mass communication,* (rev. ed.). Urbana: University of Illinois Press, 1971, pp. 209–234.

## Chapter VII:
## The Media of Communication

For general reading: H. Cantril and G. W. Allport, *The psychology of radio* (New York: Harper & Row, 1935); P. F.

Lazarsfeld, *Radio and the printed page* (New York: Duell, Sloan & Pearce, 1940); E. Katz and P. F. Lazarsfeld, *Personal influence: the part played by people in the flow of mass communications* (New York: Free Press, 1964); M. McLuhan, *Understanding media: the extensions of man* (New York: McGraw-Hill, 1966).

[1] McLuhan, *op. cit.*

[2] P. J. Deutschmann. The sign-situation classification of human communication. *Journal of Communication*, 1967, 7, 2, 63–73.

[3] D. E. Broadbent. *Perception and communication.* London: Pergamon Press, 1958. R. M. W. Travers, *et al. Research and theory related to audiovisual information transmission.* Salt Lake City: Bureau of Educational Research, University of Utah, 1966.

[4] G. W. Allport and L. J. Postman. The basic psychology of rumor. *Transactions of the New York Academy of Sciences*, II, 1945, 8, 61–81. L. Festinger and J. Thibaut. Interpersonal communication in small groups. *Journal of Abnormal and Social Psychology*, 1951, 46, 92–99.

[5] P. J. Lazarsfeld, B. Berelson, and H. Gaudet. *The people's choice.* New York: Harper & Row, 1944.

[6] A. Campbell, P. E. Converse, W. E. Miller, and D. E. Stokes. *The American voter.* New York: Wiley, 1960.

[7] P. Deutschmann and W. Danielson. Diffusion of knowledge of the major news story. *Journalism Quarterly*, 1960, 37, 345–355. B. S. Greenberg. Person-to-person communication in the diffusion of news events. *Journalism Quarterly*, 1964, 41, 489–494. Also, B. S. Greenberg and E. B. Parker, (eds.), *The Kennedy assassination and the American public: social communication in crisis.* Stanford, Calif.: Stanford University Press, 1965, ch. 1.

[8] E. M. Rogers and F. F. Shoemaker. *Communication of innovations: a cross-cultural approach.* New York: Free Press, 1971.

[9] V. C. Trohldahl. A field test of a modified "two-step flow of communication" model. *Public Opinion Quarterly*, 1966–1967, 30, 4, 609–623.

[10] B. S. Greenberg. Person-to-person communication in the dif-

fusion of news events. *Journalism Quarterly*, 1964, *41*, 490–494.

[11] Trohldahl, *op. cit.*

[12] See summary in Rogers and Shoemaker, *op. cit.*

[13] *Ibid.* See also Rogers's article, Interpersonal communication and mass media. In Pool, *et al.*, *Handbook of communication*. Chicago: Rand McNally, 1973.

[14] H. Innis. *The bias of communication*. Toronto: University of Toronto Press, 1951. Also, *Empire and communication*. Oxford: Oxford University Press, 1950.

[15] J. W. Carey, Harold Adams Innis, and Marshall McLuhan. *The Antioch Review*, 1967, *27*, 1, 5–39.

[16] *Ibid.*

## Chapter VIII:
## The Structure of Mass Communication

For general reading: chapters on the press, broadcasting, and film in *Handbook of communication*. There are many books on the individual media. An important one on the economics of communication is F. Machlup, *The production and distribution of knowledge* (Princeton, N.J.: Princeton University Press, 1962). Popular introductions are E. Emery, P. H. Ault, and W. K. Agee, *Introduction to mass communications* (New York: Dodd, Mead, 1970); T. Peterson, J. W. Jensen, and W. L. Rivers, *The mass media and modern society* (New York: Holt Rinehart & Winston, 1970); and J. L. Hulteng and R. P. Nelson, *The fourth estate: an informal appraisal of the news and opinion media* (New York: Harper & Row, 1971). A very useful book is B. H. Bagdikian, *The information machines: their impact on men and the media* (New York: Harper & Row, 1971).

[1] Machlup, *op. cit.*

[2] Bagdikian, *op. cit.*

[3] D. M. White. The "gate keeper": a case study in the selection of news. *Journalism Quarterly*, 1950, *27*, 383–390.

[4] G. E. Lang and K. Lang. The unique perspective of television: a pilot study. *American Sociological Review*, 1953, *18*, 3–12.

[5] G. Gerbner and P. H. Tannenbaum. Mass media censorship and the portrayal of mental illness: some effects of industry-

wide controls in motion pictures and television. In *Studies of innovation and of communication to the public*. Stanford, Calif.: Institute for Communication Research, 1962, pp. 203–226.

[6] Bagdikian, *op. cit.*, pp. 99 ff.

[7] W. Cronkite. *The challenges of change*. Washington: Public Affairs Press, 1971, pp. 61 ff.

[8] W. Breed. Social control in the newsroom. Reprinted from Social Forces (May 1955). In W. Schramm, (ed.), *Mass communication*. Urbana: University of Illinois Press, 1960, pp. 178–194.

[9] *Handbook of communication, op. cit.*

[10] Bagdikian's estimate is $306 (Bagdikian, *op. cit.*, pp. 207 ff.).

[11] *Ibid.*, pp. 127 ff.

[12] *Ibid.*, pp. 174 ff.

[13] *Ibid.*, pp. 211 ff.

## Chapter IX:
## Social Control and the Future of Mass Communication

For background, see Communication: control and public policy, in *International encyclopedia of the social sciences*. Also, F. Siebert, T. Peterson, and W. Schramm, *Four theories of the press* (Urbana: University of Illinois Press, 1963) and W. L. Rivers and W. Schramm, *Responsibility in mass communication*, 2d ed., (New York: Harper & Row, 1969).

On television and children, see H. Himmelweit, A. N. Oppenheim, and P. Vince, *Television and the child* (London: Oxford, 1958); W. Schramm, J. Lyle, and E. B. Parker, *Television in the lives of our children* (Stanford, Calif.: Stanford University Press, 1961); two Japanese studies that have been summed up in a volume by T. Furu, *Functions of television for children* (Tokyo: Sophia University, 1971); and G. Maletzke, *Jugend und television* (Hamburg, Darmstadt: Schroedel, 1964). A major contribution to the research on children and television is the report of the U.S. Surgeon General's study, *Television and social behavior: a technical report to the Surgeon General's Scientific Advisory Committee on Television and Social Behavior* (Washington, D.C.: U.S. Government Printing Office, 1972, 5 vols.).

[1] F. Terrou and L. Solal. *Legislation for press, film, and radio.* Paris: Unesco, 1951. Also, Siebert, Peterson, and Schramm, *op. cit.*

[2] J. Milton. *Areopagitica*, 1918 edition, p. 58.

[3] J. S. Mill. *On liberty*, 1947 edition, p. 16.

[4] Terrou and Solal, *op. cit.*

[5] *Red Lion Broadcasting Co.* v. *FCC*, 381 F2d 908, D.C., 1968; affirmed 395 U.S. 367, 1969.

[6] Federal Communications Commission. *Public service responsibilities of broadcast licensees.* Washington, D.C.: FCC, 1946.

[7] Commission on Freedom of the Press. *Toward a free and responsible press.* Chicago: University of Chicago Press, 1947.

[8] See for summary W. Schramm. *Motion pictures and real life violence: what the research says.* Stanford, Calif.: Stanford University Press, Institute for Communication Research, 1968, pp. 6 ff. Quotations are from W. H. Haines. Juvenile delinquency and television. *Journal of Social Therapy, 1,* 1955, 69–78; and R. S. Banay. Testimony before the committee to investigate juvenile delinquency, Committee on the Judiciary, U.S. Senate, 84th Congress. S. Res., April 1955, 62. Washington, D.C.: Government Printing Office.

[9] For instance, G. A. Hale, L. K. Miller, and H. W. Stevenson. Incidental learning of film content: a development study. *Child Development,* 1968, *39*, 1, 69–78. Also, E. E. Maccoby. Role-taking in childhood and its consequences for social learning. *Child Development,* 1959, *30*, 239–252; C. A. Ruckmick and W. S. Dysinger. *The emotional responses of children to the motion picture situation.* New York: Macmillan, 1933; A. E. Siegel. The influence of violence in the mass media on children's expectations. *Child Development,* 1958, *29*, 35–56; and R. C. Peterson and L. L. Thurstone. *Motion pictures and the social attitudes of children.* New York: Macmillan, 1933.

[10] For summary, see reference in note 8. Also, among others, A. Bandura, and R. H. Walters. *Social learning and personality development.* New York: Holt Rinehart & Winston, 1963. Among many published experiments the reader may be specially interested in A. Bandura, D. Ross, and S. Ross. Transmission of aggression through imitations of aggressive

models. *Journal of Abnormal and Social Psychology*, 1961, *63*, 3, 578–582; same authors, Imitation of film-mediated aggressive models. *Journal of Abnormal and Social Psychology*, 1963, *66*, 1, 3–11; D. P. Hartman. *The influence of symbolically modeled instrumental aggressive and pain cues on the disinhibition of aggressive behavior.* Doctoral dissertation, Stanford University, May 1965; A. E. Siegel. Film-mediated fantasy aggression and strength of aggressive drive. *Child Development*, 1956, *27*, 365–378; F. E. Emery and D. Martin. *Psychological effects of the western film—a study of television viewing.* Melbourne Department of Audio-visual Aids, University of Melbourne, 1957; and K. Heinrich. *Filmerleben, filmwerkung, filmerzeihung—einfluss des film und die aggresivitat bei jugendlichen experimentelle untersuchungen und ihre lernpsychologischen konsequenzen.* Hannover, Darmstadt: H. Schroedel, 1961.

[11] Berkowitz's viewpoint is expressed in L. Berkowitz. *Aggression: a social psychological analysis.* New York: McGraw-Hill, 1962. Among his many experiments and interpretative articles are: L. Berkowitz. Violence in the mass media. In *Paris-Stanford studies in communication.* Stanford and Paris: Institute for Communication Research and Institut Français de Presse, University of Paris, 1962, pp. 107–137; L. Berkowitz and E. Rawlings. Effects of film violence on inhibitions against subsequent aggression. *Journal of Abnormal and Social Psychology*, 1963, *66*, 405–412.

[12] *Television and social behavior, op. cit.*

[13] Proceedings of the U.S. Senate Commerce Subcommittee, March 21, 1972. Washington, D.C.: U.S. Government Printing Office, 1972.

[14] *Ibid.* Quoted in syndicated article by Norman Mark, *Honolulu Star-Bulletin*, April 1, 1972.

[15] B. H. Bagdikian. *The information machines: their impact on men and the media.* New York: Harper & Row, 1971, p. 247.

## Chapter X:
## The Audiences of Mass Communication

There are a few general books on media audiences. One of them is G. Steiner. *The people look at television* (New York:

Knopf, 1963). With this might be placed *The people look at educational television*, by W. Schramm, J. Lyle, and I. Pool, (Stanford, Calif.: Stanford University Press, 1963). The best sources of recent audience data are the yearbooks of the media and the various audience measurement services.

[1] These data are derived from national surveys conducted by Educational Testing Service. Survey reveals what American adults read in one day, *ETS Developments, 19*, Summer 1972, *4*, 1–4.

[2] *Television and social behavior: a technical report to the Surgeon General's Scientific Advisory Committee on Television and Social Behavior*, Vol. II. Washington, D.C.: U.S. Government Printing Office, 1972, pp. 129 ff.

[3] W. Schramm and D. M. White. Age, education, and economic status as factors in newspaper reading. *Journalism Quarterly*, 1949, *26*, 149–159.

[4] P. F. Lazarsfeld and P. Kendall. *Radio listening in America*. Englewood Cliffs, N.J.: Prentice-Hall, 1948.

[5] H. C. Link and H. A. Hopf. *People and books*. New York: Bohm Industry Committee, Book Manufacturers' Institute, 1946.

[6] Lazarsfeld and Kendall, *op. cit.*

[7] L. A. Handel. *Hollywood looks at its audience*. Urbana, Ill.: University of Illinois Press, 1950.

[8] Steiner, *op. cit.*

[9] M. E. Samuelson, R. F. Carter, and L. Ruggles. *Education, available time, and mass media use*. Seattle: University of Washington, School of Communication, 1963.

[10] See W. Schramm and S. Wade. *Knowledge and the public mind*. Stanford, Calif.: Institute for Communication Research, 1967.

[11] B. W. Roper. *A ten-year view of public attitudes toward television and other mass media*. New York: Television Information Office, 1969.

[12] *Ibid.* See also B. W. Roper. *An extended view of public attitudes toward television and other mass media, 1959–1971*. New York: Television Information Office, 1971.

[13] Report issued by the American Newspaper Publishers Association, 1967.

[14] See S. Wade and W. Schramm. The mass media as sources of public affairs, science, and health knowledge. *Public Opinion Quarterly*, 1969, *33*, 197–209, esp. p. 207.

[15] *Ibid.*

## Chapter XI:
## How Communication Has an Effect

For general reading a number of the papers in the *Handbook of communication* deal with effects. So also do many papers in the readers mentioned before. In addition, see J. T. Klapper, *The effects of mass communication* (New York: Free Press, 1960).

[1] H. Cantril. *The invasion from Mars*. Princeton, N.J.: Princeton University Press, 1940.

[2] *Saturday Review*, April 3, 1971, *54*, 14.

[3] N. Cousins. Decline and fall of Congressman Day. *Saturday Review*, May 8, 1971, *54*, 19, 18.

[4] D. Cartwright. Some principles of mass persuasion: selected findings of research on the sale of U.S. War Bonds. *Human Relations*, 1949, *2*, 253.

[5] For example, C. L. Hull. *Principles of behavior: an introduction to behavior theory*. New York: Appleton, 1943; E. L. Thorndike, *The fundamentals of learning*. New York: Teachers College Press, 1932; E. R. Guthrie. *The psychology of learning*. New York: Harper & Row, 1935; B. F. Skinner. *Verbal behavior*. New York: Appleton, 1957; N. E. Miller and J. Dollard. *Social learning and imitation*. New Haven, Conn.: Yale University Press, 1943; C. Hovland, I. L. Janis, and H. H. Kelley. *Communication and persuasion*. New Haven, Conn.: Yale University Press, 1953; C. I. Hovland, (ed.). *The order of presentation in persuasion*. New Haven, Conn.: Yale University Press, 1957; C. I. Hovland and I. L. Janis. *Personality and persuasibility*. New Haven, Conn.: Yale University Press, 1959; C. I. Hovland and M. J. Rosenberg. *Attitude organization and change*. New Haven, Conn.: Yale University Press, 1960.

[6] See also N. Maccoby and E. E. Maccoby. Homeostatic theory in attitude change. *Public Opinion Quarterly*, 1961, *25*, 535–545.

[7] For example: F. Heider. *The psychology of interpersonal relations.* New York: Wiley, 1958; T. M. Newcomb. *Personality and social change: attitude formation in a student community.* New York: Dryden, 1943; L. Festinger. *A theory of cognitive dissonance.* New York: Harper & Row, 1957; S. Schachter. *The psychology of affiliation: experimental studies of the sources of gregariousness.* Stanford, Calif.: Stanford University Press, 1959; J. S. Bruner. Social psychology and perception. In E. E. Maccoby, T. M. Newcomb, and E. L. Hartley, *Readings in social psychology.* New York: Holt Rinehart & Winston, 1958, pp. 85–93; M. B. Smith, J. S. Bruner, and R. W. White. *Opinions and personality.* New York: Wiley, 1956.

[8] Heider, *op. cit.* This was circulated for a number of years in manuscript before publication.

[9] T. M. Newcomb. An approach to the study of communicative acts. *Psychological Review*, 1953, *60*, 393–404.

[10] D. Cartwright and F. Harary. Structural balance: a generalization of Heider's theory. *Psychological Review*, 1956, *63*, 277–293.

[11] Festinger, *op. cit.*

[12] Hovland and Rosenberg, *op. cit.*

[13] C. E. Osgood, G. J. Suci, and P. H. Tannenbaum. *The measurement of meaning.* Urbana, Ill.: University of Illinois Press, 1957.

[14] See the highly useful review by W. J. McGuire. The nature of attitudes and attitude change. In G. L. Lindzey and E. Aronson, (eds.), *The handbook of social psychology.* Reading, Mass.: Addison-Wesley, 1969, pp. 136–314.

[15] P. F. Lazarsfeld and R. K. Merton. Mass communication, popular taste, and organized social action. In L. Bryson, (ed.), *The communication of ideas.* New York: Institute for Religious and Social Studies, 1948.

[16] W. A. Belson. Learning and attitude changes resulting from viewing a television series, "Bon Voyage." *British Journal of Educational Psychology*, 1956, *26*, 31–38.

[17] E. Cooper and M. Jahoda. The evasion of propaganda: how prejudiced people respond to anti-prejudice propaganda. *Journal of Psychology*, 1947, *23*, 15–25.

[18] Cantril, *op. cit.*

[19] *Ibid.*

[20] R. K. Merton. *Mass persuasion.* New York: Harper & Row, 1946.

## Chapter XII:
## Components of Effect

The best starting place for reading about attitudes and other components of effect is *The handbook of social psychology*, notably the article by McGuire. Many of the classic books in the field are mentioned in the notes that follow.

[1] G. W. Allport. Attitudes. In C. M. Murchison, (ed.), *Handbook of social psychology.* Worcester, Mass.: Clark University Press, 1935, pp. 798–844.

[2] M. Rokeach. Attitude change and behavioral change. *Public Opinion Quarterly*, 1966–1967, *30*, 529–550.

[3] M. L. DeFleur and F. R. Westie. Attitude as a scientific concept. *Social Forces*, 1963, *42*, 17–31.

[4] *Ibid.*

[5] *Ibid.*

[6] See W. Schramm. Communication in family planning. *Reports on Population/Family Planning*, April 1971, pp. 38–39.

[7] L. Festinger. Behavioral support for opinion change. *Public Opinion Quarterly*, 1964, *28*, 404.

[8] V. H. Vroom. *Work and motivation.* New York: Wiley, 1964.

[9] A. W. Wicker. Attitudes versus actions: the relationship of verbal and overt behavioral responses to attitude objects. *Journal of Social Issues*, 1969, *25*, 4, 41–78.

[10] Wicker, *ibid.*, p. 75.

[11] R. T. LaPiere. Attitudes vs. actions. *Social Forces*, 1934, *13*, 230–237.

[12] LaPiere, *ibid.*, p. 237.

[13] Q. McNemar. Opinion-attitude methodology. *Psychological Bulletin*, 1946, *43*, 289–374.

[14] C. I. Hovland. Reconciling conflicting results derived from

experimental and survey studies of attitude change. *American Psychologist*, 1959, *14*, 8.

[15] M. Fishbein. Attitude and the prediction of behavior. In M. Fishbein, (ed.), *Readings in attitude theory and measurement*. New York: Wiley, 1967.

[16] Rokeach, *op. cit.*

[17] C. I. Hovland, A. A. Lumsdaine, and F. D. Sheffield. *Experiments on mass communication*. Princeton, N.J.: Princeton University Press, 1949.

[18] I. Lorge. Prestige, suggestion and attitudes. *Journal of Social Psychology*, 1936, *7*, 386–402.

[19] C. I. Hovland and W. Weiss. The influence of source credibility on communication effectiveness. *Public Opinion Quarterly*, *15*, 635–650.

[20] H. C. Kelman and C. I. Hovland. "Reinstatement" of the communicator in delayed measurements of opinion change. *Journal of Abnormal and Social Psychology*, 1953, *49*, 327–335.

[21] K. Burke. *A grammar of motives*. Englewood Cliffs, N.J.: Prentice-Hall, 1945.

———. *A rhetoric of motives*. Englewood Cliffs, N.J.: Prentice-Hall, 1950.

[22] P. G. Zimbardo. The effect of effort and improvisation on self-persuasion produced by role-playing. *Journal of Experimental Social Psychology*, 1965, *1*, 103–120.

[23] Kelman and Hovland, *op. cit.*

[24] K. Lewin. Group decision and social change. In E. E. Maccoby, T. M. Newcomb, and E. L. Hartley. *Readings in social psychology*. New York: Holt Rinehart & Winston, 1958, pp. 197–211.

[25] D. L. Thistlethwaite, H. deHaan, and J. Kamenetzky. The effects of "directive" vs. "non-directive" communication procedures on attitudes. *Journal of Abnormal and Social Psychology*, 1955, *51*, 107–113.

[26] J. E. Dietrich. The relative effectiveness of two modes of radio delivery in influencing attitudes. *Speech Monographs*, 1946, *13*, 58–65.

[27] Hovland, Lumsdaine, and Sheffield, *op. cit.*

[28] See McGuire in *The handbook of social psychology, op. cit.*

29 F. H. Lund. The psychology of belief: IV. The law of primacy in persuasion. *Journal of Abnormal and Social Psychology*, 1925, *20*, 183–191.

30 H. Cromwell. The relative effects of audience attitude in the first versus the second argumentative speech of a series. *Speech Monographs*, 1950, *17*, 105–122.

31 C. I. Hovland and W. Mandell. Is there a "law of primacy in persuasion"? In C. I. Hovland, (ed.), *The order of presentation in persuasion.* New Haven, Conn.: Yale University Press, 1957, pp. 13–22.

32 McGuire, *op. cit.*

33 L. Festinger and N. Maccoby. On resistance to persuasive communications. *Journal of Abnormal and Social Psychology*, 1964, *68*, 359–366.

34 S. C. Menefee and A. G. Granneberg. Propaganda and opinions on foreign policy. *Journal of Social Psychology*, 1940, *11*, 393–404.

35 I. L. Janis and S. Feshbach. Effects of fear-arousing communication. *Journal of Abnormal and Social Psychology*, 1953, *48*, 78–92.

36 G. C. Chu. Fear arousal, efficacy, and imminency. *Journal of Personality and Social Psychology*, 1966, *5*, 517–524.

37 McGuire, *op. cit.*

38 H. H. Kelley and E. Volkart. The resistance to change of group-anchored attitudes. *American Sociological Review*, 1952, *17*, 453–465.

39 S. E. Asch. Studies of independence and conformity: a minority of one against a unanimous majority. *Psychological Monographs*, 1956, *70*, 9.

40 See McGuire's excellent summary in *The handbook of social psychology*, III, *op. cit.*, pp. 235–236.

41 K. Lewin. In Maccoby, Newcomb, and Hartley, *op. cit.*

## Chapter XIII:
## Some Special Effects of Mass Communication

In addition to the readings suggested for chapters XI and XII, the reader may want to look at the chapter by W. Weiss in *The handbook of social psychology*, V, pp. 77 ff.

[1] F. Wertham. *Seduction of the innocent.* New York: Holt Rinehart & Winston, 1952.

[2] This paper by Lazarsfeld and Merton, originally published in L. Bryson, (ed.), *The communication of ideas* (New York: Harper & Row, 1948), is now easily available in W. Schramm and D. F. Roberts. *The process and effects of mass communication,* rev. ed. (Urbana, Ill.: University of Illinois Press, 1971), pp. 554–578.

[3] *Ibid.,* p. 555.

[4] *Ibid.,* pp. 555–556.

[5] *Ibid.,* p. 566.

[6] *Ibid.,* p. 567.

[7] *Ibid.*

[8] *Ibid.,* p. 575.

[9] J. T. Klapper. *The effects of mass communication.* New York: Free Press, 1960, p. 8.

[10] *Ibid.*

[11] E. Katz and P. F. Lazarsfeld. *Personal influence.* New York: Free Press, 1964.

[12] See note 5, Chapter XI for a list of the principal Hovland books.

[13] R. A. Bauer. The obstinate audience: the influence process from the point of view of social communication. *American Psychologist,* 1964, *19,* 319–328.

[14] C. Zimmerman and R. A. Bauer. The effects of an audience on what is remembered. *Public Opinion Quarterly,* 1956, *20,* 238–248.

[15] See B. Rosenberg and D. M. White. *Mass culture.* New York: Free Press, 1957 (revised version, 1971).

[16] H. T. Himmelweit, A. N. Oppenheim, and P. Vince. *Television and the child.* London: Oxford University Press, 1958.

[17] J. Trenaman and D. McQuail. *Television and the political image.* London: Methuen, 1961.

[18] J. B. Stewart. *Repetitive advertising in newspapers.* Boston: Division of Research, Harvard Graduate School of Business, 1964.

[19] S. Fujitake. In *Studies of Broadcasting,* Tokyo: NHK, 1963, 156–160.

[20] U.S. Information Agency. The impact of Hollywood films abroad. PMS-50, 1961.

[21] P. W. Holaday and G. W. Stoddard. *Getting ideas from the movies.* New York: Macmillan, 1933.

[22] See W. Schramm and S. Wade. *Knowledge and the public mind.* Stanford, Calif.: Institute for Communication Research, Stanford University Press, 1967, pp. 27 ff.

[23] H. H. Hyman and P. B. Sheatsley. Some reasons why information campaigns fail. *Public Opinion Quarterly,* 1947, *11,* 413–423.

[24] D. J. Boorstin. *The image: a guide to pseudo-events in America.* New York: Harper & Row, 1964.

## Chapter XIV:
## The Political Impact of Mass Communication

General reading in this area includes: D. Boorstin, *The image: a guide to pseudo-events in America* (New York: Harper & Row, 1961); D. Nimmo, *The political persuaders* (Englewood Cliffs, N.J.: Prentice-Hall, 1970); S. Kraus, (ed.), *The great debates: background, perspective, effects* (Bloomington: Indiana University Press, 1962); and D. O. Sears' review of political behavior in (G. Lindzey and E. Aronson, (eds.), *Handbook of social psychology,* V, Reading, Mass.: Addison-Wesley, 1969), pp. 315 ff.

[1] Robert Samuelson, Washington Post Service, June 18, 1971.

[2] Washington Post Service, June 20, 1971.

[3] Nimmo, *op. cit.* Also J. McGinnis. *The selling of the President, 1968.* New York: Trident Press, 1969.

[4] Nimmo, *op. cit.*

[5] W. L. Rivers, T. Peterson, and J. W. Jensen, (eds.). *The mass media and modern society.* San Francisco: Rinehart Press, 1971, p. 246.

[6] Quoted in Rivers, Peterson, and Jensen, (eds.), *op. cit.,* p. 136.

[7] *Ibid.,* pp. 136–137.

[8] B. R. Berelson, P. F. Lazarsfeld, and W. N. McPhee. *Voting: a study of opinion formation in a Presidential election.* Chicago: University of Chicago Press, 1954.

[9] D. O. Sears. Political behavior. In Lindzey and Aronson, (eds.), *op. cit.,* 315–458.

[10] T. M. Newcomb. *Personality and social change: attitude formation in a student community.* New York: Dryden, 1943.

[11] A. Bandura. Social learning through imitation. In M. R. Jones, (ed.), *Nebraska Symposium on Motivation.* Lincoln, Neb.: University of Nebraska Press, 1962, pp. 211–269.

[12] M. Rowan. Candidates aren't packaged—you are. *Politeia,* 1971, *1,* 2, 7–10.

[13] *Ibid.,* p. 9.

[14] *Ibid.,* p. 10.

[15] K. Lang and G. E. Lang. The television personality in politics: some considerations. *Public Opinion Quarterly,* 1956, *20,* 103–112.

[16] Berelson, Lazarsfeld, and McPhee, *op. cit.*

[17] W. Schramm and R. F. Carter. The effectiveness of a political telethon. *Public Opinion Quarterly,* 1959, *23,* 121–127.

[18] R. F. Carter. Some effects of the debates. In Kraus, *op. cit.,* pp. 253–270.

[19] P. J. Deutschmann. Viewing, conversation, and voting intentions. In Kraus, *op. cit.,* pp. 232–252.

[20] Kraus, *op. cit.,* p. 14.

[21] K. Lang and G. E. Lang. Reactions of viewers. In Kraus, *op. cit.,* pp. 313–330.

[22] For a summary of the data behind these pages on the events following the Kennedy assassination, see W. Schramm. Communication in crisis. In B. Greenberg and E. B. Parker, (eds.), *The Kennedy assassination and the American public.* Stanford, Calif.: Stanford University Press, 1965, pp. 1–25.

## Appendix:
## A Note on Models

[1] C. E. Shannon and W. Weaver. *The mathematical theory of communication.* Urbana, Ill.: University of Illinois Press, 1949.

[2] C. E. Osgood, G. J. Suci, and P. H. Tannenbaum. *The measurement of meaning.* Urbana, Ill.: University of Illinois Press, 1957. See esp. pp. 228 ff.

[3] B. Westley and M. MacLean. A conceptual model for communication research. *Journalism Quarterly,* 1957, *34,* 31–38.

[4] T. Newcomb. An approach to the study of communicative acts. *Psychological Review*, 1953, *60*, 393–404.

[5] A good place to read a simple exposition of the "gatekeeper" concept is Lewin's article, "Group decision and social change." In E. E. Maccoby, T. M. Newcomb, and E. L. Hartley, (eds.), *Readings in social psychology*. New York: Holt Rinehart & Winston, 1958, pp. 200–201.

# Indexes

# Index of Names

# Index of Subjects

9420

73 74 75 76   9 8 7 6 5 4 3 2 1

## DATE DUE

| | |
|---|---|
| 9. 25. '80 | |
| 6. 06. '85 | |
| MAR 0 1 '99 | |